KURT
VONNEGUT

WRITINGS BY

INTRODUCTION BY NANETTE

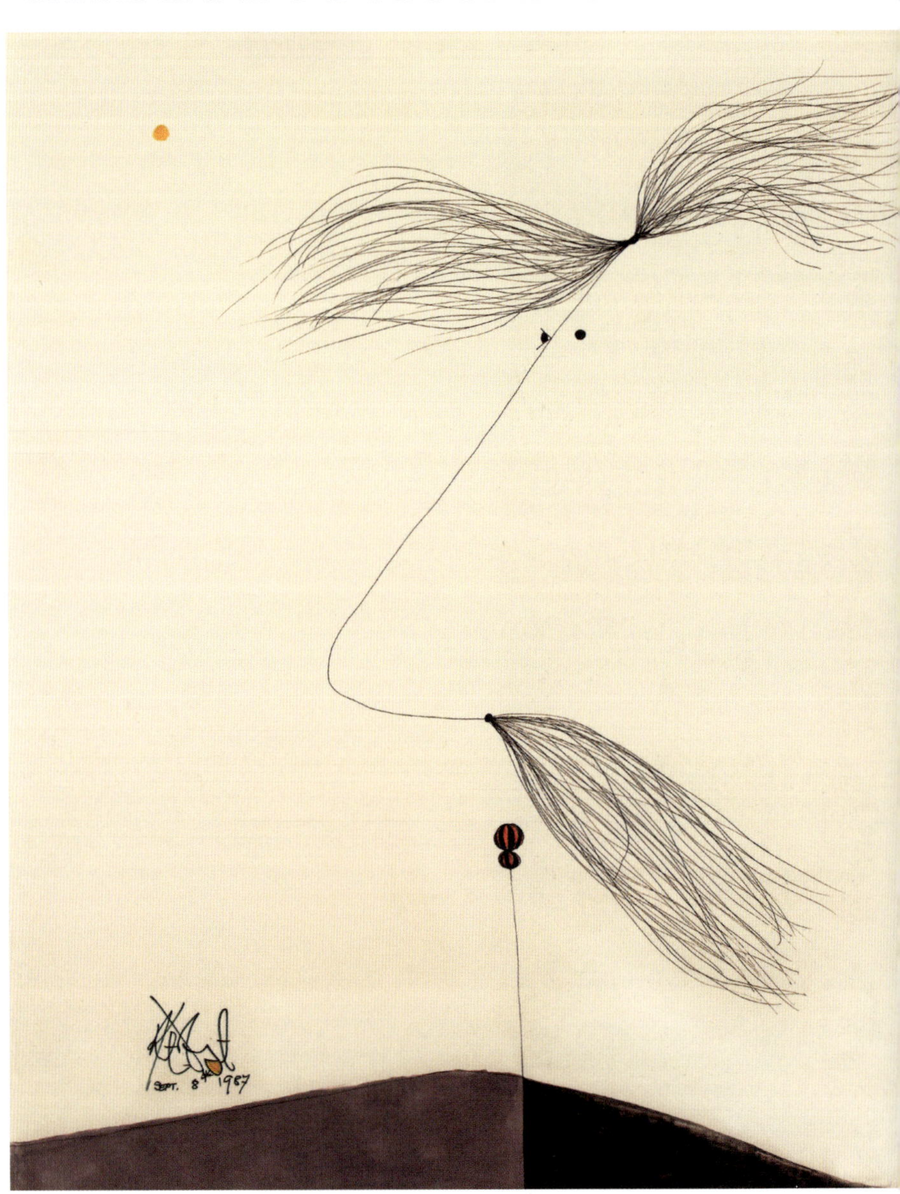

ESSAY BY PETER REED

KURT VONNEGUT

DRAWINGS

M

Phaidon Press Limited
2 Cooperage Yard
London E15 2QR

Monacelli
A Phaidon Company
111 Broadway
New York, NY 10006

Phaidon SARL
55, rue Traversière
75012 Paris

phaidon.com/monacelli

Reprinted 2026

ISBN 978-1-58093-377-3

Library of Congress Control Number 2013955283

Production by Michael Vagnetti
Designed by Misha Beletsky

Printed in China

COVER: Self-portrait, February 19, 1985
p. 2: Untitled, September 8, 1987 (see p. 151)
p. 6: Untitled, 1985 (see p. 137)
p. 12: Untitled, n.d. (see p. 118)

CONTENTS

INTRODUCTION

My Father, The Doodler
Nanette Vonnegut
6

ESSAY

The Remarkable Artwork of Kurt Vonnegut
Peter Reed
12

DRAWINGS & TEXTS

Self-portraits
21
Abstraction
26
Women
39
Letters
46
People
64
Faces
96
Looking at Things
126
Lines
133
Things
156
Words
170

MY FATHER, THE DOODLER

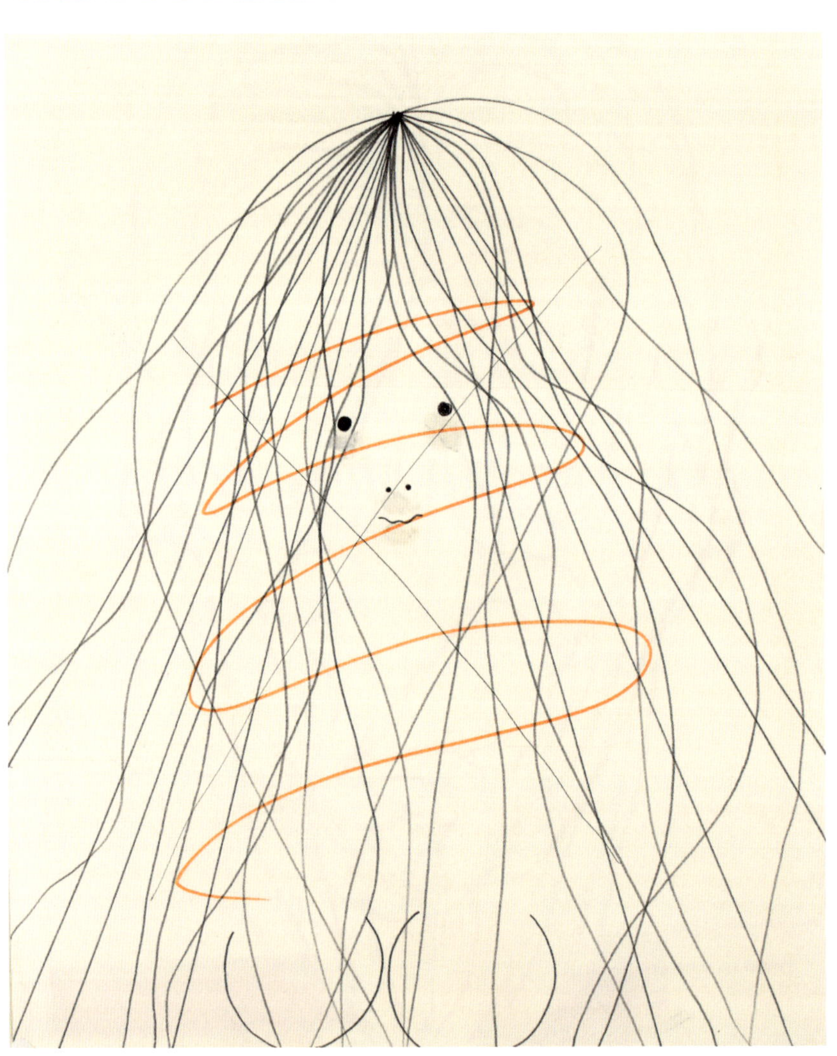

NANETTE VONNEGUT

My father once suggested that I make a piece of artwork and then burn it, as a spiritual exercise. I wanted to say, but didn't, "Go burn all that writing you did this morning!"

During one visit with me in New York City, my father sat down to finish a drawing he was working on. It was spread out on a coffee table and sprinkled with cigarette ashes. Without looking up, he said, "This isn't very good, is it?" I answered without hesitation, "Burn it, dad, it's no good!" Beaming in appreciation, he quietly said, "Yeah, you're right." He wadded up the drawing and dropped it on the floor, next to the trash can.

We were talking shop, and he was listening. He said he was tired of having to hit home runs all the time as a writer. A few days later he sent me a postcard: "Darling Daughter—I have always believed you to be a poet, so Please start writing poems, but *rhyme* them. No fair tennis without a net. Love—Dad"

About these drawings: I received them in two unwieldy shipments sometime in the mid-1990s, not long after I had ordered dad to burn his drawing. He called to make sure they had arrived safely; otherwise he had no advice as to what I might do with them. In the throes of child-rearing, I stored them in flat files in my studio and spent little time with them. Honestly, at the time, I thought myself a bona fide artist because I went to Art School. I thought dad should stay in his writing corner, where he belonged, and I would stay in mine.

Remembering my father and the house on Cape Cod where I grew up conjures up a cartoon tornado, a spinning funnel with dozens of floating Siamese cats, two dogs, a piano, a bucket of baby-blue paint, a grandfather clock, a garden hose, my mother wearing an apron, and my father holding a cigarette and a lit match.

My father was more than a writer: he was the guy who never wore socks with his off-white, banged-up sneakers, who rarely left the house and was very regular about disappearing into a forbidden part of the house called "the study." There were two doors you had to go through to get there. No one tried to pass through the second one. If you did, you'd turn to ash because the room was booby-trapped with something having to do with *creation*. My father had proven himself worthy to be in that room, although I always worried about what was happening to him in there. I could hear the rapid-fire rat-a-tat-tat-tat of his typewriter and knew he was trying to wrestle big thoughts onto small pieces of paper, rat-a-tat-tat-tat . . . tat . . . tat-tat-tat . . . At day's end, he emerged from his study and charged headlong toward the sound of my mother frantically cracking ice for his predinner cocktail.

The days my father got his hands dirty were happier days. With vigor and rhythm, he'd stomp a shovel into dirt with one flimsy, sneaker-shod foot to make way for bricks, shrubbery, and trees. Over a period of days, he built a large patio and turned our yard into a little Eden. To finish it off, he installed an old, eroded cement fountain he found at the dump and rigged it with a garden hose so water came burbling out of the lion's mouth. Whatever work he was doing, he kept the white noise of Muzak playing in the background.

When my father did leave the house, it was usually a trip to the dump, where he salvaged beautiful old planks of wood and slabs of marble. Into one plank he carved these words: "'Beware Of All Enterprises That Require New Clothes,' Thoreau," and turned it into a six-foot-long coffee table. He chiseled into marble the last words of Molly Bloom's soliloquy in James Joyce's *Ulysses*, "and his heart was going like mad and yes I said yes I will Yes." In the heat of carving, he often nicked himself. Amused by his own scabbed-up hands, he explained, "Jesus, that stuff was slippery and that blade was sharp!"

"Ye Shall Love One Another" was painted on the mantel of our dining room fireplace one day. The next day, "Go Love Without The Help of Anything On Earth" and "God Damn It, You've Got To Be Kind" showed up on other walls. The script was bold and elegant, lined in black and gold. My father's creativity inspired my older sister to follow suit. In the large, curving stairwell she painted an epic scene of Satan wrestling an angel down to the pits of hell. Simultaneously I wrote, "Shit, Fuckitty Shit" in black magic marker on my bedroom wall, copying my father's distinctive script.

Not long after my father died in 2007, I visited his childhood home in Indianapolis. His father, Kurt Vonnegut Sr., otherwise known as "Doc," designed and helped build the large, brick Craftsman/Art Deco–style house in 1923. As I walked through it, I noted my grandfather's artistry everywhere. I was struck by the beauty of a leaded-glass panel, set into the heavy, wooden front door, with their monogram, "K & E" (Kurt & Edith), cradled by a much larger, gently curved "V." There was something very familiar in Doc's lettering—it was the same lettering I was copying when I wrote "Shit, Fuckitty Shit" on my bedroom wall.

There were more similarly designed leaded-glass panels inside the house. The designs were elegant yet simple and complemented the Craftsman-style tile and woodwork throughout the house. I felt my grandfather's spirit in every nook and cranny. A tremendous wave of affection for my grandfather, for his *style*, washed over me. I had never known him until then. At the rear entryway, I found the concrete slab Doc had poured that displays five Vonnegut handprints, arranged vertically according to age. My father's baby handprint, at the bottom, includes the knitted cuff edge of his tiny sweater. Like the monogram on the front door, the handprints are dated 1923. The small wishing pond Doc created, which once held frogs and water lilies, and the remnants of an old garden in the big backyard were still there. I was electrified by the recognition that I had discovered my father's *origins*.

My father once said, "Where is home? I've wondered where home is, and realized, it's not Mars or someplace like that, it's Indianapolis when I was nine years old. I had a brother and a sister, a cat and a dog, and a mother and a father and uncles and aunts. And there's no way I can get there again."[1]

According to my father, his big brother Bernard, the science prodigy, designed weather systems in the basement of their home and sometimes sent rockets ripping through the dining room floor. I examined the dining room floor for telltale traces of mayhem, and was satisfied by a slight discoloration in one spot. I know little about my grandmother Edith, beyond the fact of her unhappiness, the legendary bathtub that she special-ordered to accommodate her extraordinary height, and her serious attempt at writing short stories for ladies' magazines to bring in much-needed money.

Doc taught his daughter, Alice, how to throw a pot and glaze it and the art of lettering, and he instilled in her a love of craft and design. There is a surviving piece of work they made together, displaying my grandfather's skill and Alice's budding promise as an artist. "Oscar Bug," painted on an old piece of battered wood, is a terrifically silly cross between a mouse, a June bug, and a lobster, wearing giant boots, striped underpants, and a big bow tie. I imagine my father as a young boy, standing at Alice's side, watching her create worlds out of mud and thin air and never wanting it to end.

"We do, doodley do, doodley do, doodley do . . ."

Alice grew up to be a private "Master Grand Doodler," creating art for her own pleasure and for her children in the form of family scrapbooks: black-and-white photos of her family, half-melted birthday candles, relics of a day, bordered by her distinctive, playful script, all in white ink on black paper. She painted decoratively on wood and usually included odd and poetic words. She once said, "Just because you have talent doesn't mean you have to do something with it."[2] This magnificent "underachiever" died before her time, at age forty-one, of breast cancer. My father quietly said to me while giving me a tour of Indianapolis in the early 1990s, "My sister would have been such a wonderful old woman."

My father also said this about Alice: "I had never told her so, but she was the person I had always written for. She was the secret of my technique. Any creation which has any wholeness and harmoniousness, I suspect, was made by an artist or inventor with an audience of one in mind."[3]

Doc was a "Master Grand Doodler" not just because he left his mark as an architect all over Indianapolis but also because he found time to create "Sidney the Seahorse," the first logo for the Children's Museum in Indianapolis. My grandfather was a "Master Grand Doodler" because he fashioned whimsical, original objects of beauty out of thin air and mud.

"What we must, muddily must, muddily must, muddily must; . . ."

In 1930, the house was lost to the Depression. By then, my father had downloaded everything he needed: Doc and Alice's visual whimsy, Bernard's mad-scientist's view from the clouds, his mother's wild idea that writing might be a means to make money, and the secret joy of doodling in a dreadfully serious world.

My own enchantment with art began in our living room on Cape Cod where all the art books were kept. It took all the strength I had to pull Al Hirschfeld's humongous book of pen and ink drawings off the middle shelf and onto my lap. I spent hours looking for the artist's daughter's name, "Nina," cleverly hidden in the drawings. More than that, the characters he drew were so animated that they welcomed me into their lives. I kept going back to visit them. I cannot think of Hirschfeld without thinking of my father. I imagine he sat me on his lap once, flipped through this art book, page-by-page, saying, "See darling? This is Stan Laurel and Oliver Hardy. They are my angels." I reached for the next-fattest art book, Paul Klee, and then I found William Blake. I would've reached for anything. Those were the books that were there, and for better or worse, they made me want to be an artist.

My father believed in Art and in his dog. Wherever he went, his tick-riddled, shaggy mutt Sandy was with him. Whether it was music, literature, theater, or the visual arts, he believed practicing the arts saved lives. He once told me that he thought people worked out their neuroses through art. I thought recounting the death and destruction of World War II was a bit more than working out a neurosis. What I saw growing up was a man fighting for his life, and to keep food on the table.

"We are broke!" were the three words I heard my father repeat regularly, over the years. The words were like a fire drill, usually late at night, intended for my mother's ears only. I could hear the alarm through the radiator hole in my bedroom floor. The next morning, the house was always miraculously intact.

There was just one instance that I can remember when my father traded art for money. In the early 1960s, he was commissioned to make a large sculpture for a cocktail lounge wall at Logan Airport. The assembly of the sculpture took place in our kitchen, since the thirty-foot-long sculpture would never have made it through the tiny doors and hallways of our ancient, labyrinthine house. *Comet* was made out of rods of bent steel with a large cement orb jammed on one end, to represent a comet. I remember a lot of swearing and everyone staying clear as he and a friend maneuvered the thing out the door. The project inspired little joy, mainly the promise of $600. But not long after, we piled into the station wagon to go see *Comet* bolted to a wall in the cocktail lounge. He was as pleased as I have ever seen him.

Dad thought being a full-time visual artist would have been much more fun than being a writer, even if it meant lopping off a finger or two. "And may I say parenthetically that my own means of making a living is essentially clerical, and hence tedious and constipating. Intruders, no matter how ill-mannered or stupid or dishonest, are as refreshing as the sudden breakthrough of sunbeams on a cloudy day. The making of pictures is to writing what laughing gas is to the Asian influenza."[4]

I believe my father forgot about the War when he doodled.

"Muddily do, muddily do, muddily do, muddily do, . . ."

Saul Steinberg was a friend and neighbor of my father's on Long Island and happened to be the artist I admired more than any other, living or dead. In the summer of 1975, my father arranged for a studio visit for the two of us. I was relieved to hear from dad that Steinberg didn't talk much, which meant I wouldn't have to be clever, that I could just look. Steinberg was quiet but welcoming; his hands stayed firmly planted in his pockets and his smile was a steady, crooked line. He was compact and square, except for his round glasses. The studio was a cavernous, expanded piece of his artwork; it was clean, white, and full of gorgeous trickery. At one point on the tour, I thought I was looking at a drafting table, except everything appeared slightly thick and slanted. In fact, it was a carved wooden replica of a drafting table. The ink bottle, the stacks of paper, the pens, and brushes were all carved out of wood, painted, and glued down. This mixed-media piece was so exquisitely executed and so delicately funny, tears welled up in my eyes in gratitude.

My father seemed unusually quiet and deferential in Steinberg's company. On our drive home, he admitted Steinberg made him feel stupid. But the respect they had for one another was palpable and absolutely mutual. I felt something *good* was agitating my father; a new bar had been set. Stupid or not, he was ready to play with ideas, line, and color, like his pal, Saul.

Had my father been granted two lifetimes, I have no doubt he would have mastered some aspect of the visual arts. And he would have cursed it and wished he had chosen to be a poet instead.

When my father admired a work of art, he shared it. He was never predictable or stuffy about it. The work of art could be a joke involving bird poop, or Goldie Hawn dancing on *Rowan & Martin's Laugh-In*, or an art book like *Amphigorey* by Edward Gorey. We all gave it to each other on Christmas of 1972. Like my father, Gorey crossed into very dark, hilarious territory, drawing demented-looking children in black ink, using a few choice words that, on the surface, were not disturbing, but whose juxtaposition with the drawings was something new, something brilliant, and quietly shocking. Though I never heard him say so, I think Gorey left his mark on my father.

Not long after my father died, I looked at the drawings he had given me again and was thunderstruck by how good they are. My favorite one is a self-portrait created by one, continuous, fat, squiggly line. I see hints of blueprints, tile work, leaded-glass windows, William Blake, Paul Klee, Saul Steinberg, Al Hirschfeld, Edward Gorey, my mother's wasp waist, cats and dogs. I see my father, at age four, forty, and eighty-four, doodling his heart out. I see Doc, Edith, Alice, and Bernard, smiling. I see myself in that house in Indianapolis, thanking them, while my six-year-old father, future Master Grand Doodler, streaks out the back door to play hide-and-seek with his neighborhood friends in the twilight of his little Eden.

"Until we bust, bodily bust, bodily bust, bodily bust."[5]

1. "The World According to Kurt," *The Globe and Mail*, Toronto, October 11, 2005.
2. J. C. Gabel, "The Melancholia of Everything," interview with Kurt Vonnegut, *Stop Smiling*, issue 27: *Ode to the Midwest*, August 2006.
3. Kurt Vonnegut, *Slapstick, or, Lonesome no More!* (New York: Delacorte Press/S. Lawrence, 1976), 15 (prologue).
4. Kurt Vonnegut, *Fates Worse Than Death: An Autobiographical Collage of the 1980s* (New York: G. P. Putnam's Sons, 1991), 45.
5. Kurt Vonnegut, *Cat's Cradle* (New York: Random House, 1963), chap. 119.

THE REMARKABLE ARTWORK OF KURT VONNEGUT

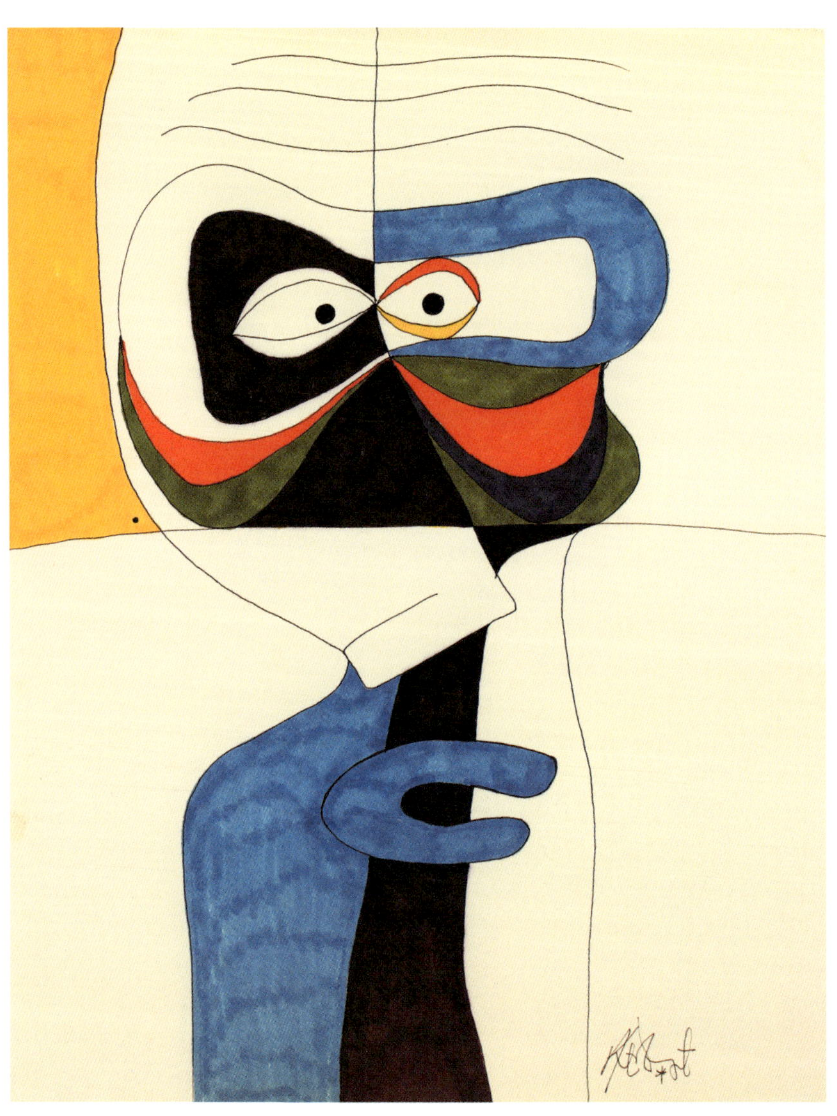

ESSAY BY PETER REED

When I first met Kurt Vonnegut in 1972, soon after I had published a book about his first six novels, I was unaware of his creativity in the graphic arts. Soon after, he began using profile drawings, like the one at the end of *Breakfast of Champions* (1973), as a kind of signature. In the following years, we talked about art at various times. I remember that we touched on the Armory Exhibition, Paul Klee, Georges Braque (whom he liked), and Willem de Kooning (whom he didn't much like). We discussed his essay on Jackson Pollock, "Jack the Dripper," when it appeared in *Esquire* in 1983. About that time was when I saw early drawings he had given to his close friend Loree Rackstraw.

In later years we met a couple of times in the Lexington, Kentucky, studio of Joe Petro III, who silkscreened drawings Kurt had made on sheets of acetate. I watched Kurt work in this medium in his apartment in Northampton, Massachusetts, in October 2000, when his exhibition, "The Art of Kurt Vonnegut," was mounted at the R. Michelson Gallery. My interest in his drawings led to my writing a couple of short essays about them.

The drawing of the locket bearing the "Serenity Prayer", slung between Montana Wildhack's breasts in *Slaughterhouse-Five* (1969), is the first appearance of Vonnegut's artwork in one of his novels. *Breakfast of Champions*, however, with its whimsical drawings of everything from beavers to cobras, first drew attention to Vonnegut as a graphic artist. Montana's pendant and the *Breakfast of Champions* drawings seemed whimsical, part of the flaunting of "serious" novelistic rules that he often enjoyed. Yet Vonnegut had been painting and drawing for many years previously, from landscapes and seascapes in oils in the 1950s when he lived on Cape Cod, to doodles in the margins of manuscripts of his early narratives. None of the early landscapes have been shown publicly, but examples of his doodling can be seen in *Armageddon in Retrospect* (2008).

The *Breakfast of Champions* drawings came as a surprise at the time, first as being an unusual addition to a novel, but also for their frank, seemingly naïve, and simply funny qualities. The drawings frequently emphasize the ludicrous disparities that often exist between words as signifiers and what they signify. Others simply function as embellishments or even punchlines of jokes. In their almost childlike simplicity of line, they have a certain ironic propriety in a novel where the central event is an arts fair. Above all, they are part of—and draw attention to—the guileless, even adolescent, perspective from which Vonnegut deconstructs and demystifies American culture and society in this novel.

Vonnegut continued drawing, frequently making doodles with a felt-tip pen on pages of discarded manuscript. From these he evolved what he called "felt-tip calligraphs," abstract faces drawn with felt-tip pens.[1] He was invited to enter a show where artwork by writers, including Norman Mailer and Tennessee Williams (both accomplished painters), were exhibited. He said, "I've drawn all my life, on the edges of manuscripts and things like that. But I started thinking, 'This is the amateur approach.'... So I decided to take myself seriously as an artist... My father was an artist, my grandfather was an artist, and I have three children who are accomplished artists."[2]

Larger drawings ensued, often similar in style to those drawn on manuscript pages, but making use of color. Some thirty of these were exhibited in a one-man show at the Margo Fiden Gallery in Greenwich Village, which opened on October 15, 1983. The drawings in the present collection that are dated were made mainly from 1985 to 1987. Significantly, this is the period when, having published *Galapagos* in 1985, Vonnegut was at work on *Bluebeard* (1987), the novel about painter Rabo Karabekian. The collection comes from some 150 drawings Vonnegut gave to his daughter Nanette and her husband, Scott Prior, both of them accomplished artists.

These drawings were made on heavy paper, or Bristol board, measuring either 26 by 19 inches or 18 by 14 inches. Vonnegut drew with thick magic markers of various colors, with black usually used for outlining and color to fill in. As in his later work silkscreened by Joe Petro, he made extensive use of the white space of the paper or board. There is an obvious kinship between these drawings and the earlier faces drawn on manuscript pages, although the kinds of self-caricature profiles that he was to elaborate on repeatedly in the later silkscreened work are conspicuously absent here. The collection of images here, many never exhibited or published, covers a remarkably broad range of subjects.

The technique he was to use in his later graphics had its origin in a request by an old friend from Vonnegut's days as a public relations writer at General Electric. In 1993 Ollie Lyon, once a fellow "flack" at G.E., who had gone on to reside in Lexington, Kentucky, and had become chair of the Development Council for Midway College, invited Vonnegut to assist in the dedication of a college library. Vonnegut was asked to perform one of his "How to Succeed in a Job Like Mine" evenings as a fund-raiser for the new library. Vonnegut additionally created one of his profile self-portraits for a poster advertising the event. Here began his connection with Lexington artist Joe Petro III, who silkscreened Vonnegut's graphic for the poster. Subsequently, Vonnegut and Petro continued their collaboration, with Vonnegut producing images on large sheets of acetate, which Petro then silkscreened onto 30-by-22–inch sheets.[3] Faces may be the most frequent subjects in Vonnegut's art. Once, as we walked in New York, he remarked that one can recognize someone at a distance when the face appears as little more than the three dots of eyes and mouth. "The human face is the most interesting of all forms," he told an interviewer. "So I've just made abstracts of all these faces. Because that's how we go through life, reading faces very quickly."[4] His curly-haired profile self-portrait, used in its simplest form to accompany his signature, but also subject to many elaborations, remains his most familiar image. As already mentioned, it does not appear in this collection, though there are full-face self-portraits that are in a similar style.

One face that does appear here is a surprise—a self-portrait that is a rare example of realism (p. 24). He is smoking the inevitable cigarette, dressed in suit jacket and tie, leaning forward, as if at a podium. He seems pensive, a suggestion of skepticism in the expression, listening to a questioner perhaps. It represents a pretty chubby Vonnegut, and is anything but flattering! Worth noting is that while most of his drawings were spontaneously composed with marker, particularly the later images on acetate, this one has been first roughed out in pencil. Two other self-portraits are characteristically humorous. In one he appears as a brightly colored clown face (p. 22), while another is an ingenious creation of one continuous line, weaving together artist and flowerpot (p. 25). Kurt would have enjoyed playing with that kind of puzzle.

Closest to that self-portrait in its realism is the profile of a man with a high forehead, glasses, and longish hair or a wig (p. 97). The half-veiled eye seems to look down and slightly askance, an expression perhaps condescending or guarded, giving the impression of a rather imperious intellectual. The unusual red background adds weight, or a touch of grandeur, and to me there seems a hint of the Martin Droeshout engraving of William Shakespeare or some other historical portrait. The nose, mouth, mustache, and eye-bags all become purely geometric (as opposed to the more realistic head, eye, and glasses). Sharply colored, they draw the observer's attention to the subject's eye. There are in effect two profiles here, one that curves down from the hairline to the eyebrow, and one that mounts nose, mustache, and glasses, but ends abruptly where the vertical line divides the head. Double profiles appear elsewhere among Vonnegut's faces.

The portrait on page 99 appears to be one of the earlier, less abstract drawings. It is a step away from the realism of the self-portrait, almost cartoonish in its strong lines and simplified features. Again, there has been preliminary sketching in pencil, which is not found in his later work, and also far more color and color blending, particularly in the bushy hair. The busy-ness and heavy coloring evident here are characteristics not found in the more spare later works, such as those in the Vonnegut-Petro portfolio. Nevertheless, certain features seen here are characteristic of the later work. For example, the face can be seen as two faces: a three-quarter view, with a central dividing vertical creating a face in profile. The horizon line in the background is a frequent feature of the later work, as is the heavy frame but with content appearing outside of it. The multicolored, checkerboard areas at the top of the forehead, in the eyebags, and at the neck and throat reappear. They add an abstract geometric element to the semi-realistic face. Elsewhere one sees Vonnegut do the reverse, inserting curlicued human features into geometric, "cubist" drawings.

When I watched Vonnegut draw, he began with a vertical line, and then a horizontal one. It was almost as if he were about to draw a graph. That approach is most apparent in those drawings one might loosely call "cubist," where vertical and horizontal lines bisect the image. (He once told me he was intrigued by what the cubists did in "breaking up the chaotic into geometric forms, pleasing shapes."[5] The faces seen on pages 100 and 106 are key examples of this technique and are almost identical. There are differences in lines, however, as well as in coloring and background. There is the familiar creation of a profile within a full face, and a rather ambiguous doubling of lips and chin. Here the geometric effect is emphasized by the triangles against the left side of the face, but also counterbalanced by the curls around the eyes and nostril.

The geometric obviously fascinated Vonnegut at this stage, and the works on pages 108–111 use intersecting lines to create rectangular patterns without actually treating the face in the "cubist" fashion of the drawings on pages 100 and 106. The drawings on pages 108 and 109 were made back to back, and each shows through the other. Perhaps that captures Peeping Tom on page 108 spying on the bare-breasted damsel on page 109! The squares surrounding those heads create the effect of the subjects being seen through a window or opening of some kind. Vonnegut's dating of this pair, November 19, 1985 (a week after his sixty-third birthday), emphasizes their connection. While quite similar, the piece on page 111 is starker in line and lacks color. The tall hat might suggest a chef, whereas the costumes of the previous two look medieval. Vonnegut does not use the kind of tight grid of squares seen here in his later works, but he often uses a few colored rectangles to emphasize space.

One unusual portrait is the striking female profile with a rainbow of colored bands across the eye (p. 103). Is there not something suggestive of ancient Egyptian masks with their painted eyes? The bands call attention to the eye, which is looking sideways, toward the viewer. One band turns down, cuts across the others, and leads into the nose, reinforcing the profile, whose strength is emphasized by its broadening dark brown coloring and also by the space behind it. The red lips counterbalance the eye. In essence there is still a basic vertical intersected by a horizontal here, but that structure is subsumed by the grace of line and color, making this one of the softest and most appealing drawings in this set.

Vonnegut's sense of humor, which shows up in many of his drawings, is evident in the almost identical pair with a woman in profile exposing one breast (pages 40 and 41). The sideways look might be saying, "How's that?" These two are about as identical in line as could be done freehand, yet there is a striking difference in expression. The one on page 40 appears stark, with a straight-ahead line from the eye to the asterisk. In her companion there is softer coloring, the line from the eye points upward, and she has red lips and soft contour lines in her face. The line from the eye does make a difference; her upward look and red lips make the expression more inviting. In a later work, titled "Astronomy," the line to an asterisk helps suggest an astronomer looking at a star. In this pair it may mostly be whimsy. Kurt had fun playing with the variations of devices he hit on from time to time.

There is a pair of nudes in this collection. One (p. 44), viewed from the rear, is perhaps a precursor of *Wasp Waist,* a silkscreen in several colors in the Vonnegut-Petro collection. The weight of the image is in the lower third, with its dark red floor, the generous gluteals, and the shading and black outline of buttock and thigh. The movement flows upward following the dark spine, through the heart-shaped back, to the tiny black head. The architecture follows the familiar formula, the vertical being the curving line of the backbone. There is a grace of line, particularly in the upper back and arms. This nude seems to celebrate yet mock the genre at the same time.

More deconstruction of the nude genre is seen on page 45. Angular hips, distended abdomen, spiderlike navel, and pincerlike sagging breasts replace the grace of line and proportion characteristic of nude studies. The tiny alien head seems to watch the viewer, whose eye is drawn to the weight and color of abdomen and shaded pelvic triangle. The pattern of this piece, with its black background and jigsaw puzzle lines, adds to its rather forbidding tone. This drawing is at once comic but unfriendly and vaguely misogynistic.

Two other nude sketches, on pages 66 and 67, are much lighter in tone despite sharing some similar characteristics. The similar figures have enlarged, pregnant bellies and heavy thighs, small upper bodies, and scarcely have heads. In each the figure carries a swath of cloth, and the posture and the effect of the swiftly drawn sketches evoke a light, even celebratory tone.

Vonnegut draws a hooded, cloaked figure in many variations. The figure on page 65 might be a monk or servant carrying a plate with an apple. The frame within the borders of the work reappears here, and the stripes and the large amount of color are noteworthy. The cloak of the figure on page 72 is magnificently colored and patterned, set off by its dramatic black and gold front. The posture, the grandeur of the cloak, and even the abstract blankness of the face, seem to radiate assurance. No doubt Vonnegut had fun with that cloak. On pages 69 and 71 the hooded figure has become pure abstraction, although the former appears to depict a couple looking down at a swaddled child. The liquid lines of the minimal figures, looking somewhat like cartoon ghosts, are set off by the rectangular lines of the frame on page 69 and the furniture on page 71. The frame seems to make the figure in the upper right of page 69 both a participant and a face in a picture, a reminder of the self-reflexivity of much of Vonnegut's work (graphic and written). It is art that declares and embraces its own artifice, and also sometimes pokes fun at it.

The five faces beginning on page 79 will come as a surprise to those acquainted with Vonnegut's abstractions and doodles, or with the Vonnegut-Petro catalogue. These five faces seem more conventional, but nevertheless feature typical Vonnegut traits. For all his minimalism, he enjoyed playing with detail, such as the hat on page 80, whose rectangular patterns are deployed elsewhere. The curled nostrils seen on pages 79, 80, and 82 also are familiar, as are the eyes of the faces on pages 79 and 80. In one of his stories, Vonnegut mentions "deedleballs," and what fun he must have had drawing those on page 82. Three of these characters appear to be historical, judging from their costumes. Yet characteristic traits, like curlicue noses and the frame-within-a-frame setting, emphasize artifice, participating in the sort of post-modern interplay of genres, usually with humorous effect, found in Vonnegut's fiction.

Five of the drawings display various ways of depicting groups of people (pp. 73–77). The composition of the first of these depends on the color of the one curved neck and the black dot eyes. But while the five mouths smile cheerily and there are ten eyes, the drawing teases us. The eyes' placement calls attention to a sixth head created by their overlapping, or to different possible numbers of eyes per head. There is more fun on page 74, where the middle of the three eyes might be shared by either profile. There are three eyes and two profiles on page 77 also, where the dramatic mouths suggest masks of comedy and tragedy. It is evident that Vonnegut is concerned with pattern in both of these works, and that is also apparent in the 1987 drawing on page 76. The figures' comic expressions are created chiefly by placement of the black eyeballs. From left to right they might be designated Indignation, Circumspection, and Accusation. Outside this little drama is the more dramatic pattern of the composition, emphasized by the bold contrast of black, red, and yellow. Page 75 harks back to the "cubism" seen earlier and also is reminiscent of the silkscreen *Cheops* of the Vonnegut-Petro collection. This drawing seems to portray Youth and Age, or perhaps Comedy and Tragedy, the one emboldened by ruby lips, the other anguished with heavy eye bags and mournful mouth.

The still life of a window with flowerpot and window shade (p. 157) resembles some later work in its simplified realism. Strings, and things hanging from strings like the shade pull and ornaments, appear in a number of his works. Some drawings, reminiscent of Calder, are made up largely of "things on strings," including parts of faces (see pp. 153–155). Vonnegut also seems to have enjoyed suggesting perspective in the flowerpot drawing. Whereas his early work mostly shows a straight horizontal line or horizon, later works may show a recess or corner, which here provides the effect of a frame within the overall image. The attractively blue sea and the black shade provide strong horizontal bands, mediated by the verticals of the flower and the strings. It makes a friendly, balanced scene.

Vonnegut made several drawings of apparently solid shapes with parts gauged or scooped out, as on page 127. (A later graphic has a roundly curved vase with a segment cut out, which he punningly titled *Vasectomy*.) In this one the shapes are abstract, but the cutouts with their shading, as well as the dark background seen through the cutouts, give the impression of depth and solidity. The smaller right-hand figure, presumably a similar object at a distance, adds to the sense of depth. The blue barbell-like gadget seems necessary to a figure that might seem too static and blank without it.

Here and there in this collection one may see echoes of earlier artists, such as the cubists and Calder already mentioned, or of Joan Miró, Paul Klee, or Georges Braque, whom he called "a special hero." Like his architect father and grandfather, both also artists, these painters were part of the culture he was raised in, and their influence was absorbed like the oxygen he breathed. Vonnegut saw no point in avoiding their influence if he saw in their work something he wanted to try. "The notion that someone can make a big discovery and then nobody can make use of it would be very poor science," he said, letting his science training speak.[6] Yet Vonnegut's drawings are scarcely derivative, and they are wildly various.

Over the years, Vonnegut used more subjects in his art works than have been mentioned here. There are faces made of many thin descending lines (e.g., pp. 136 and 137), which contrast with the bold-lined faces and groups noted earlier. There are geometric abstracts that play with patterns, some resembling mosaics, and others with curlicue conch-like designs. There are swirling abstract figures, some even resembling stylized letters of the alphabet, attractively colored and luxuriant in their loops and curves. Many are essentially doodles, but they are elevated by their sense of design and color. They illustrate beautifully a creative mind at play.

As we have mentioned, Vonnegut began his collaboration with Joe Petro III, in 1993. He drew on acetate, which he bought in twelve-foot rolls. Once I watched him cut off about a three foot square, put it on an easel, and go to work with his long, slightly jerky lines. He still enjoyed experimenting with a particular pattern or image. One was the drawing of grained wood, such as floorboards, which he said he enjoyed and suggested I try. Joe Petro silkscreened many of the acetate drawings, sometimes with color variations, and made prints of them that are still available. Among the later works were several that referred to his writing, with titles like *Trout in Cohoes* and *Tralfamadore #1*. *Gilded Cage* refers to Kilgore Trout's parrot Bill, who wisely stays put when the cage door is opened. Other titles evoke ironic interplay with the illustration, as with *Prozac*, *Egyptian Architect*, and *Astronomy*. The use of titles and references to the fiction add an extra dimension to those works.

Vonnegut found that writing came less easily. *Galapagos* (1985) presented scientific as well as literary challenges, and his labors with *Timequake* (1997) extended for several years. Painting, on the other hand, he found fun. As he described it, writing is labor, and the writer's reward arrives when he or she hands the manuscript to the editor and says, "It's yours." The painter, he said, "gets his rocks off while actually doing the painting. The act itself is agreeable."[7] When he spoke about drawing, it was always the sheer joy of it that he emphasized. I believe he hoped to gain some recognition as an artist, but he never had the kind of stake in it that he did in his writing, where, in his last years, he feared a falling off in his abilities as well as his energy. Vonnegut's career remains one of the longest and most productive in American literature, extending nearly half a century. Yet his artwork shows that he retained the imaginative playfulness and the almost adolescent undercutting of pomposity and established convention that characterizes *Cat's Cradle* and many other of his novels.

The great value of this collection is that Vonnegut's artwork gives us another perspective on his restless imagination and his creative genius. So far his art has drawn relatively little critical attention, but in time it may lead to a deeper understanding of his personality and added insight into his fiction. There are constraints in writing that even the iconoclastic Vonnegut felt, but in his art he seems wholly uninhibited. Many of the faces have tight, sucked-in mouths and weary eye-bags, reminding us that for all the joy he may have found in art, Vonnegut's life was extraordinarily burdened by death, loss, and suffering. Obviously, as Nanette shows in her beautiful tribute to her Doodler Dad, she feels close to him as she looks at these pictures. And I must say I do, too, in a way different from reading his words. With the artwork we were always more interactive, more relaxed, perhaps, than we both were when talking about his writing. Though not very talented, I drew cartoons for him and seasonal greeting cards with figures from his work, at least one of which he actually framed. He thought that was fun, and on the last picture he ever sent referred to me as a "fellow artist," which was a charitable exaggeration. I hope that others viewing this book will also feel the presence of a man who was as abundant in his kindness and generosity as he was in his remarkable talent.

1 Two doodles on manuscript and one example of felt-tip calligraphy are reproduced in Peter Reed, "Kurt Vonnegut," in *Dictionary of Literary Biography: Documentary Series*, Volume 3 (Detroit: Bruccoli Clarke/Gale Research, 1983), 321–76.
2 Anonymous art review, *Horizon*, October 10, 1980, 5.
3 An account of Lyon's role in introducing Vonnegut and Petro, their working relationship, and descriptions of some of the artwork appear in the 1993 interview and "The Graphics of Kurt Vonnegut" in Peter Reed and Marc Leeds, *The Vonnegut Chronicles*, Westport, CT: Greenwood Press, 1996, 35–44, 205–222.
4 Telephone interview of Kurt Vonnegut by Peter Reed, October 18, 1995.
5 Ibid.
6 Telephone interview of Joe Petro III by Peter Reed, October 16, 1995.
7 Interview of Vonnegut, October 18, 1995.

I myself make pictures from time to time. I actually had a one-person show of drawings a few years back . . . in Greenwich Village, not because my pictures were any good but because people had heard of me.

SELF-PORTRAITS

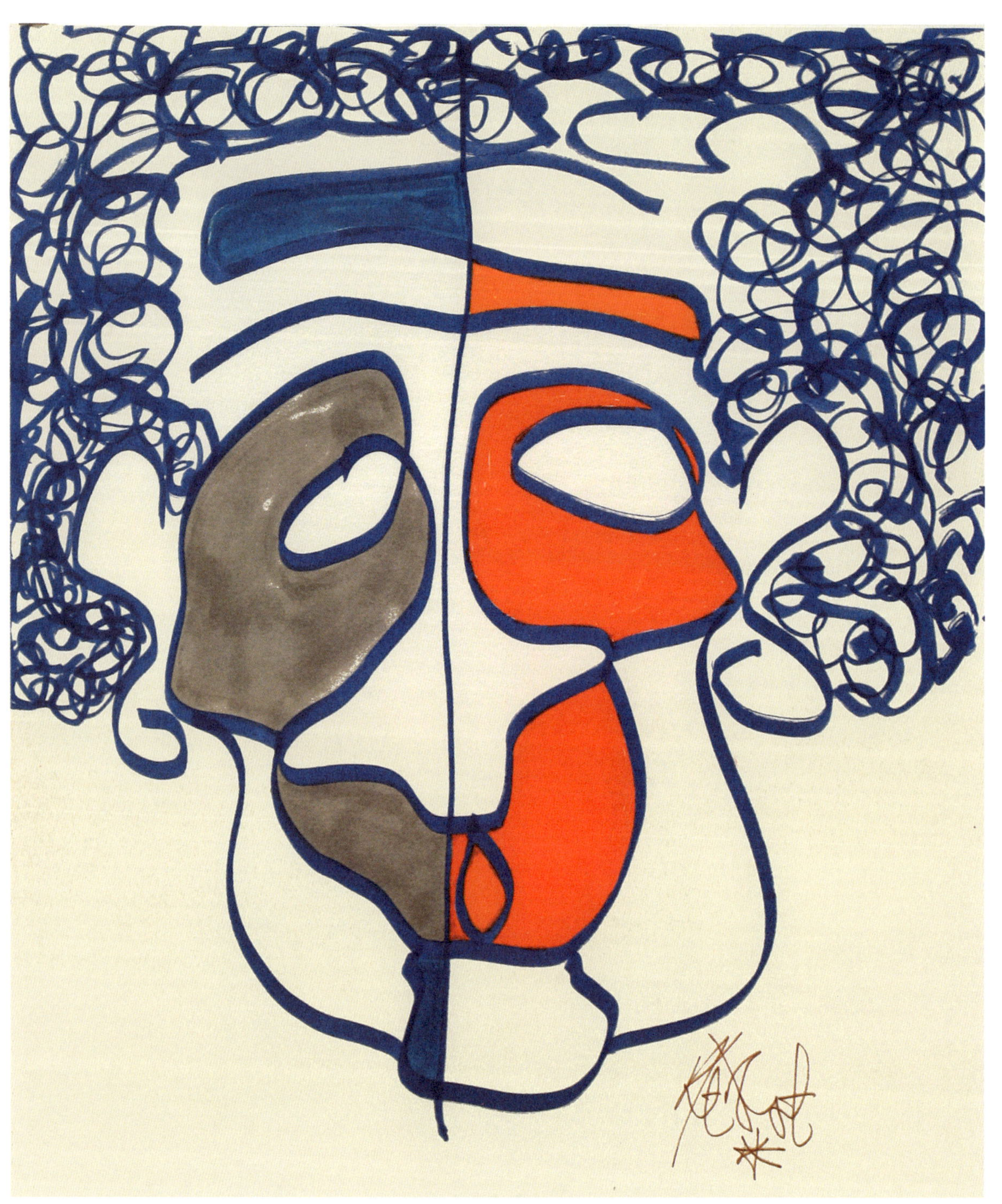

Self-portrait, n.d.

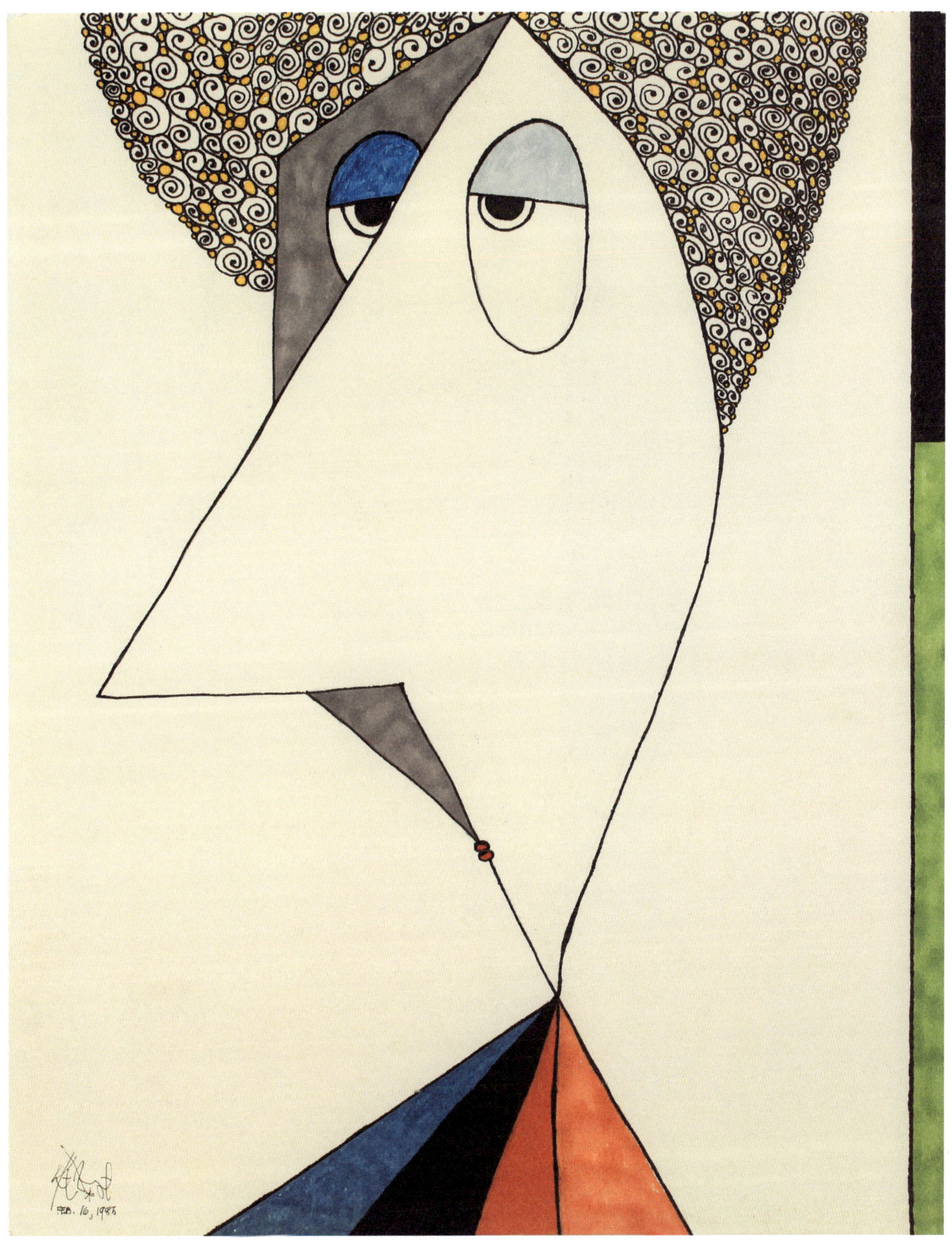

Self-portrait, February 16, 1985

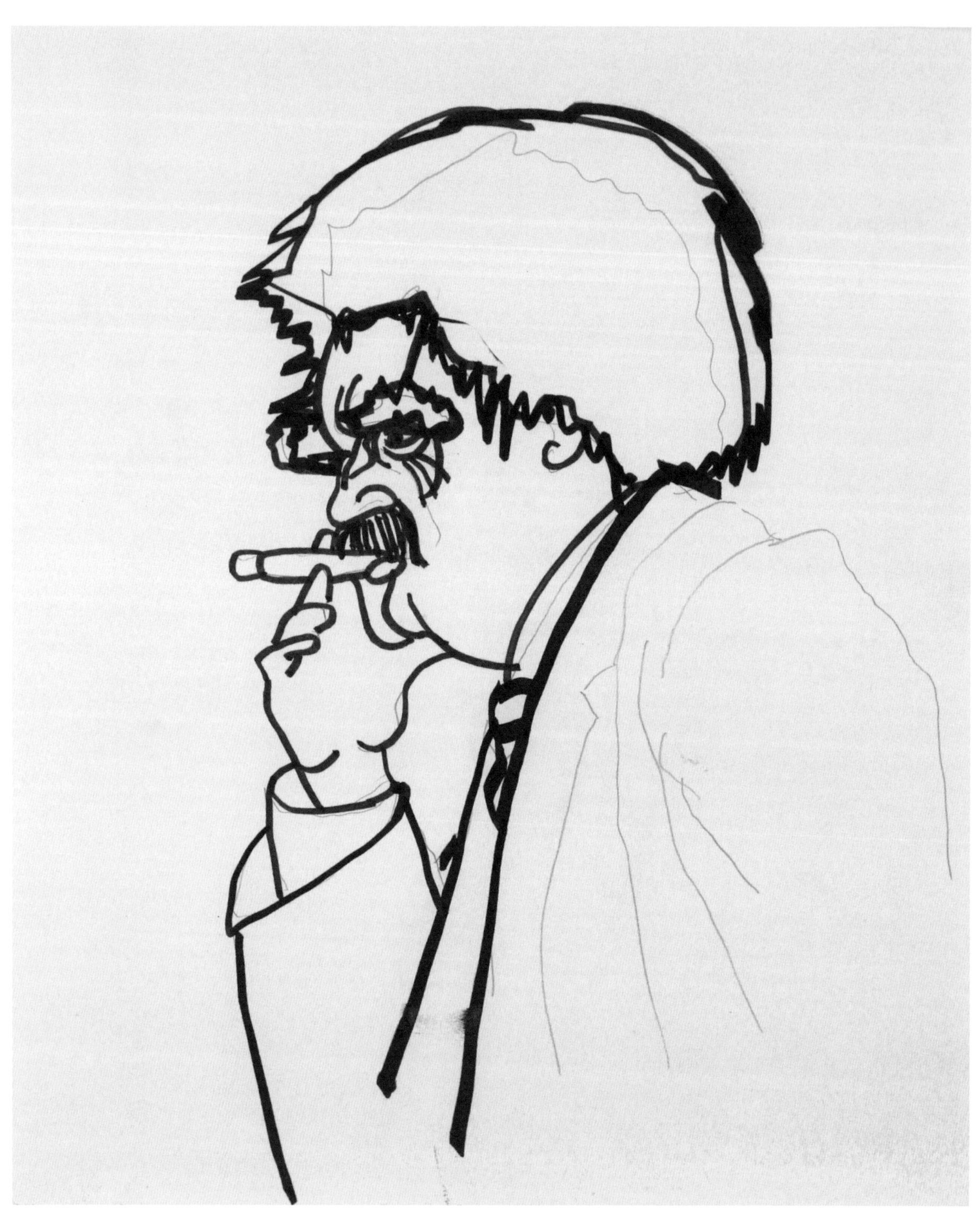

Self-portrait, n.d.

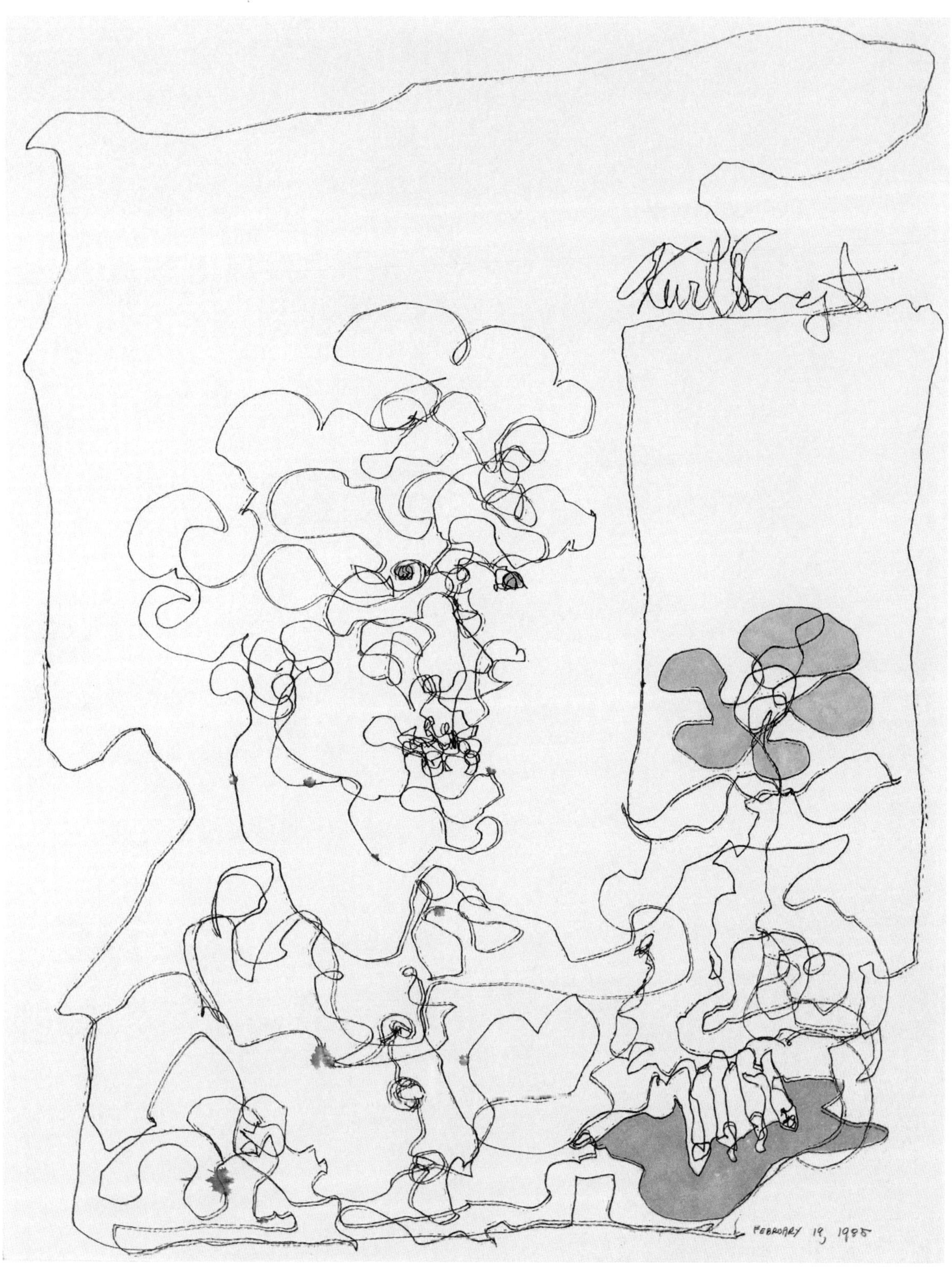

Self-portrait, February 19, 1985

The canvas, which is to say the unconscious, considers [the painter's] first stroke, and then it tells the painter's hand how to respond to it—with a shape of a certain color and texture at that point there. And then, if all is going well, the canvas ponders this addition and comes up with further recommendations. The canvas becomes a Ouija board.

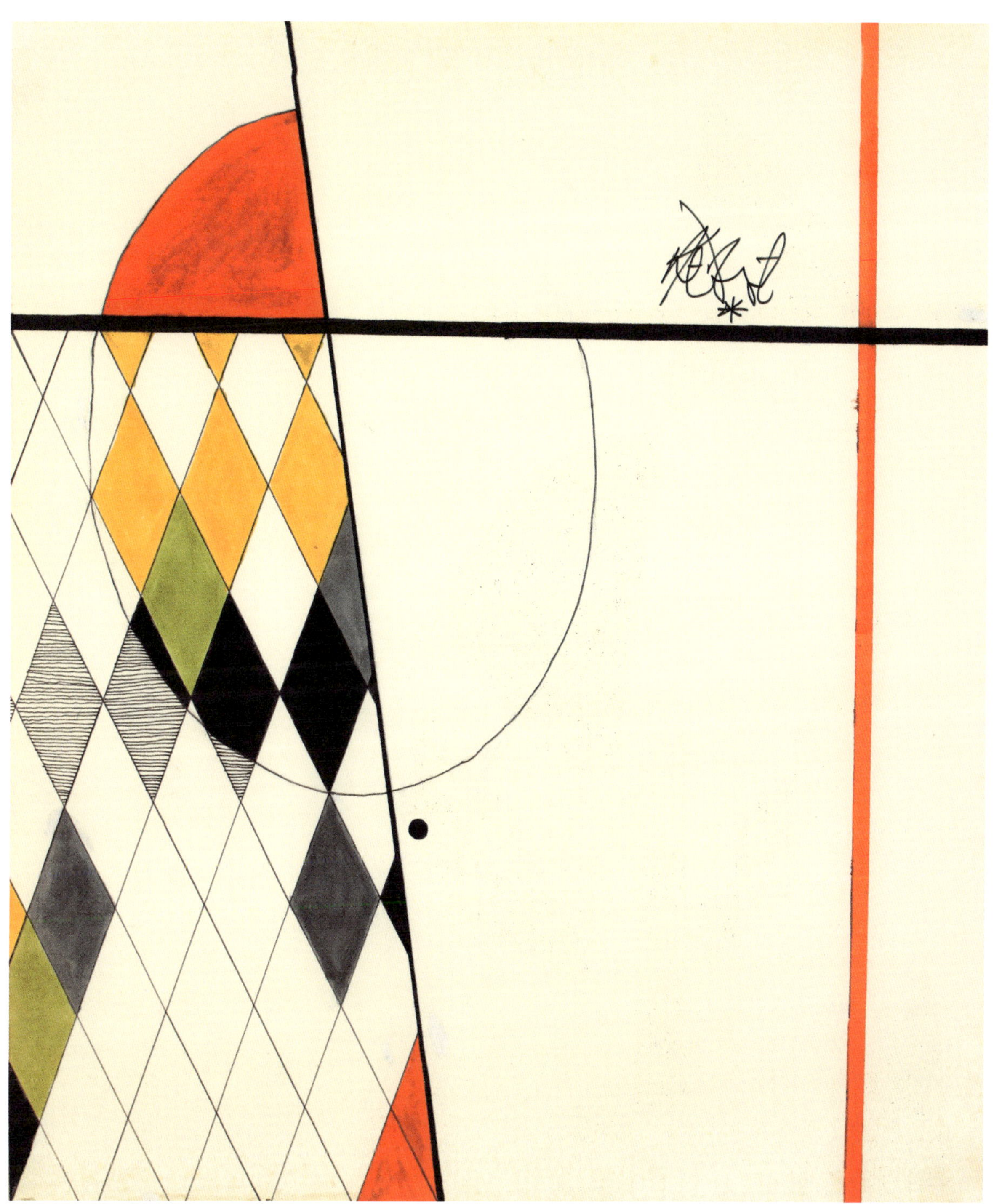

Untitled, n.d.

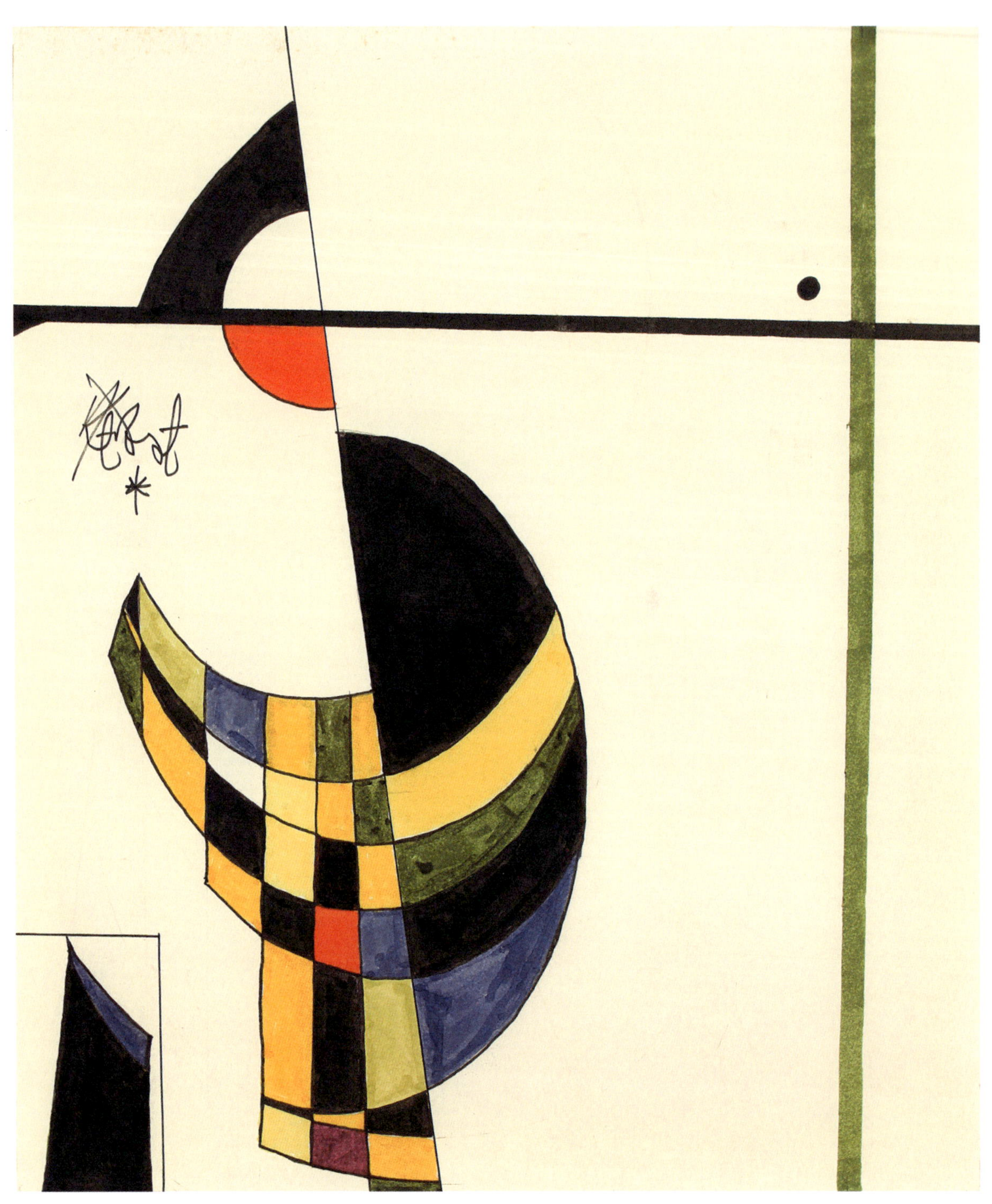

Untitled, n.d.

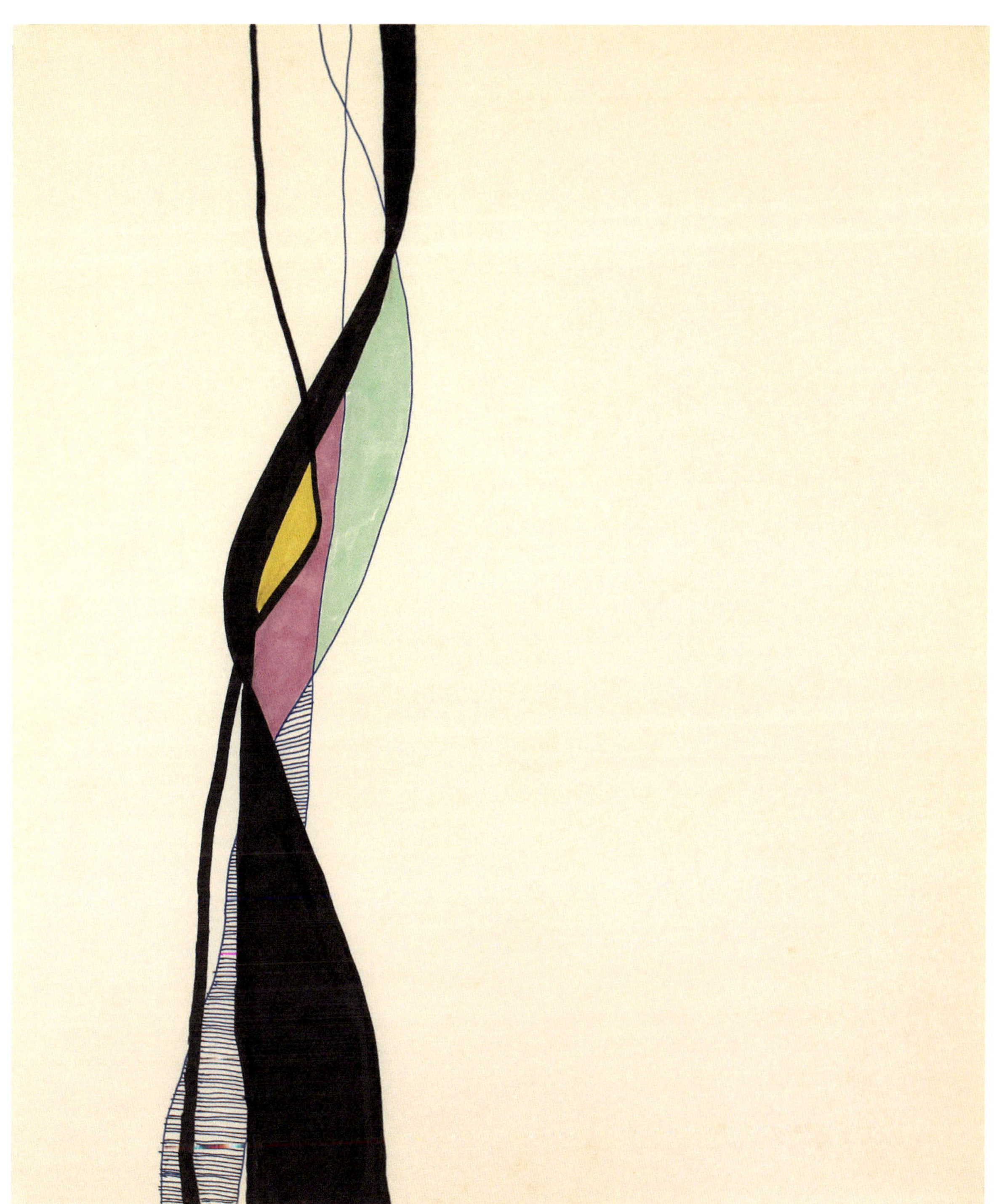

Untitled, n.d.

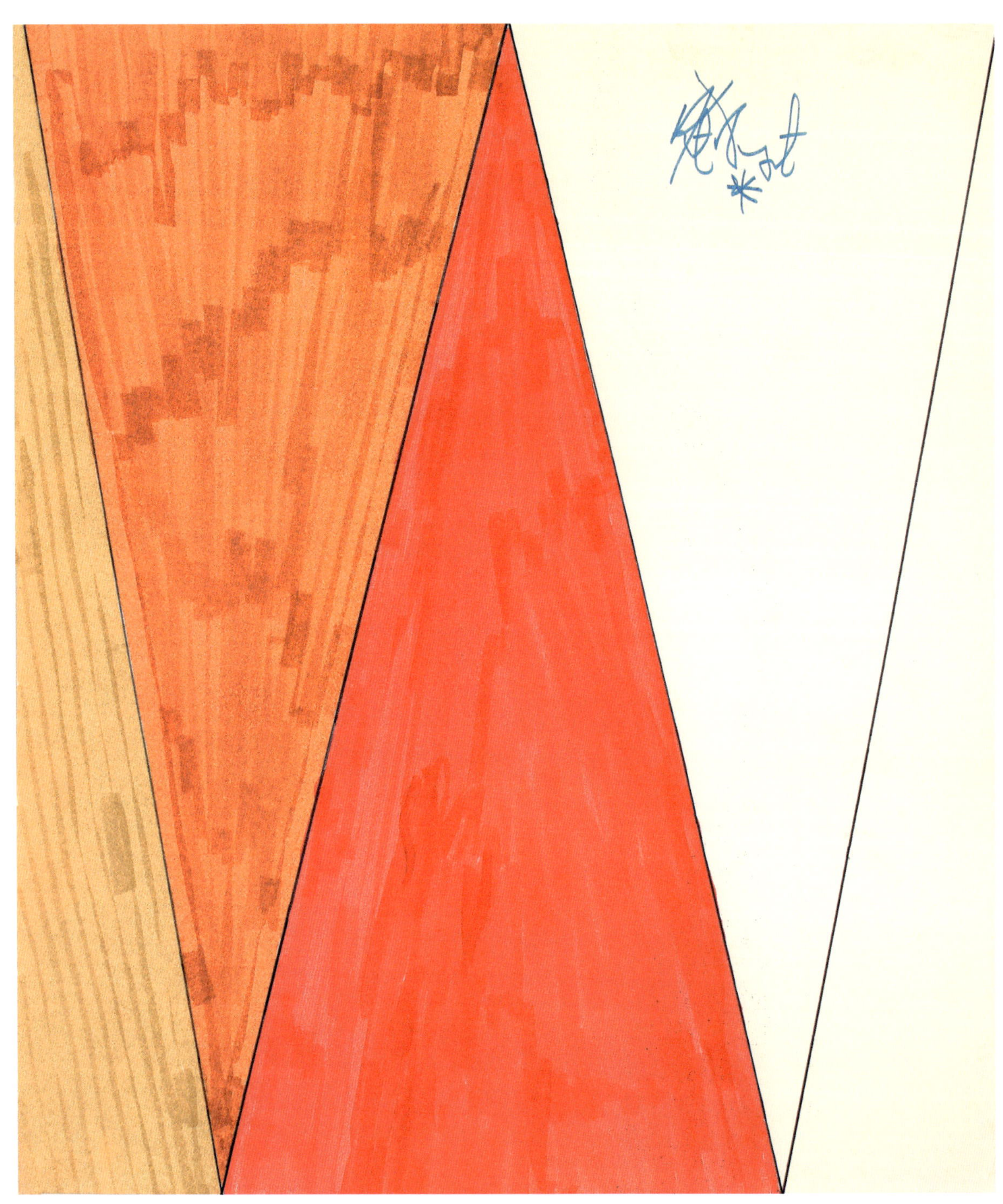

Untitled, n.d.

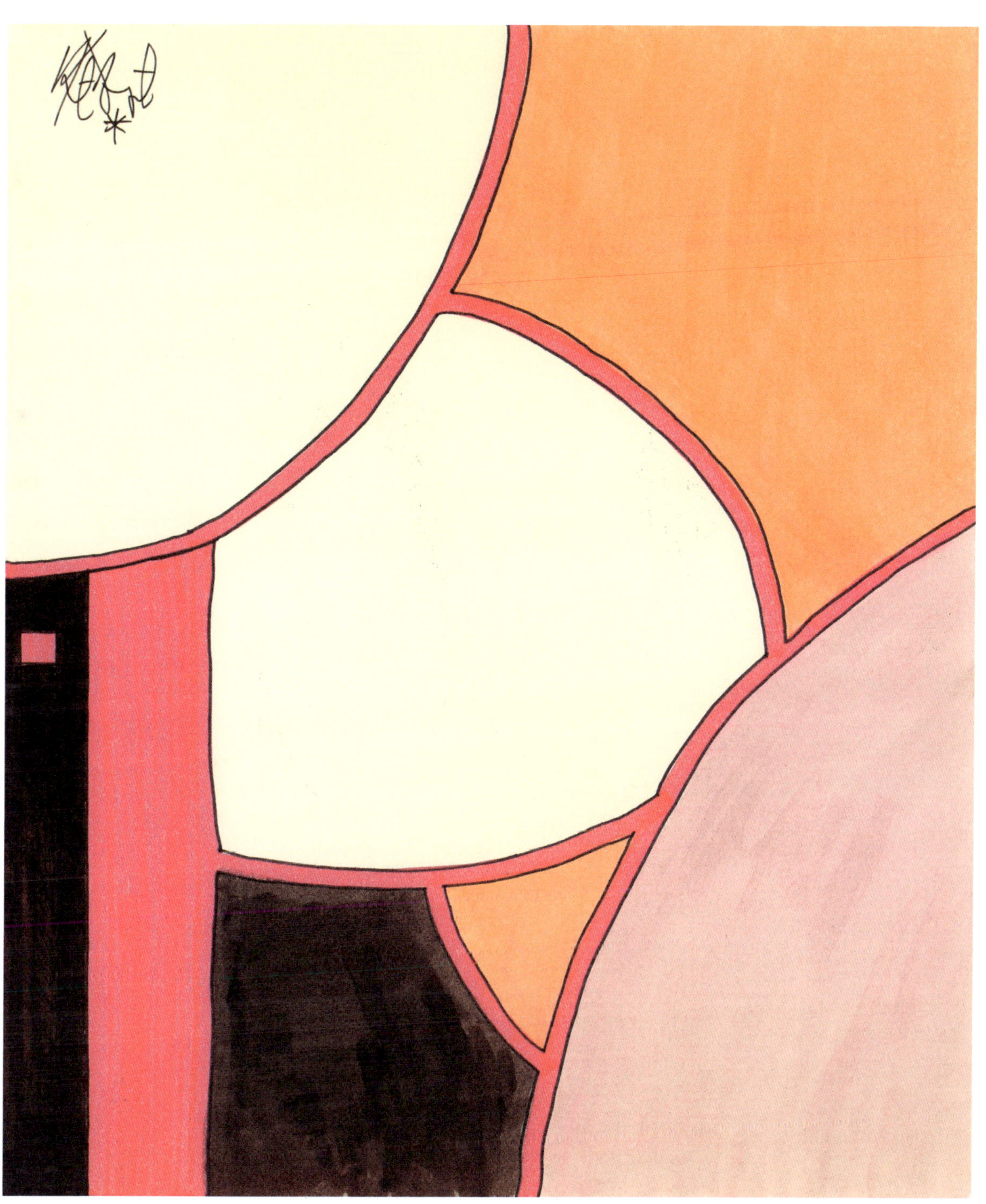

Untitled, n.d.

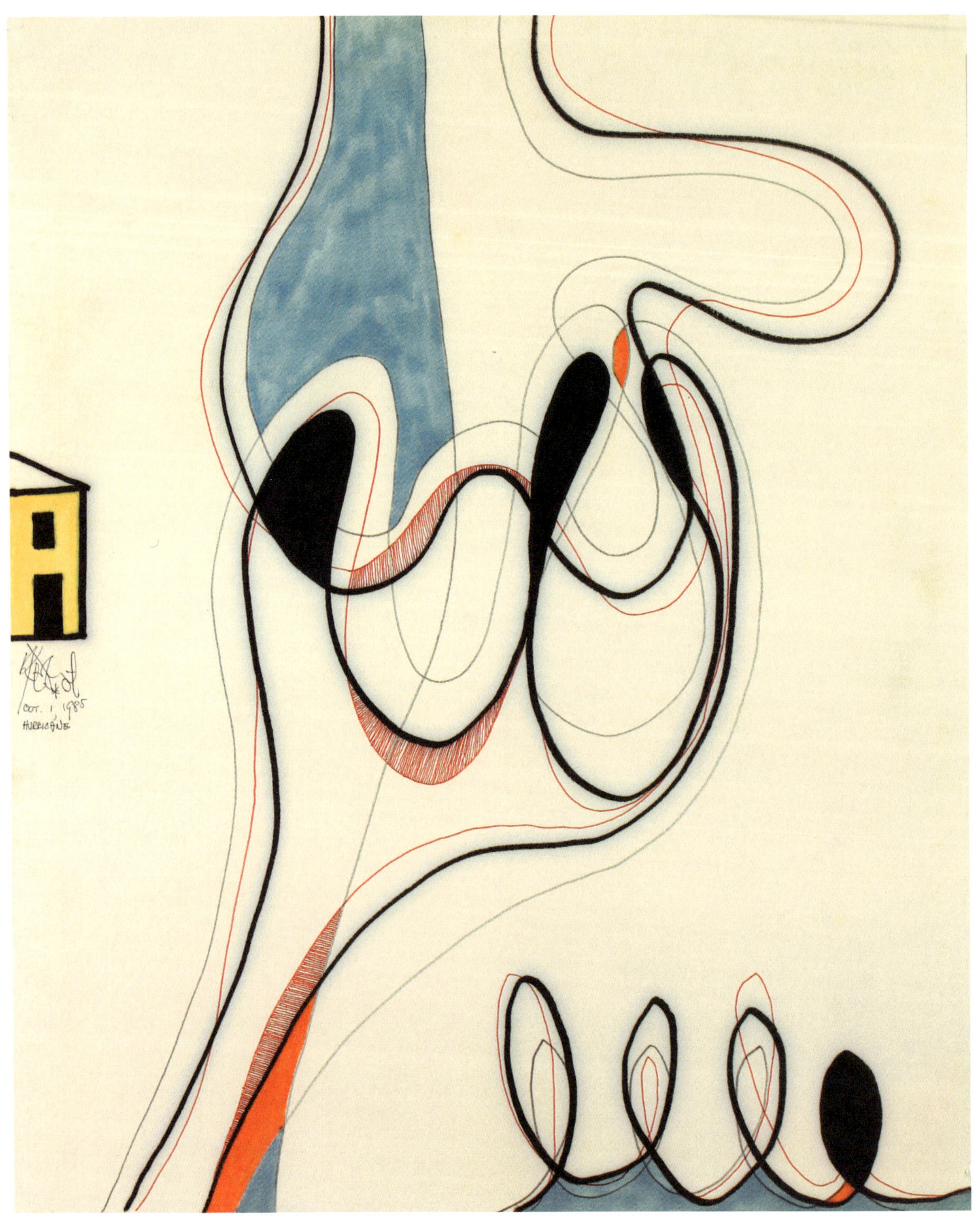

Hurricane, October 1, 1985

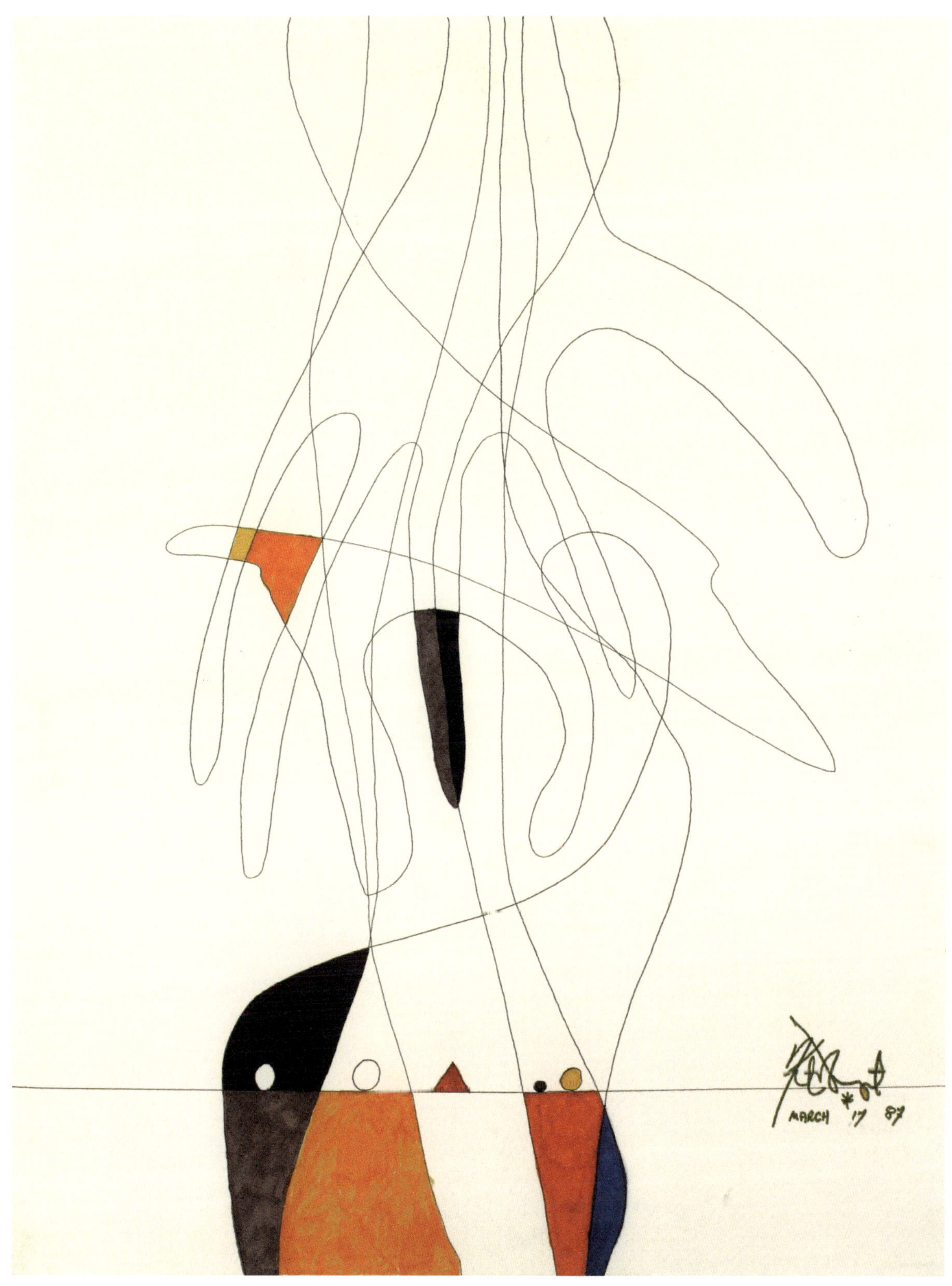

Untitled, March 17, 1987

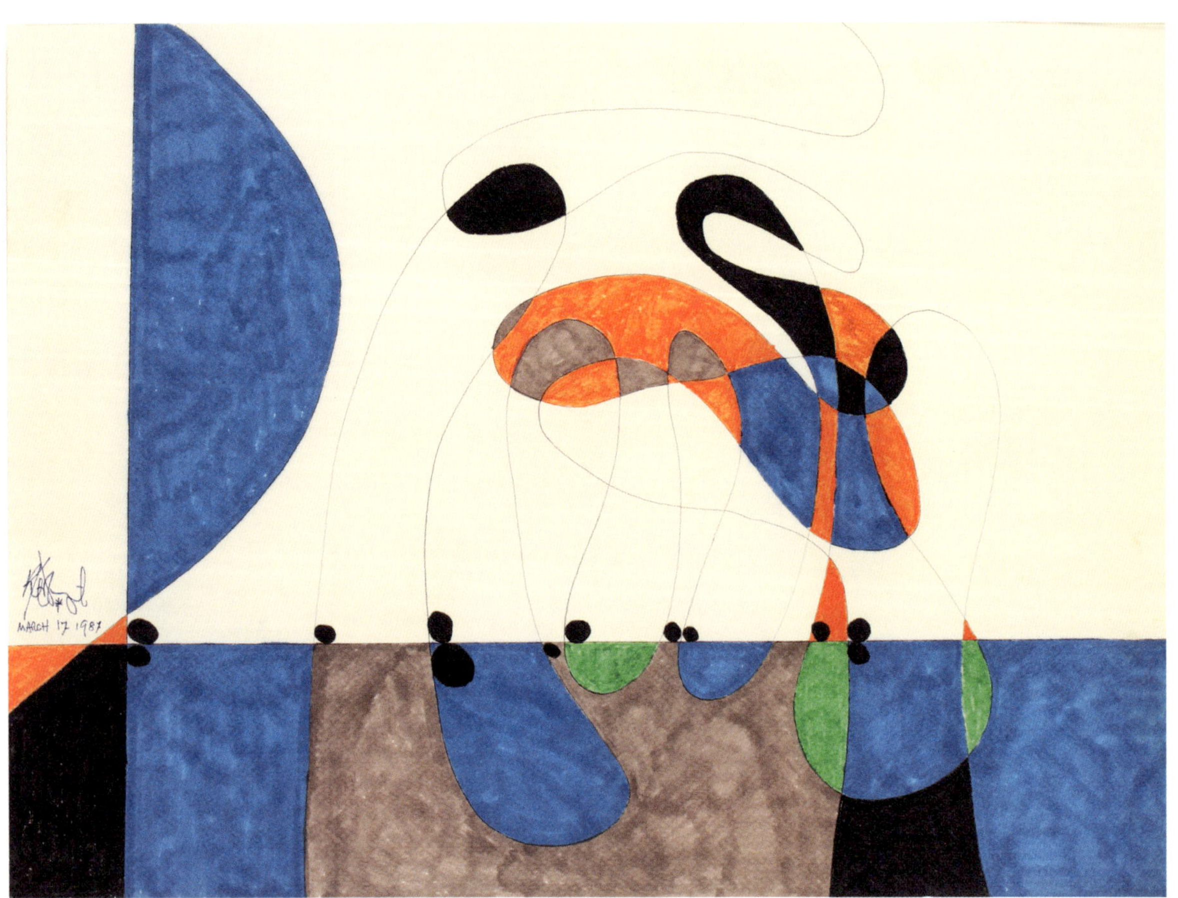

Untitled, March 17, 1987

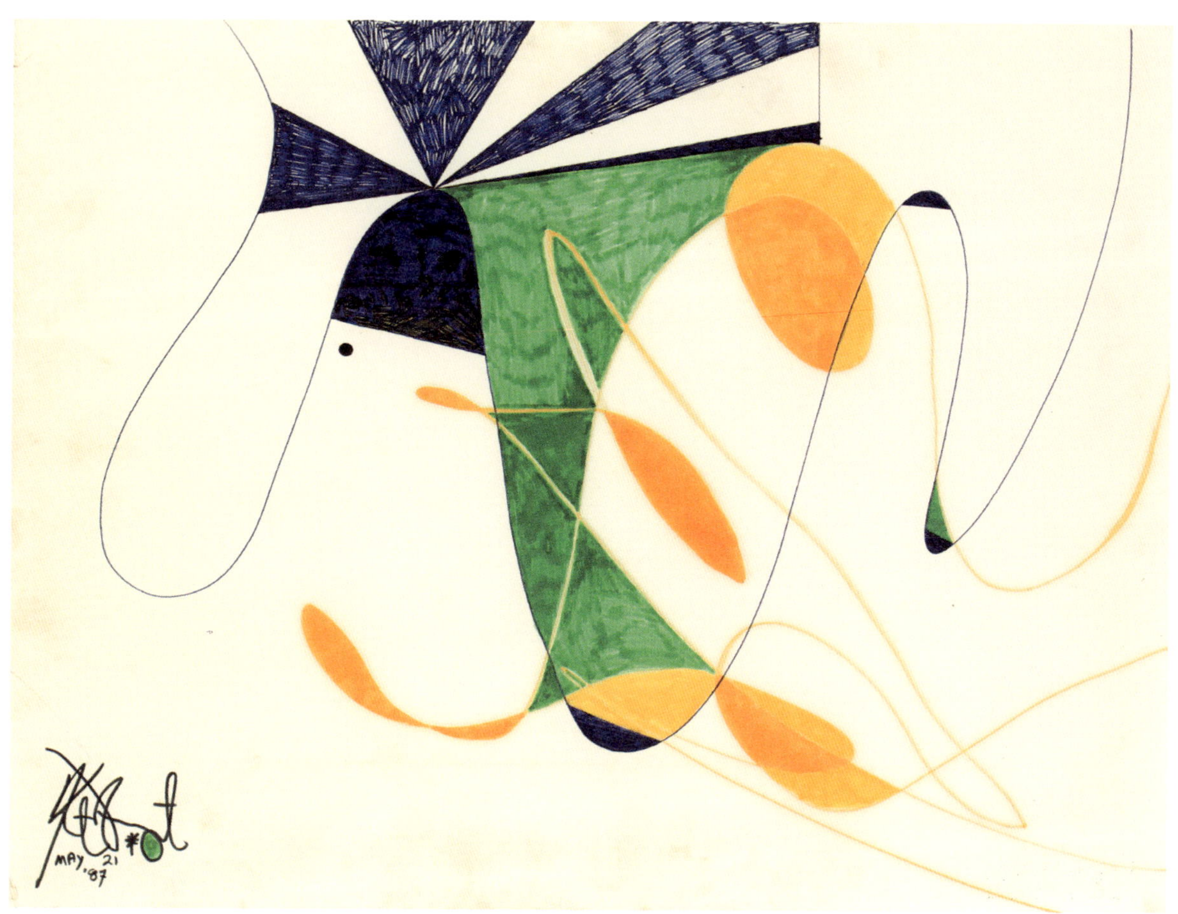

Untitled, May 21, 1987

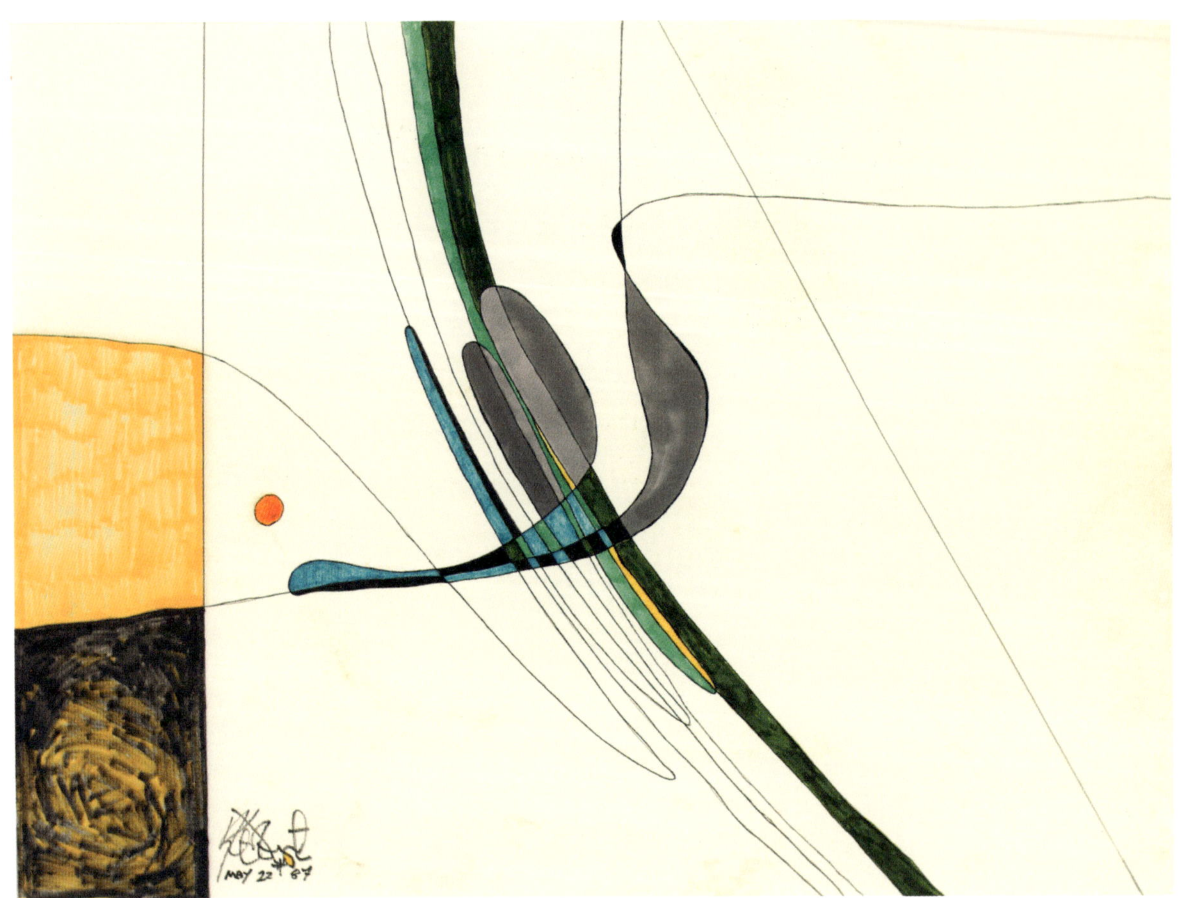

Untitled, May 22, 1987

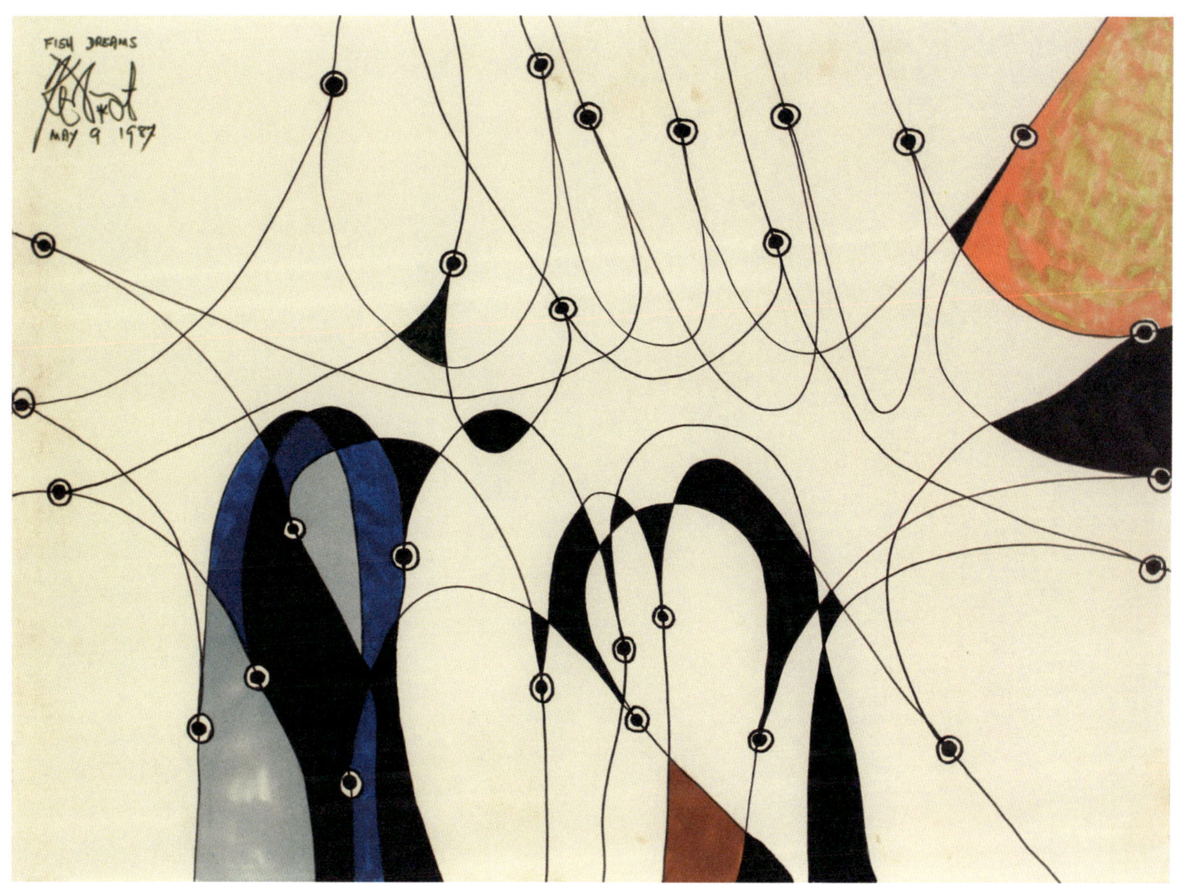

Fish Dreams, May 9, 1987

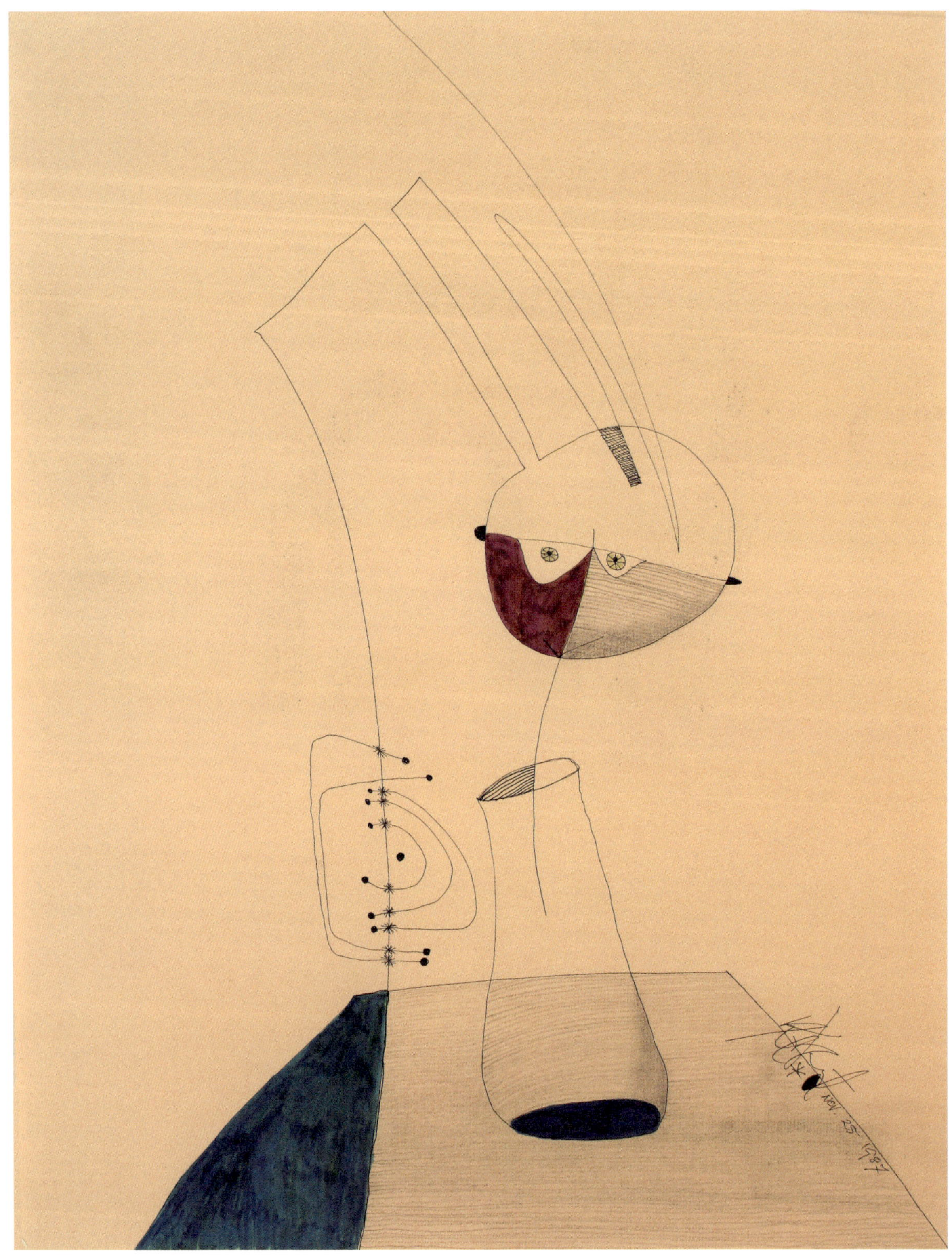

Untitled, November 25, 1987

I [wrote] a book about a painter, Bluebeard. I got the idea for it after Esquire *asked me for a piece about the Abstract Expressionist Jackson Pollock. The magazine was putting together a fiftieth-anniversary issue to consist of essays on fifty native-born Americans who had made the biggest difference in the country's destiny since 1932. I wanted Eleanor Roosevelt but Bill Moyers already had her.*

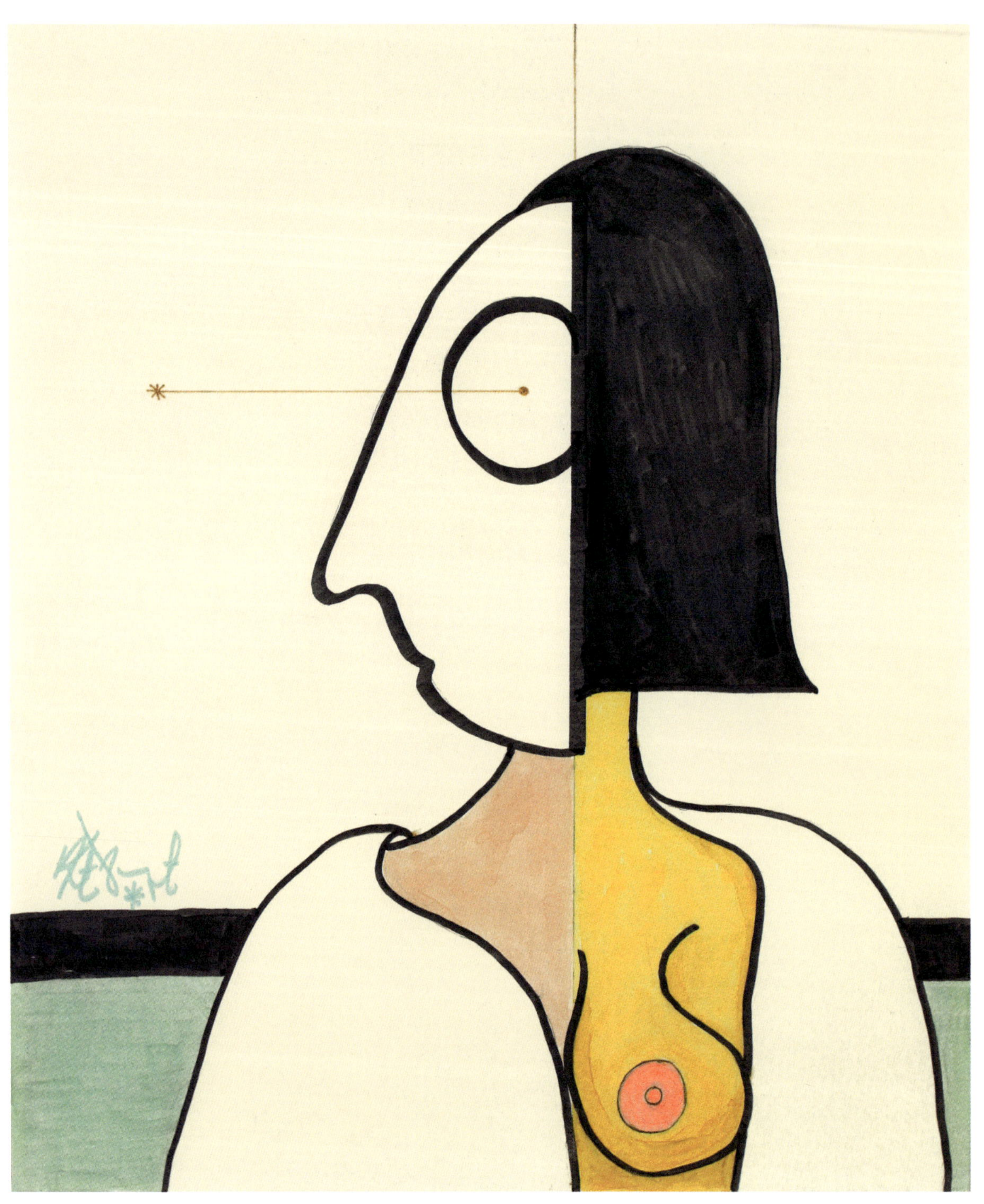

Untitled, n.d.

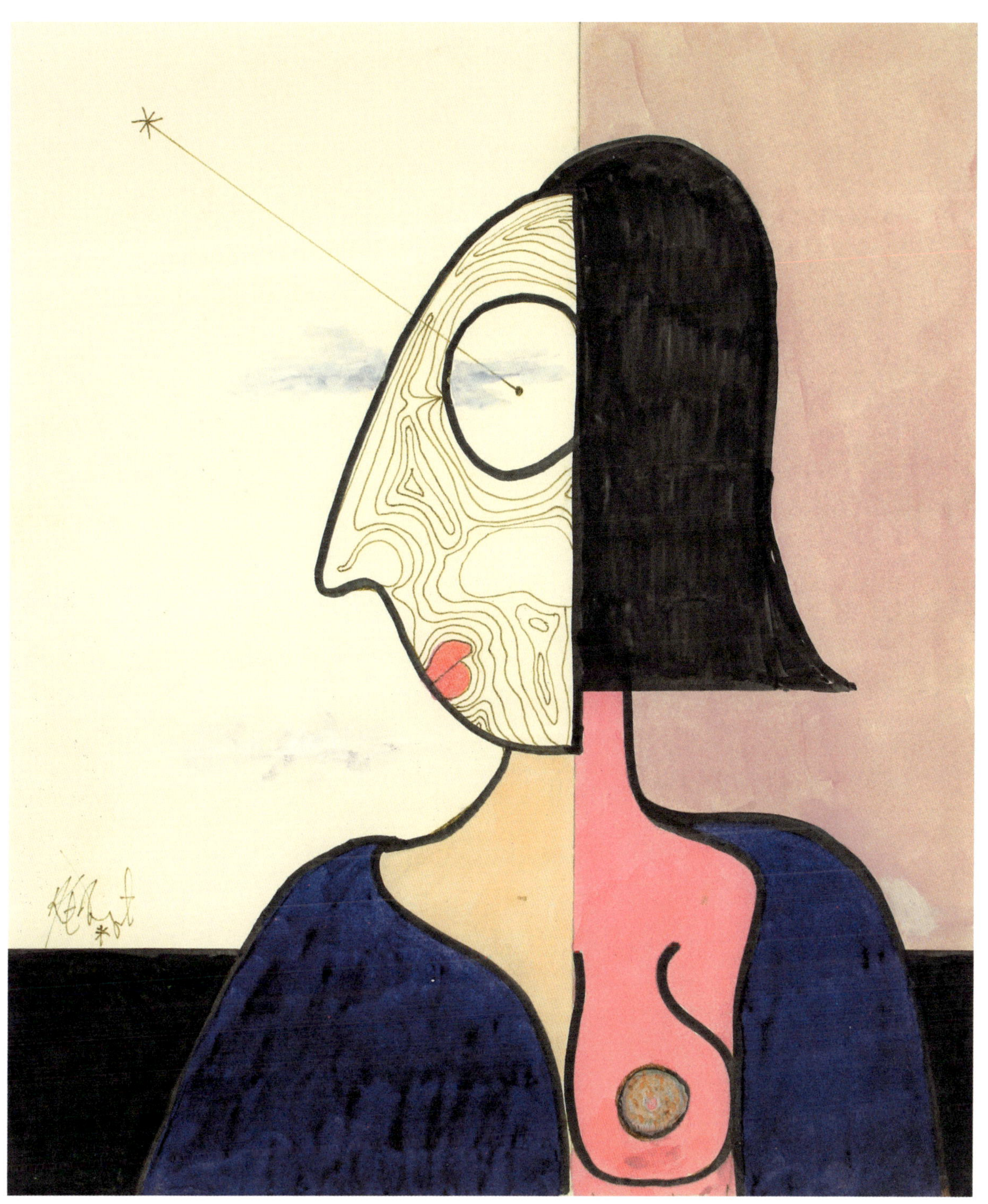

Untitled, n.d.

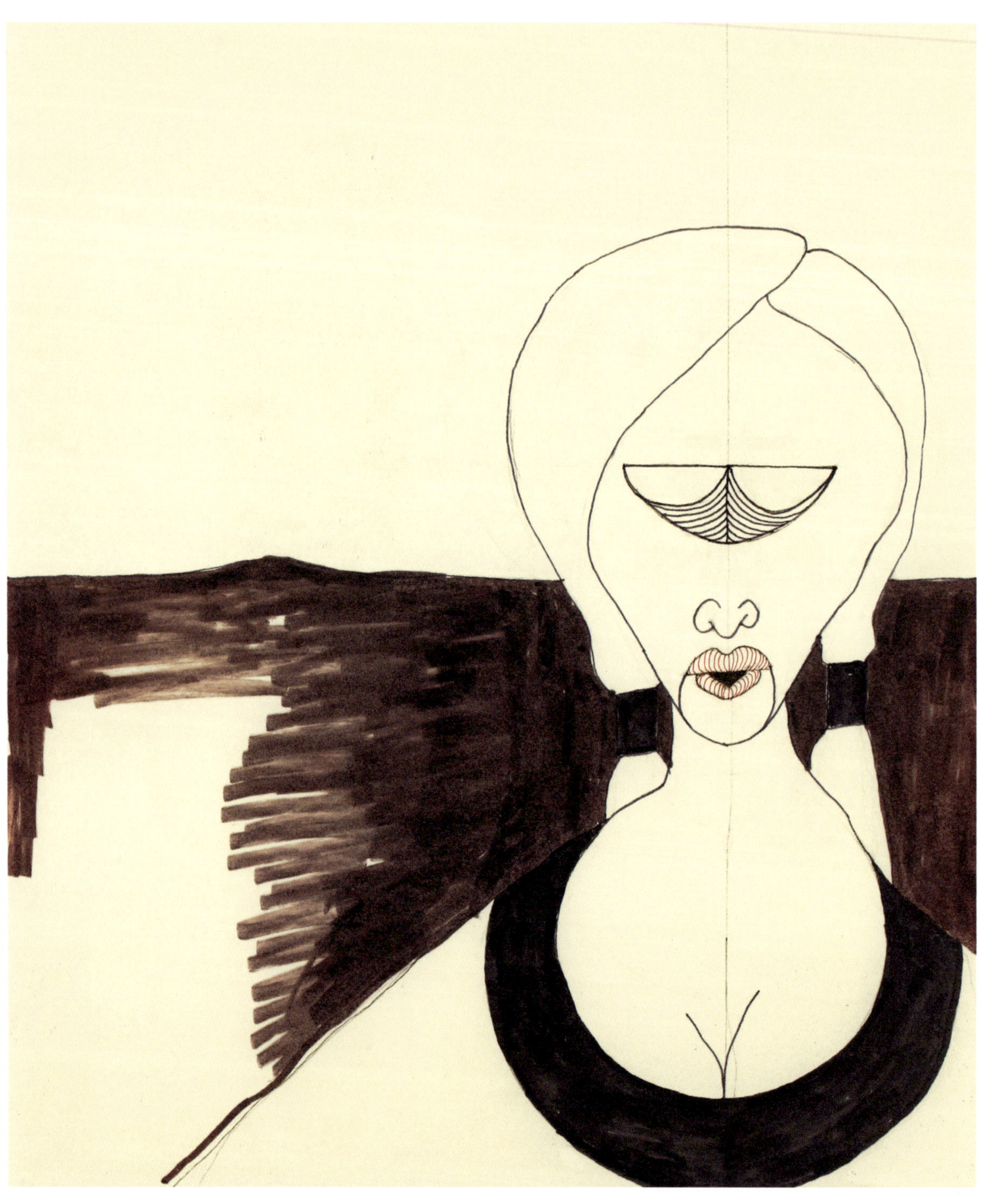

Untitled, n.d.

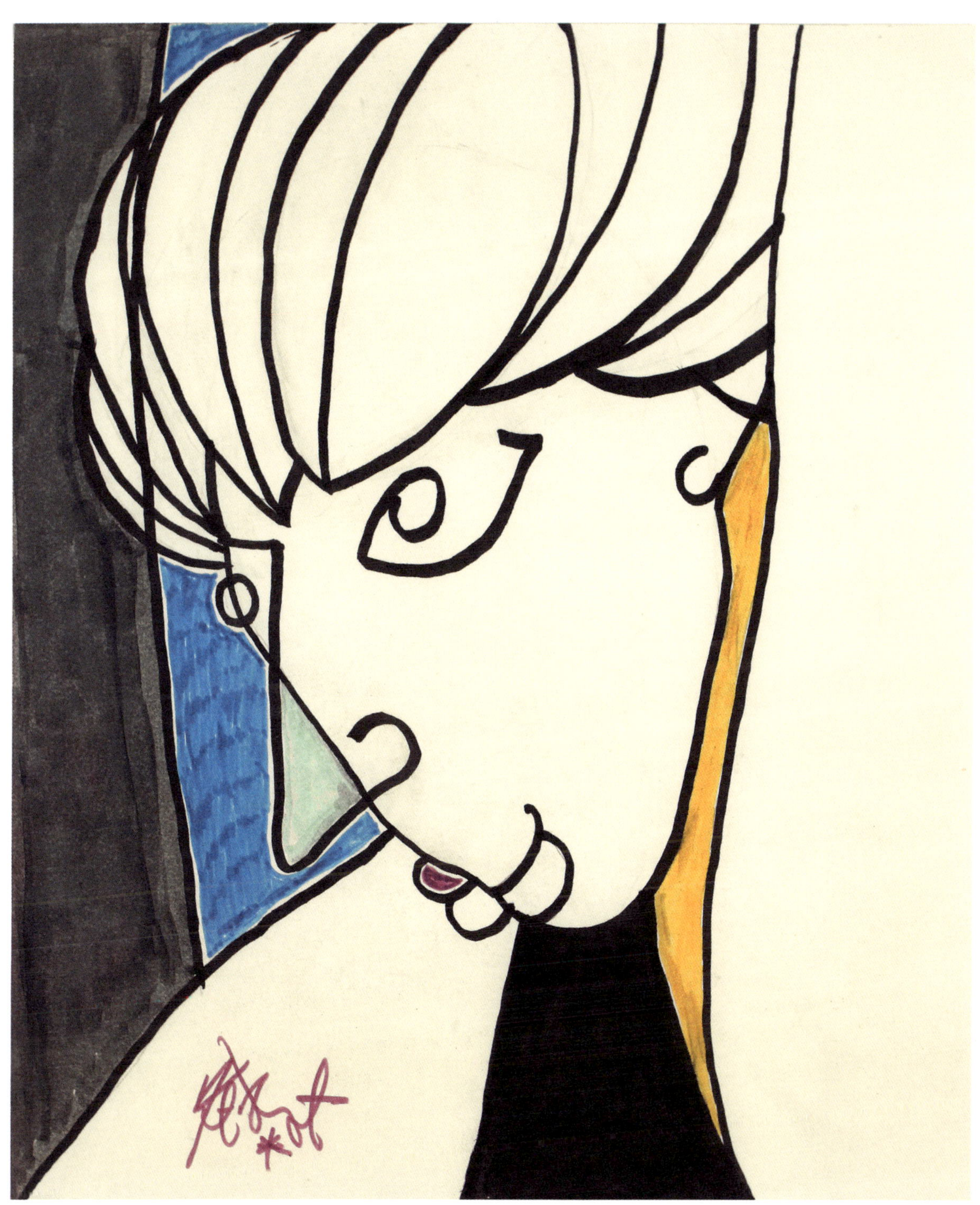

Untitled, n.d.

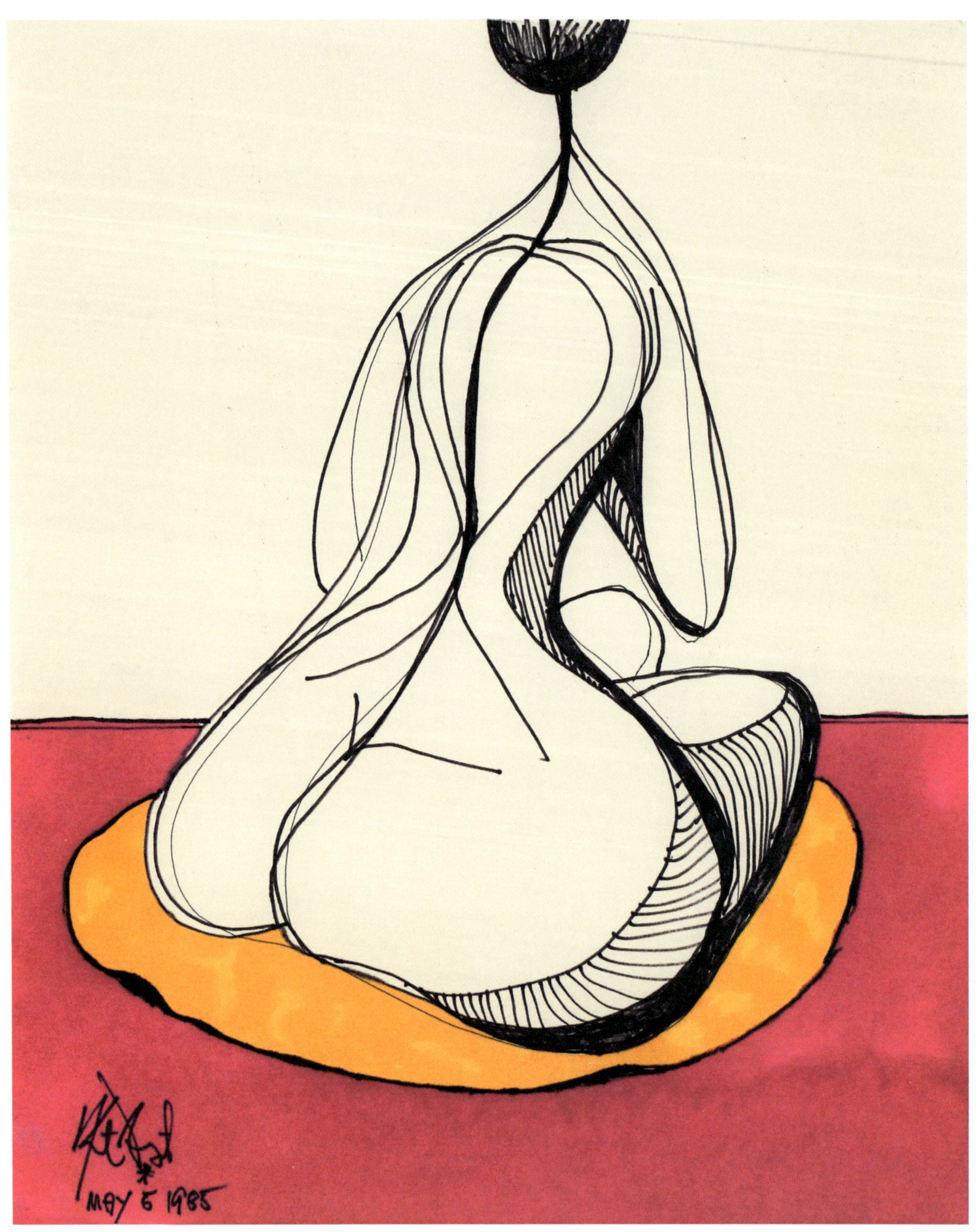

Untitled, May 5, 1985

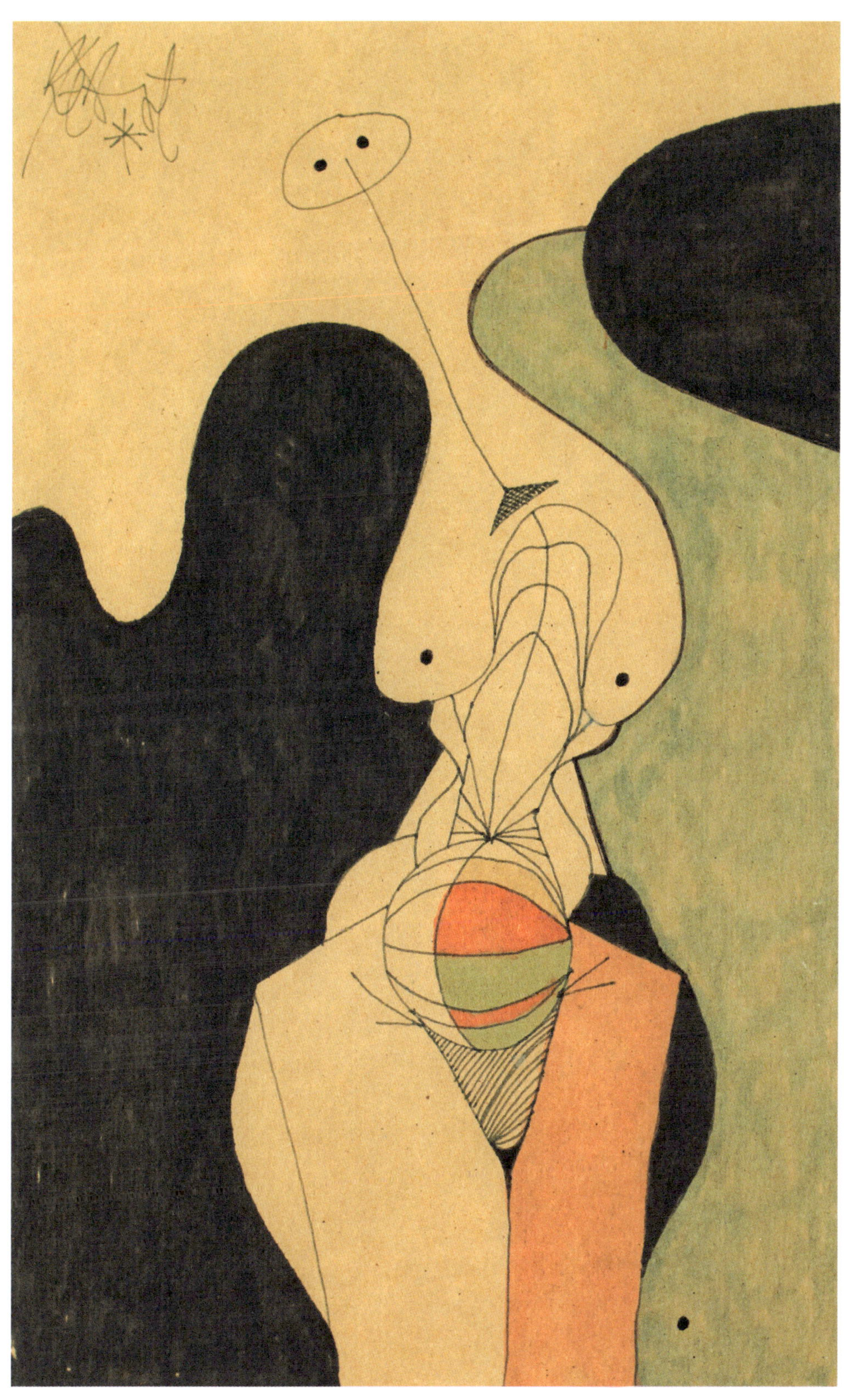

Untitled, n.d.

The making of pictures is to writing what laughing gas is to influenza.

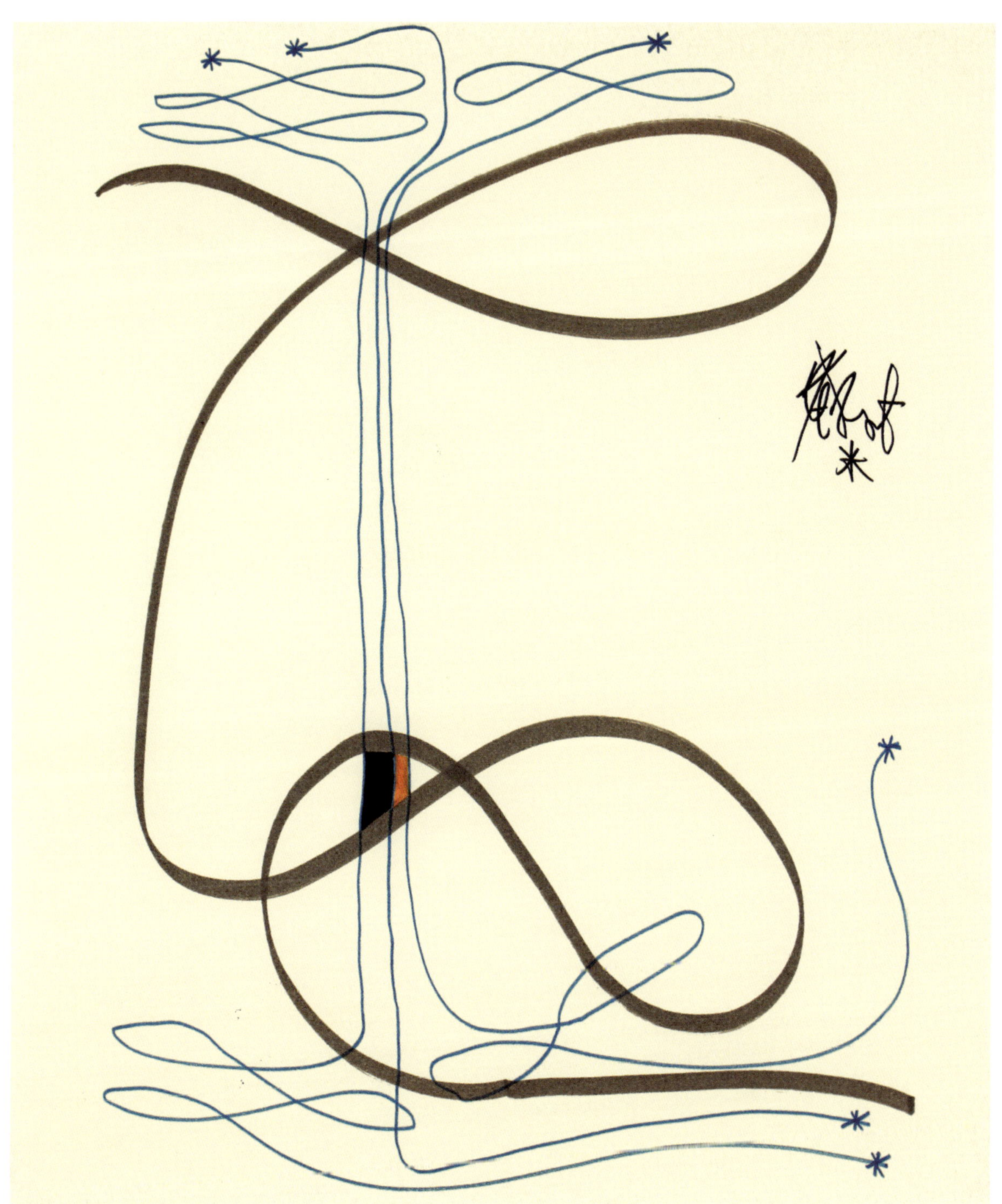

Untitled, n.d.

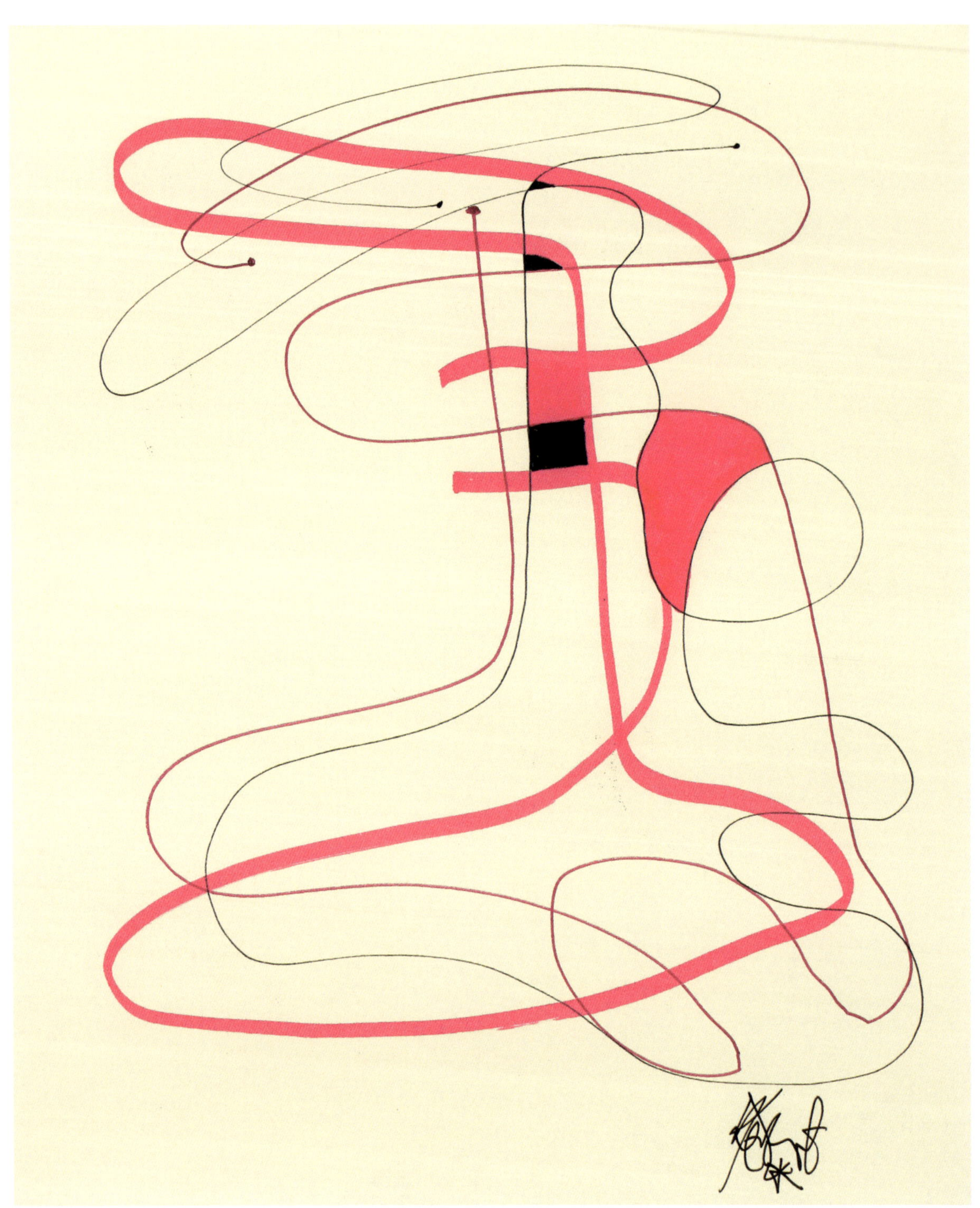

Untitled, n.d.

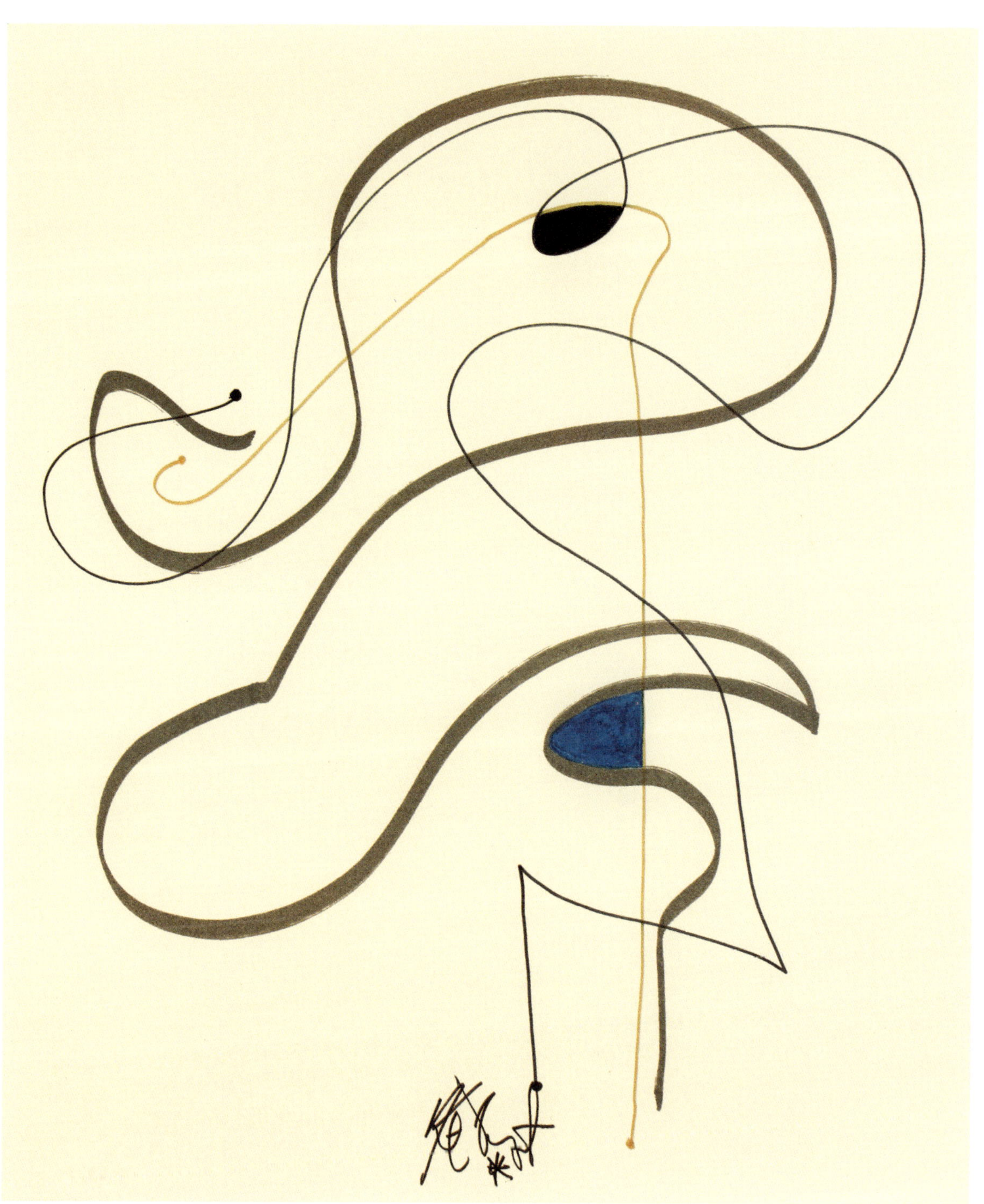

Untitled, n.d.

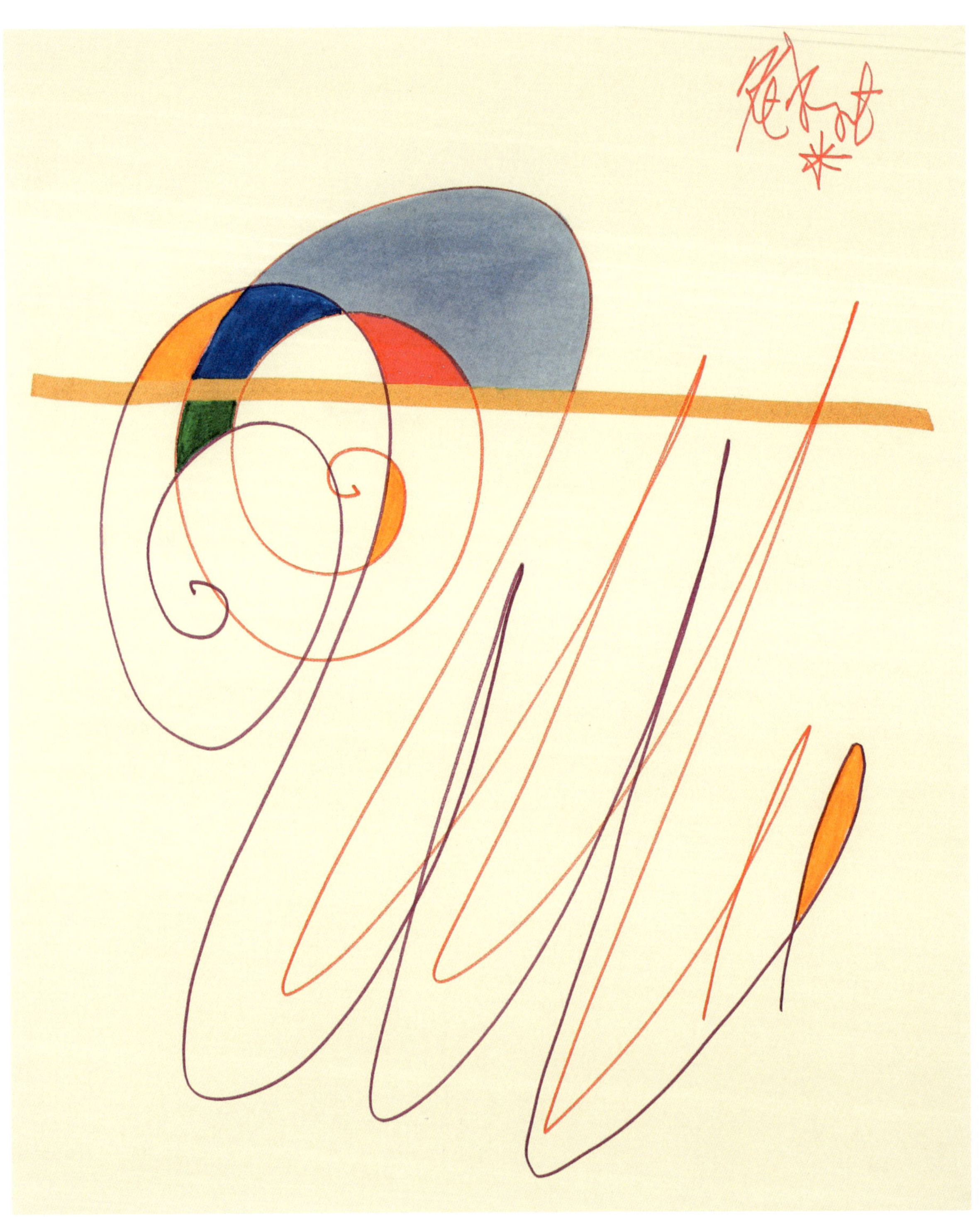

Untitled, n.d.

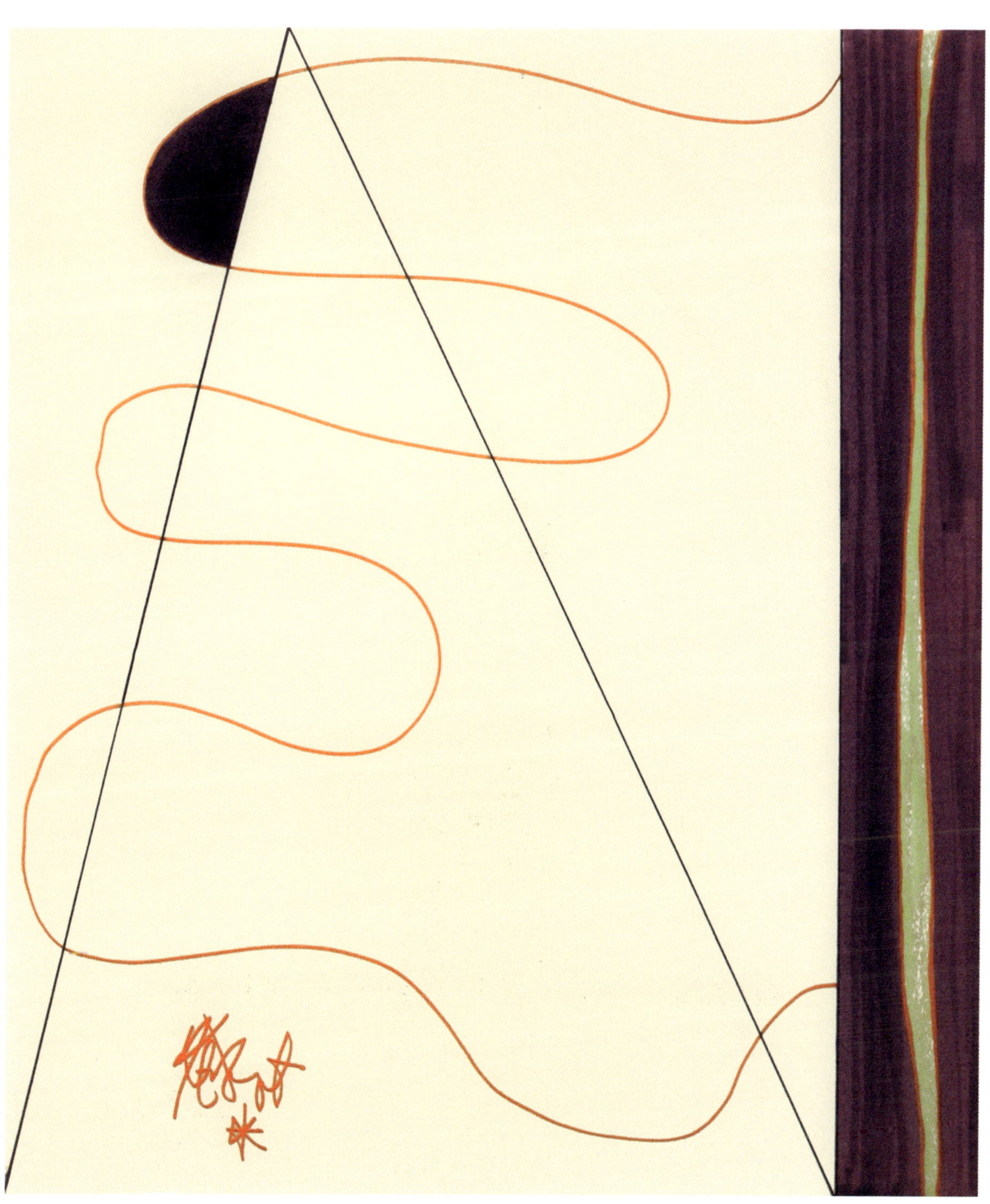

Untitled, n.d.

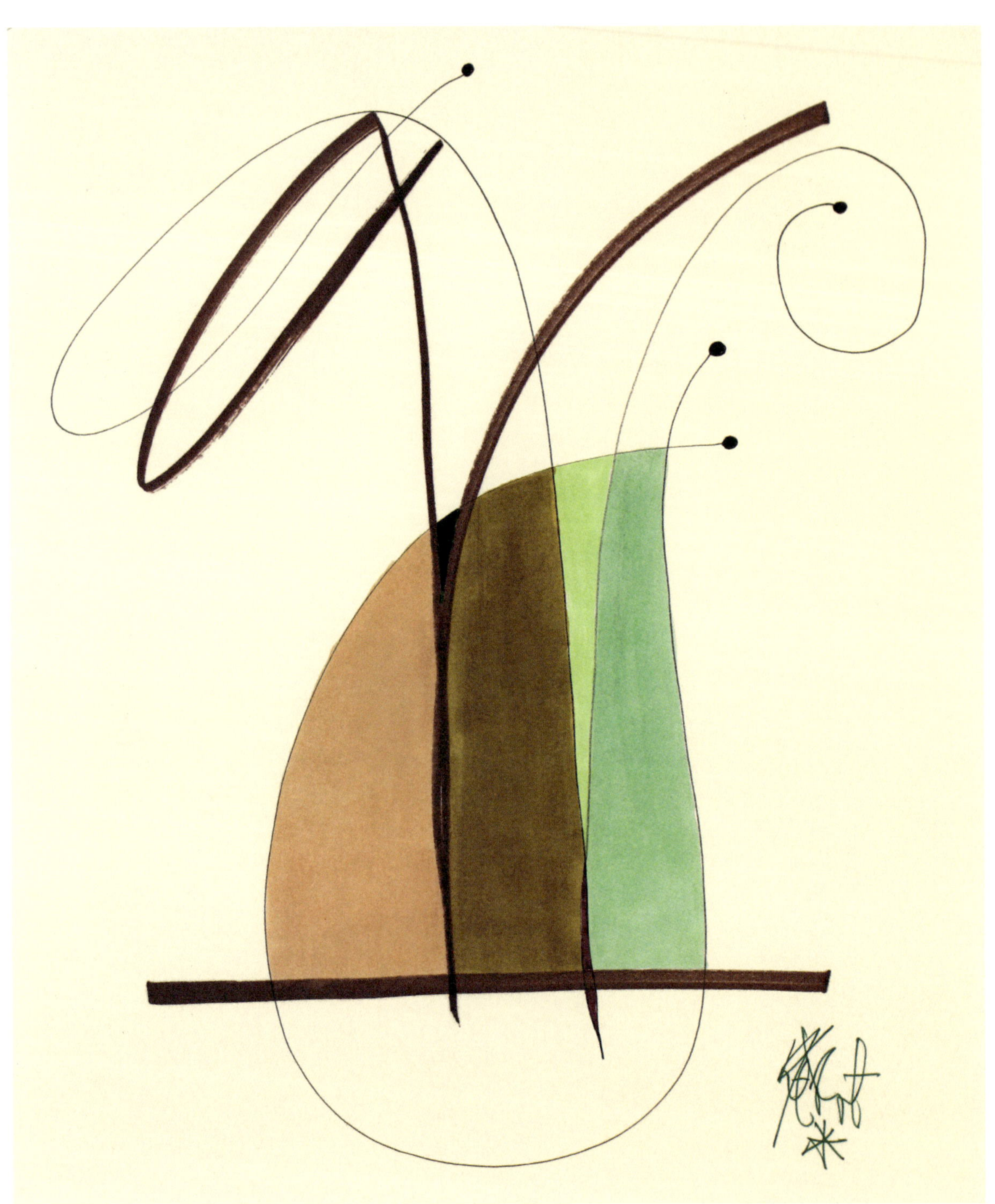

Untitled, n.d.

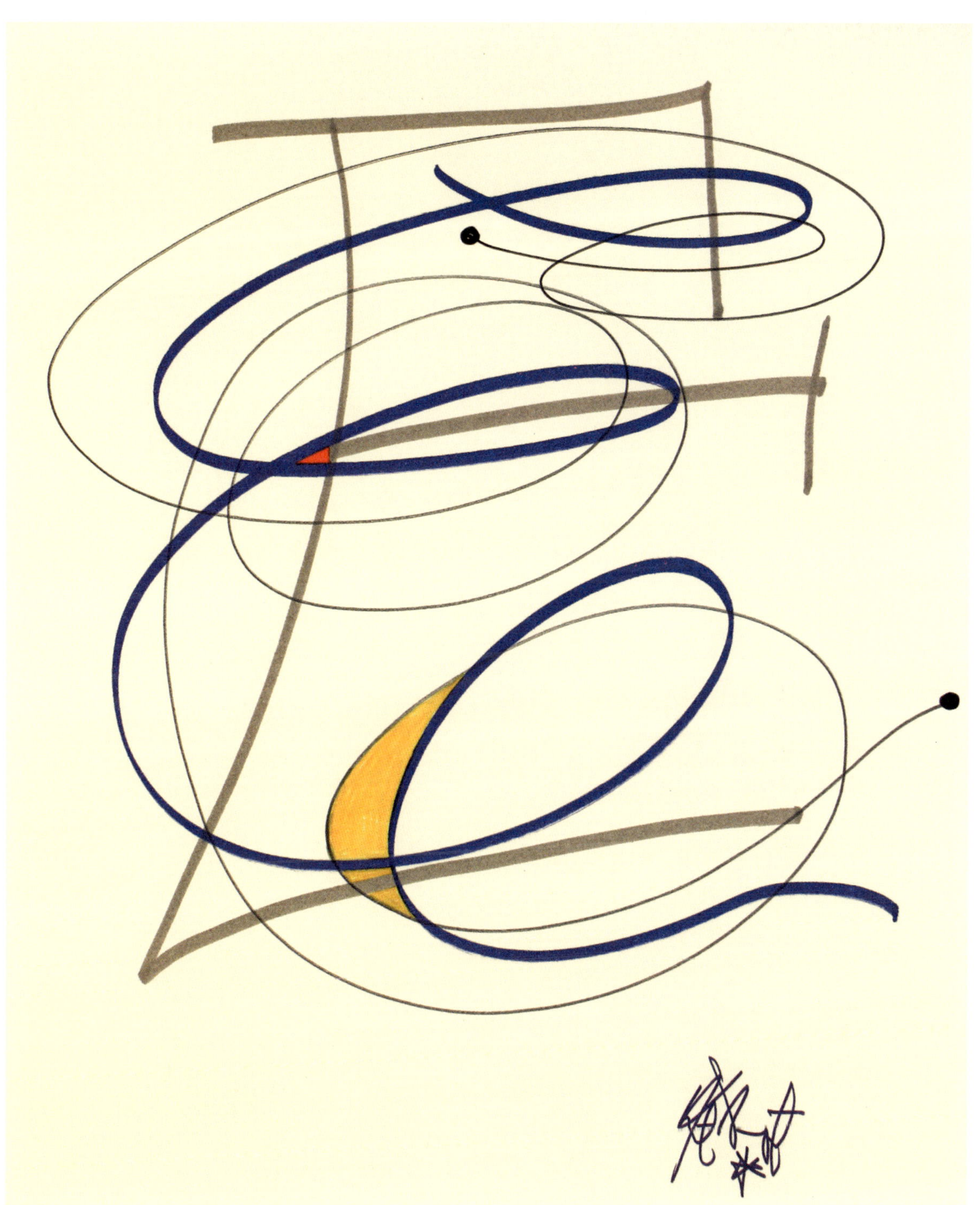

Untitled, n.d.

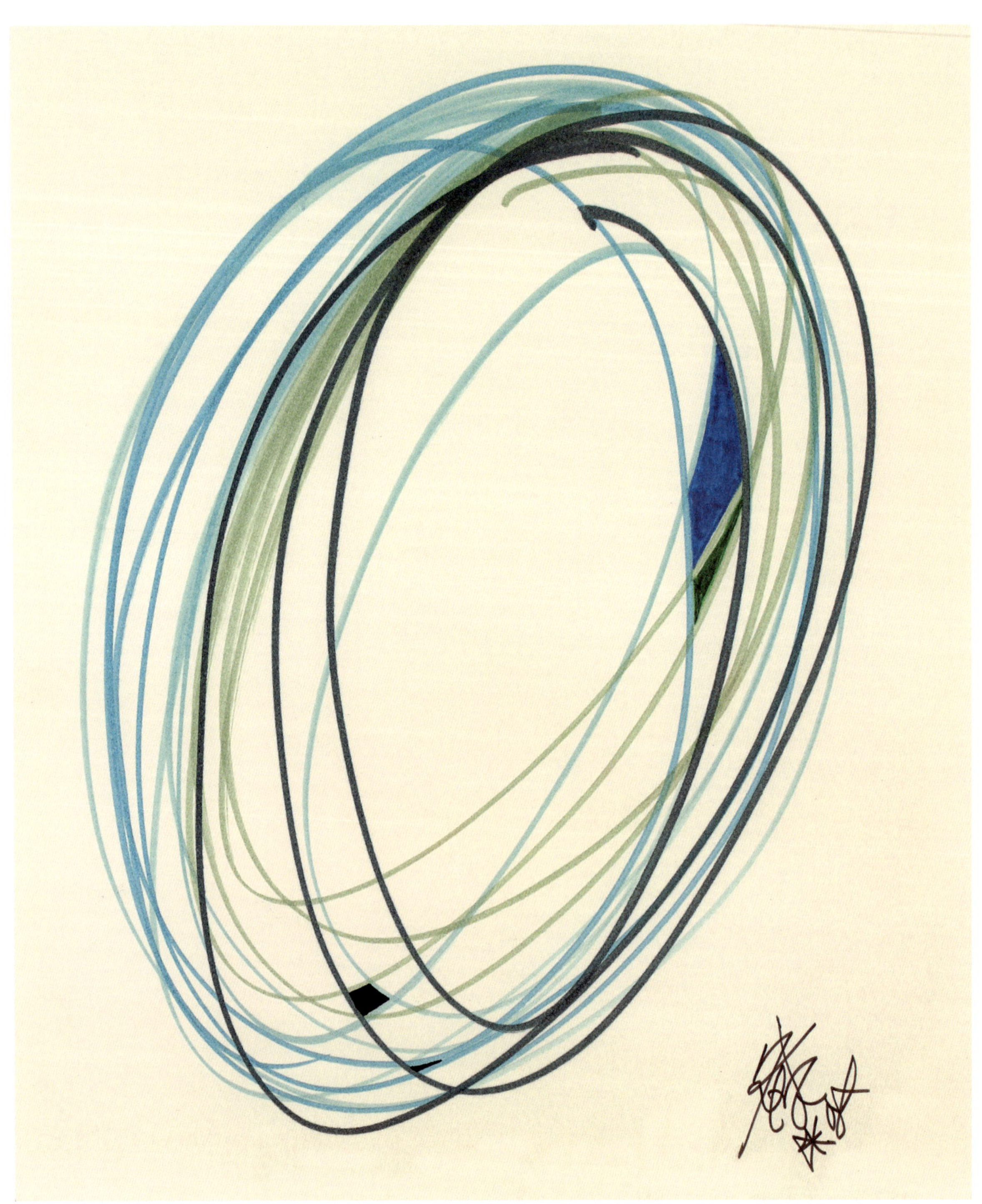

Untitled, n.d.

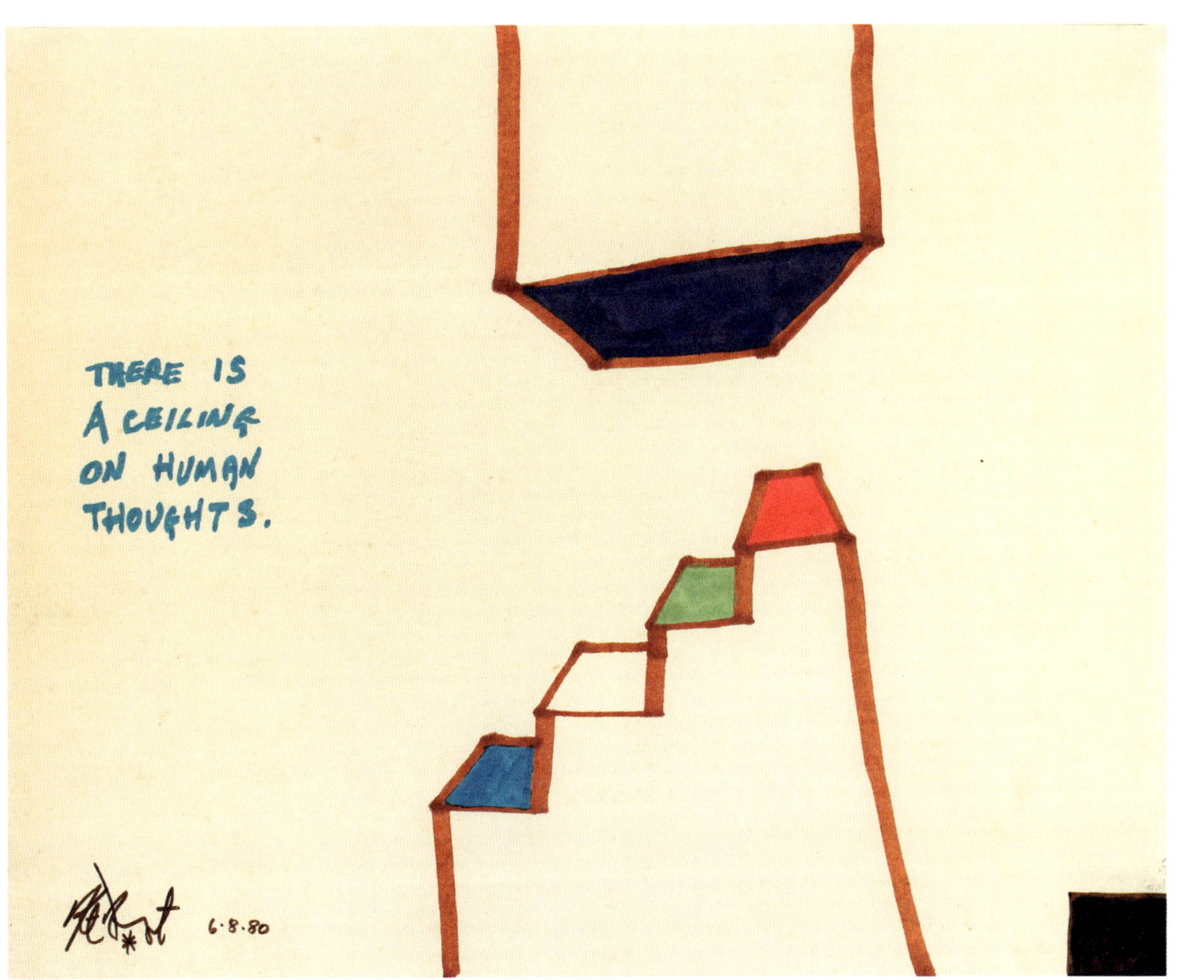

There Is a Ceiling, June 8, 1980

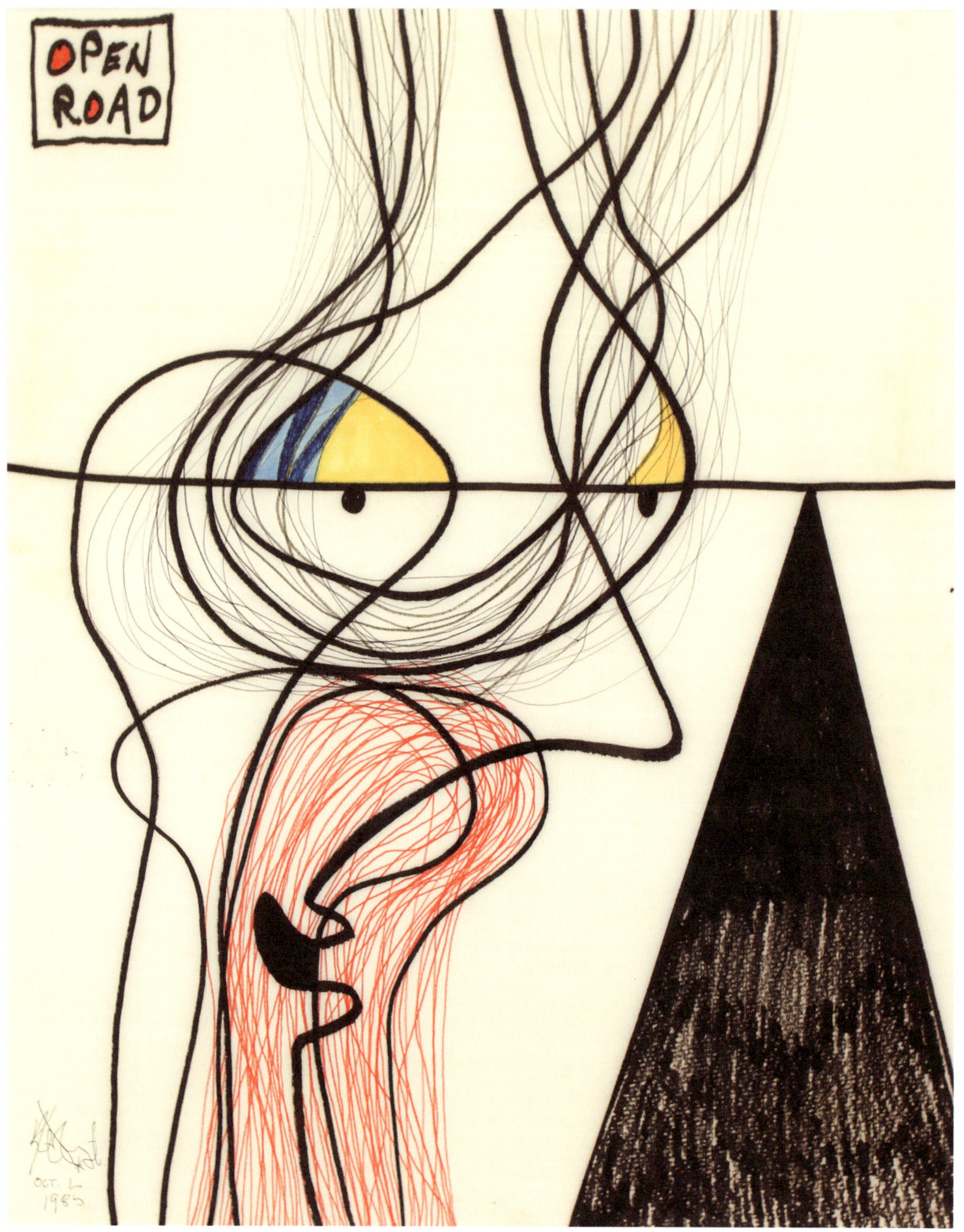

Open Road, October, 1985

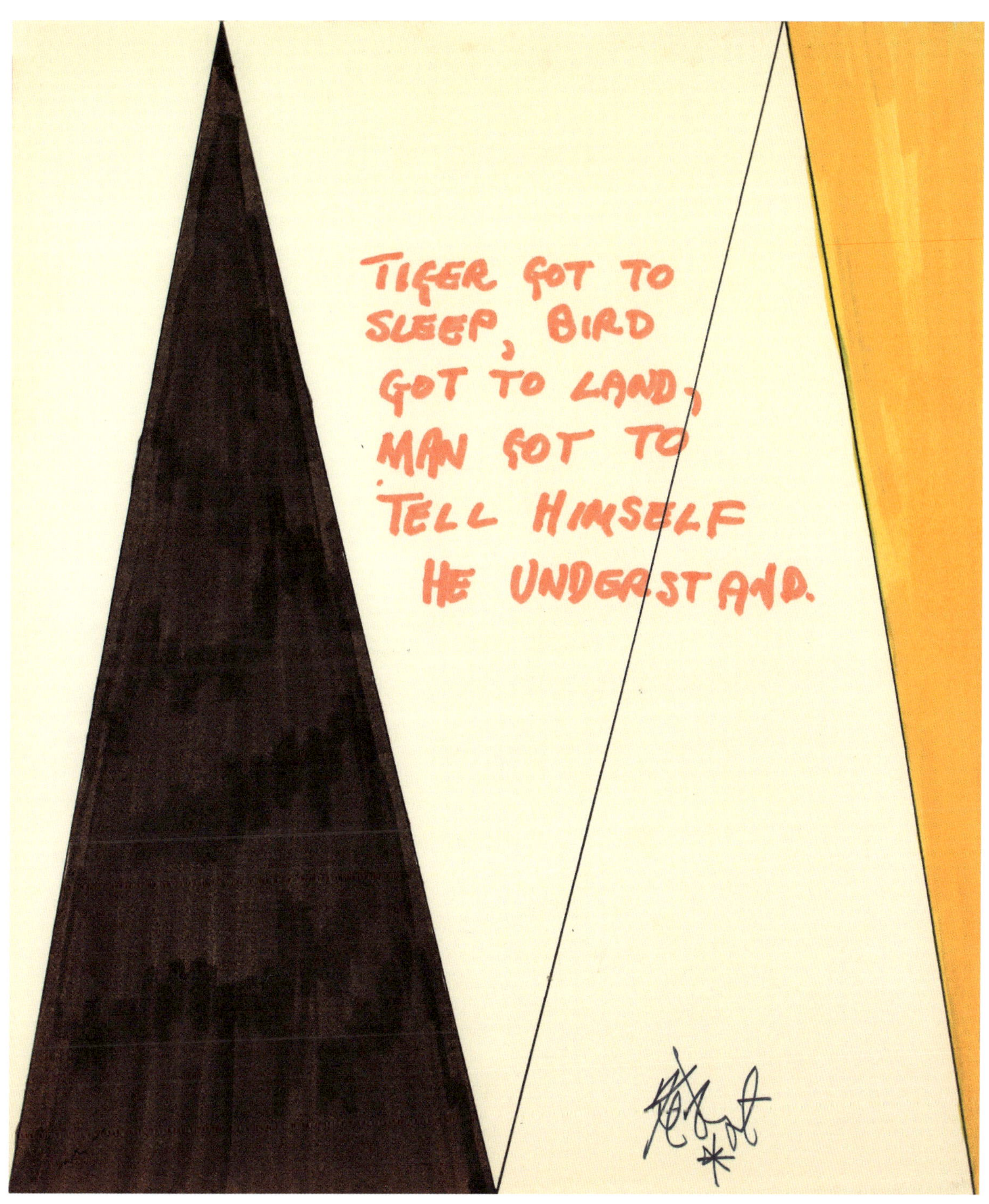

Tiger Got to Sleep, n.d.

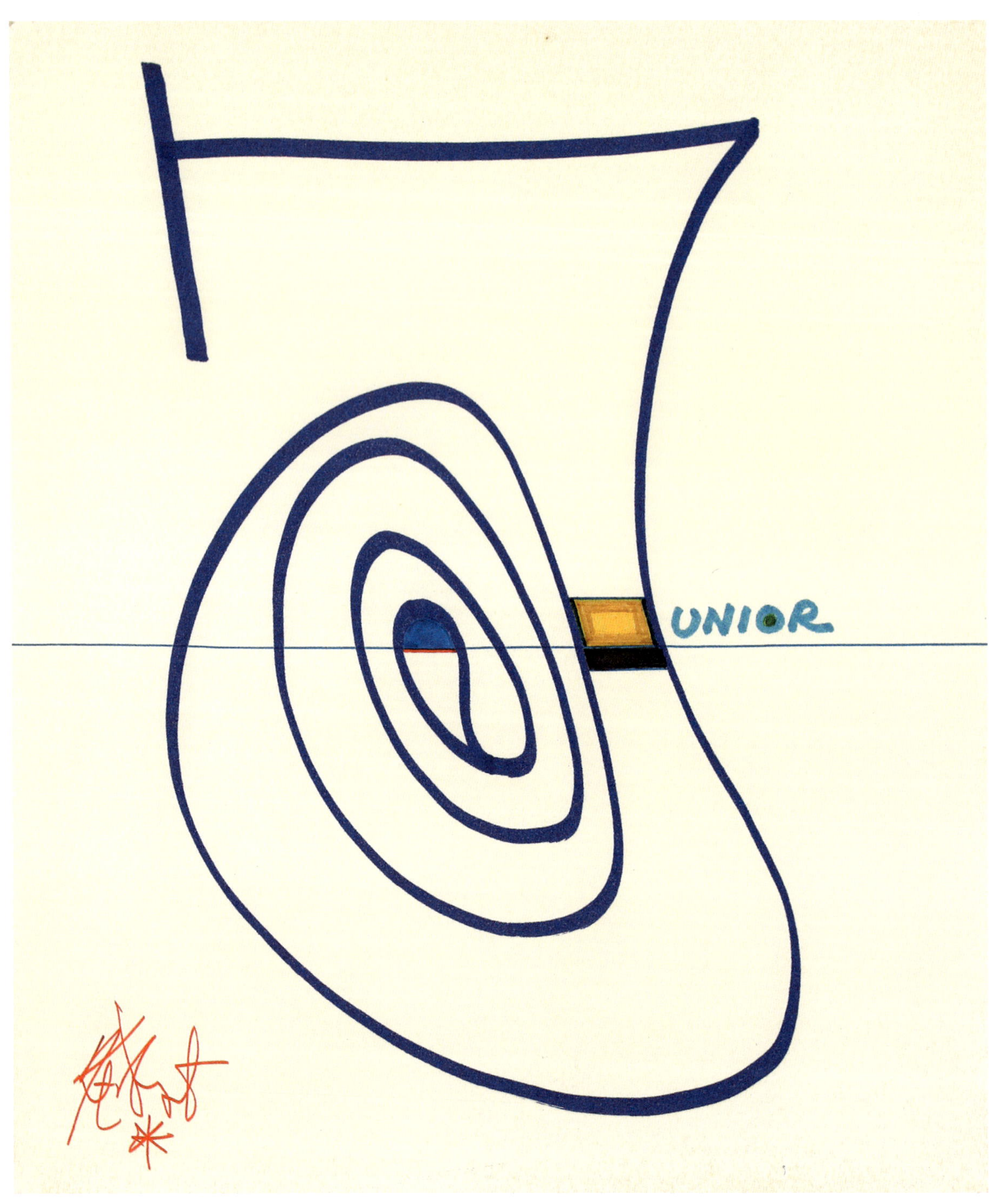

Junior, n.d.

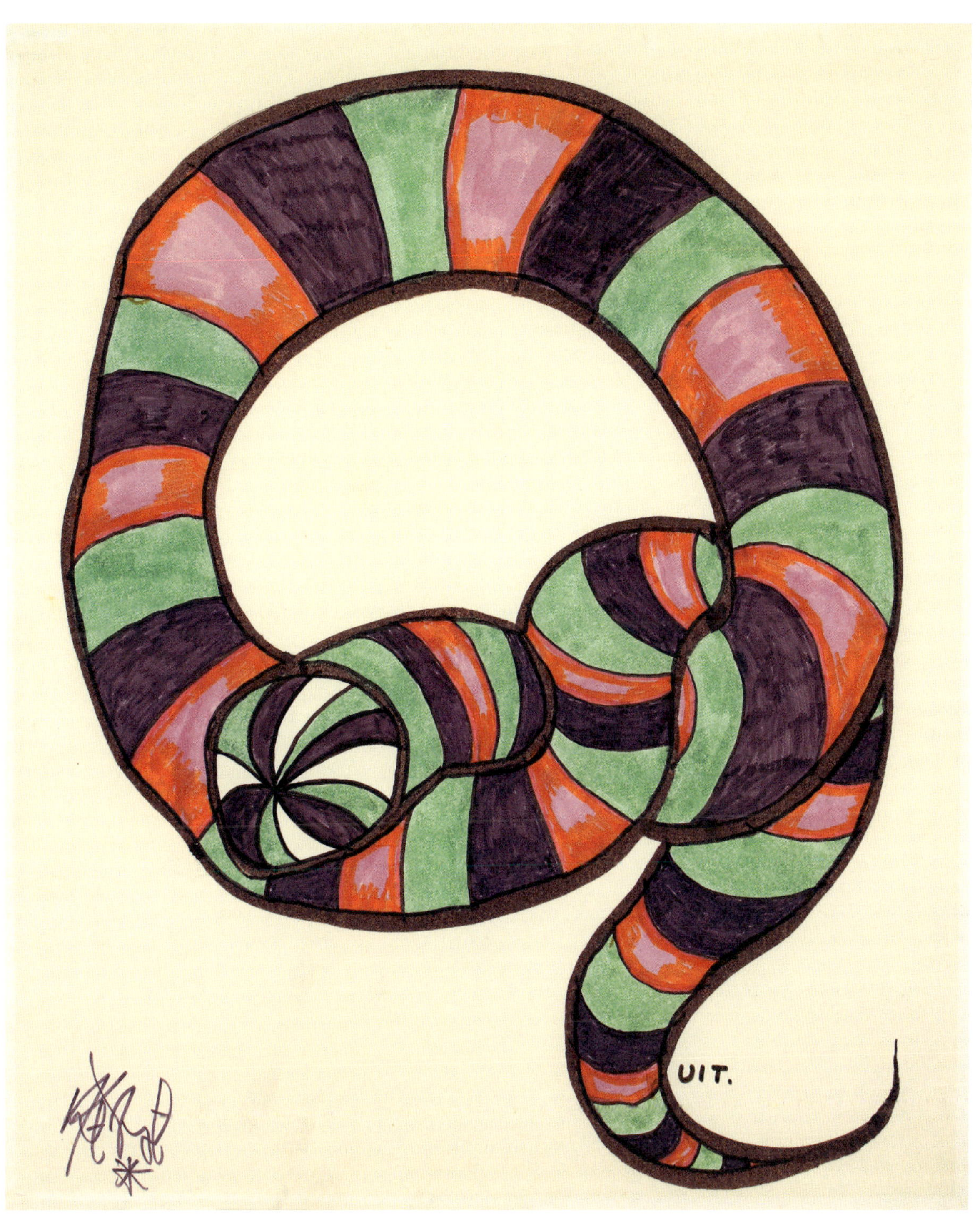

Quit, n.d.

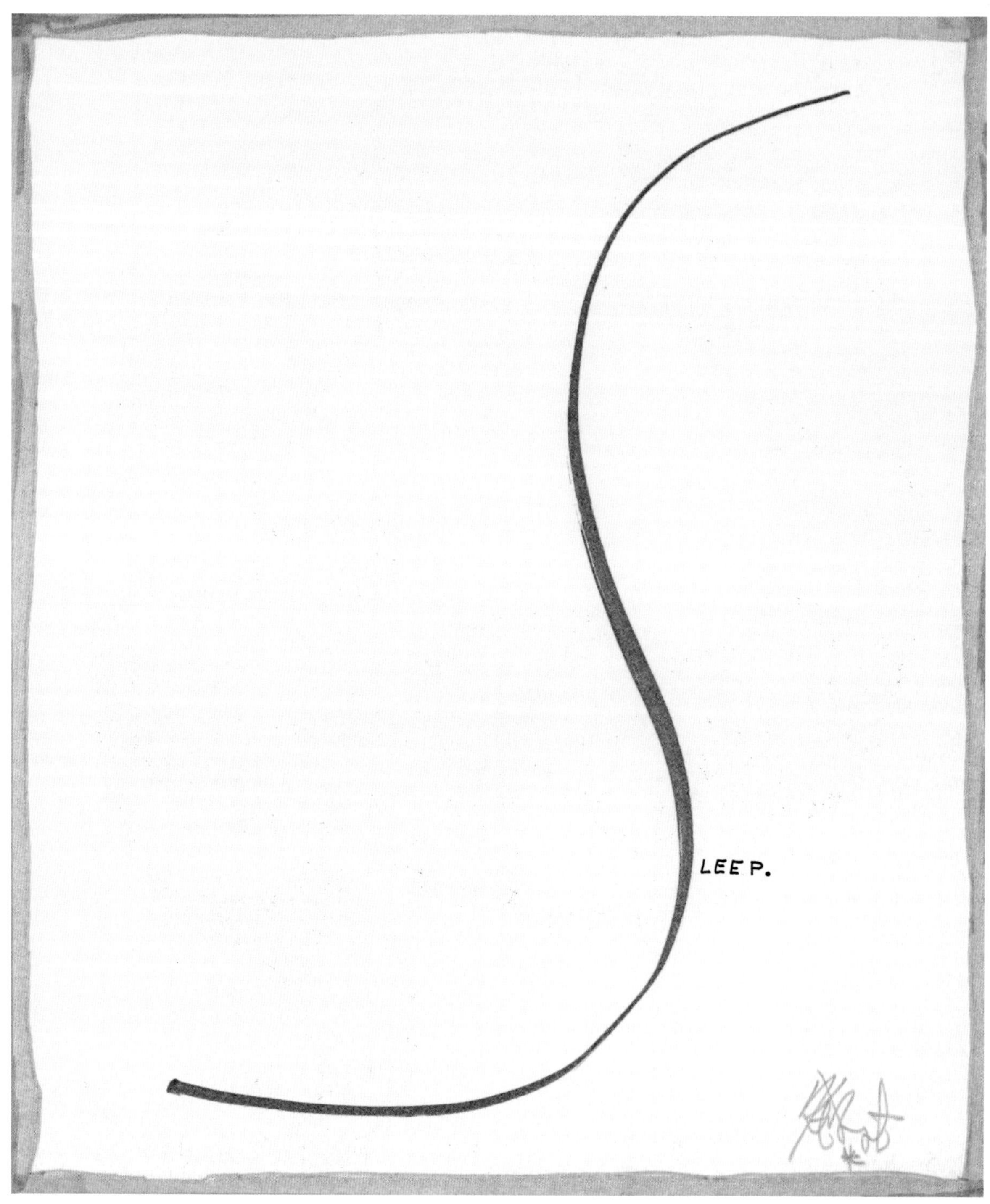

Sleep, n.d.

The imagination circuit is taught to respond to the most minimal of cues. A book is an arrangement of twenty-six phonetic symbols, ten numerals, and about eight punctuation marks, and people can cast their eyes over these and envision the eruption of Mount Vesuvius or the Battle of Waterloo.

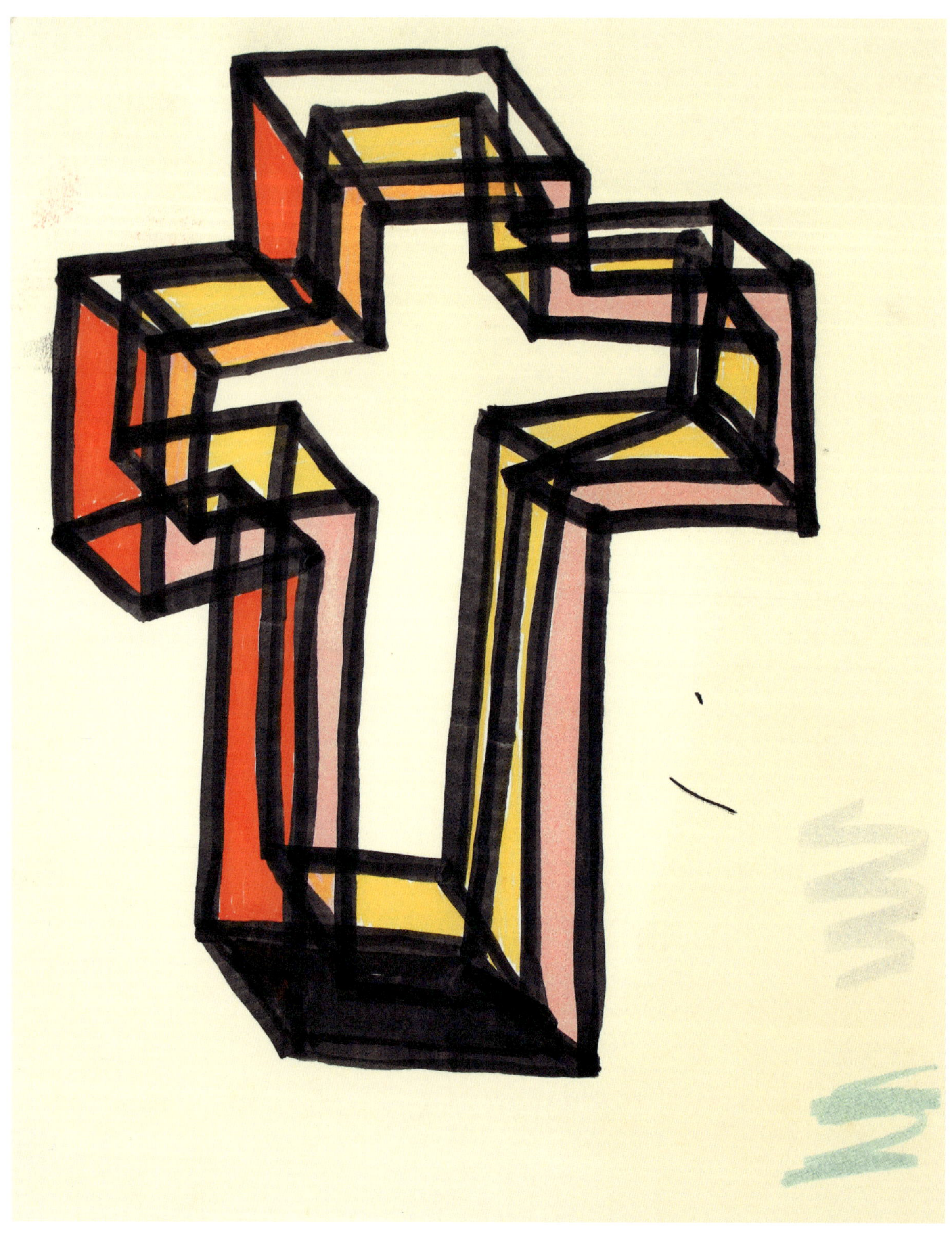

Untitled, n.d.

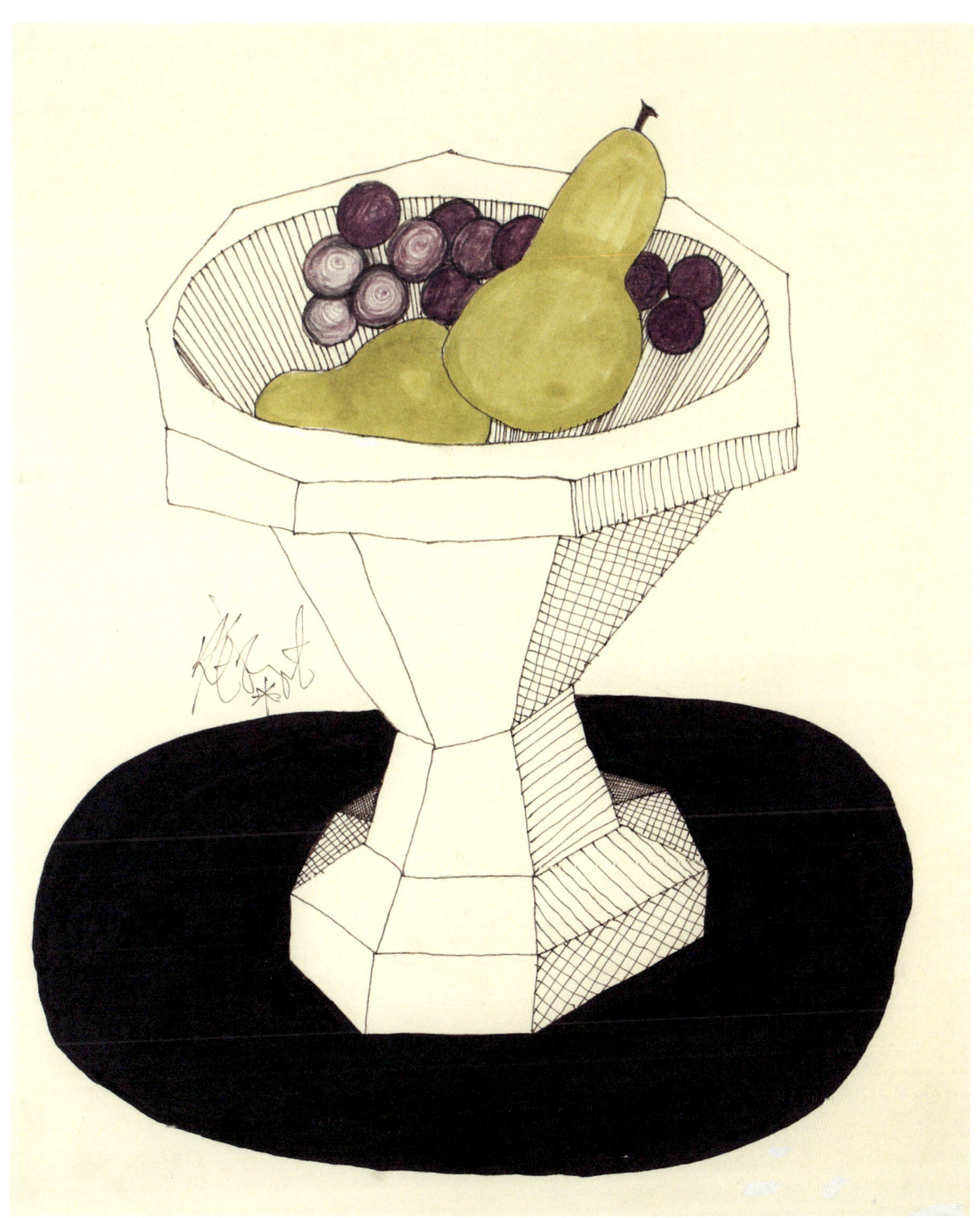

Untitled, n.d.

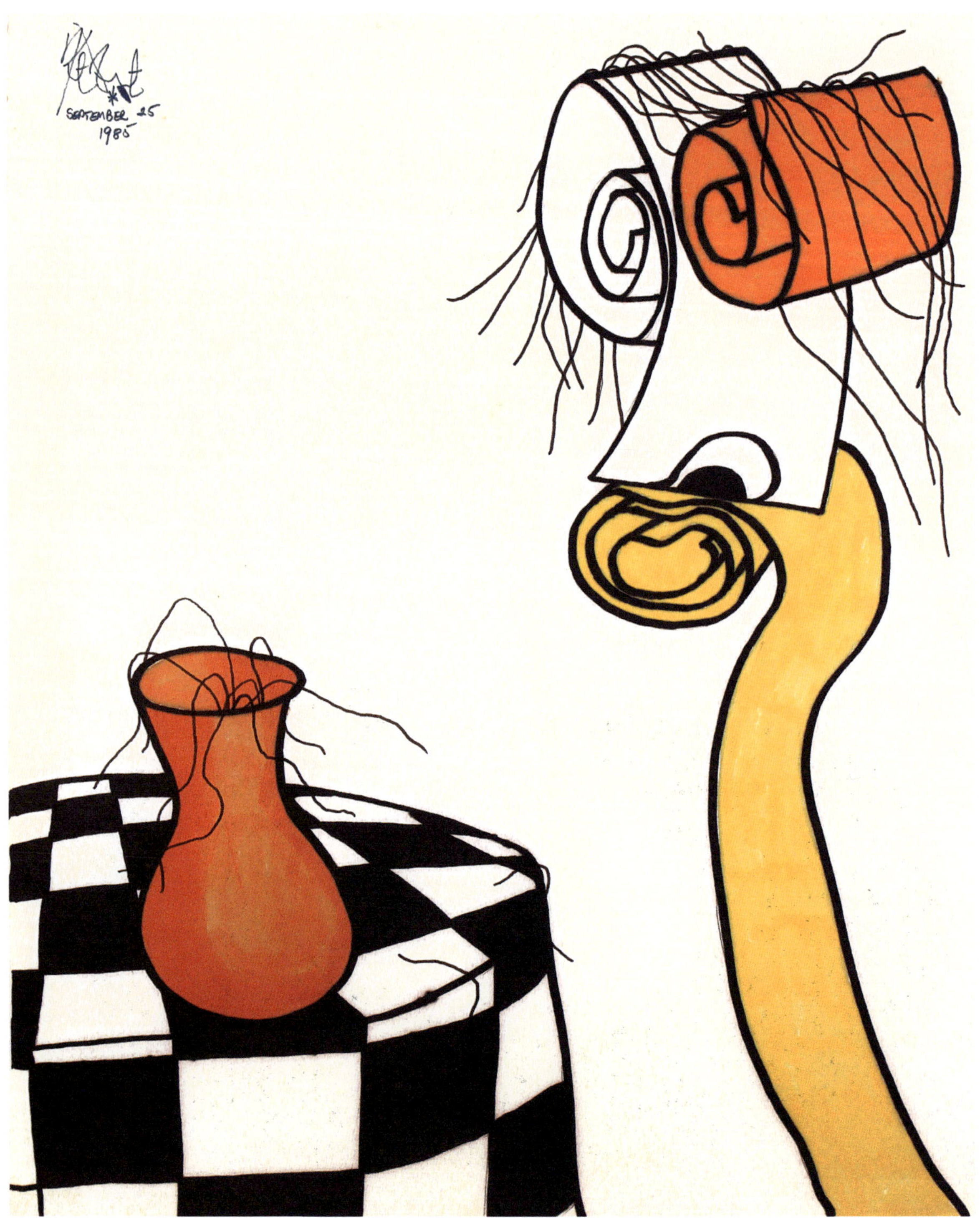

Untitled, September 25, 1985

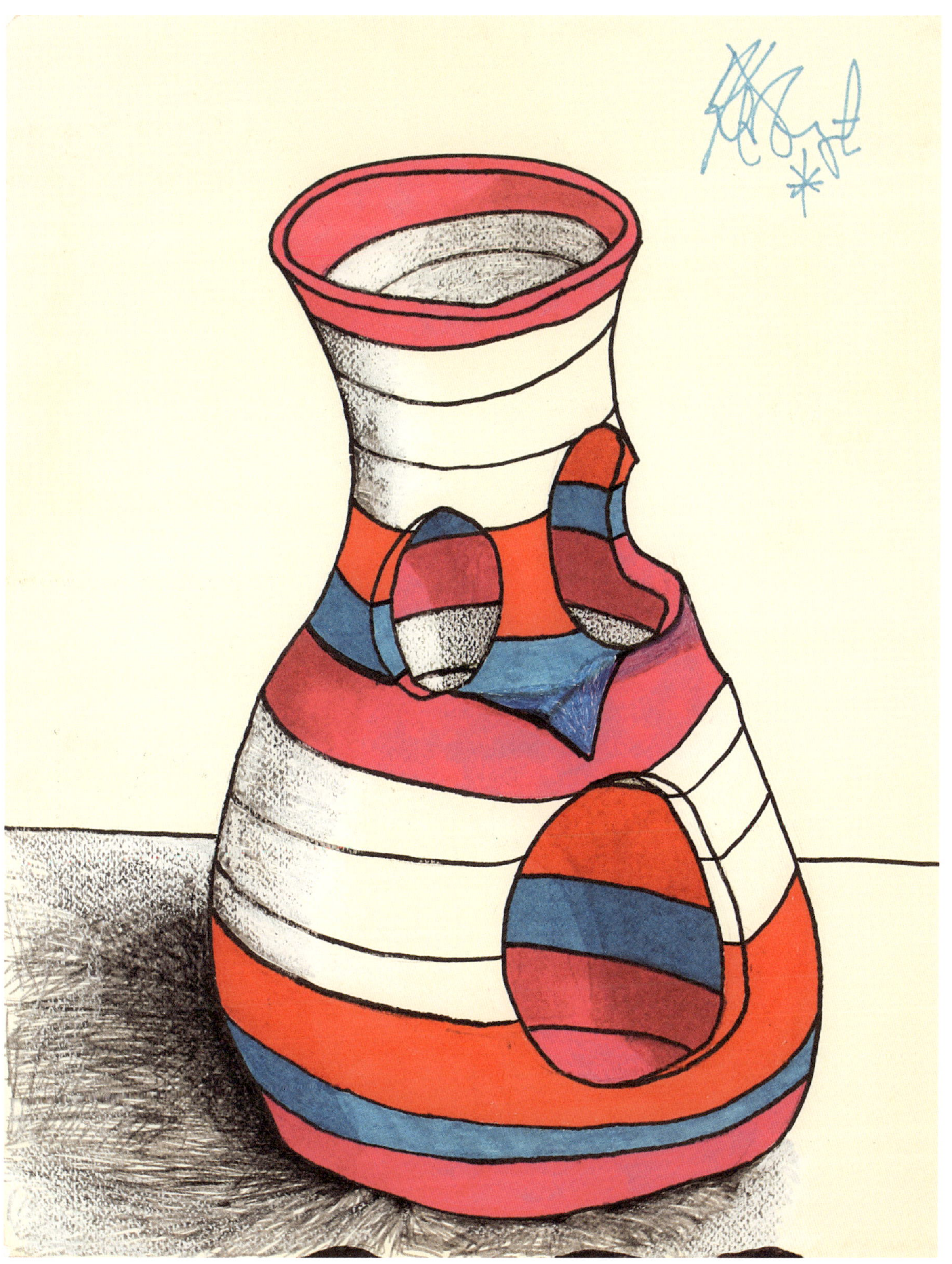

Untitled, n.d.

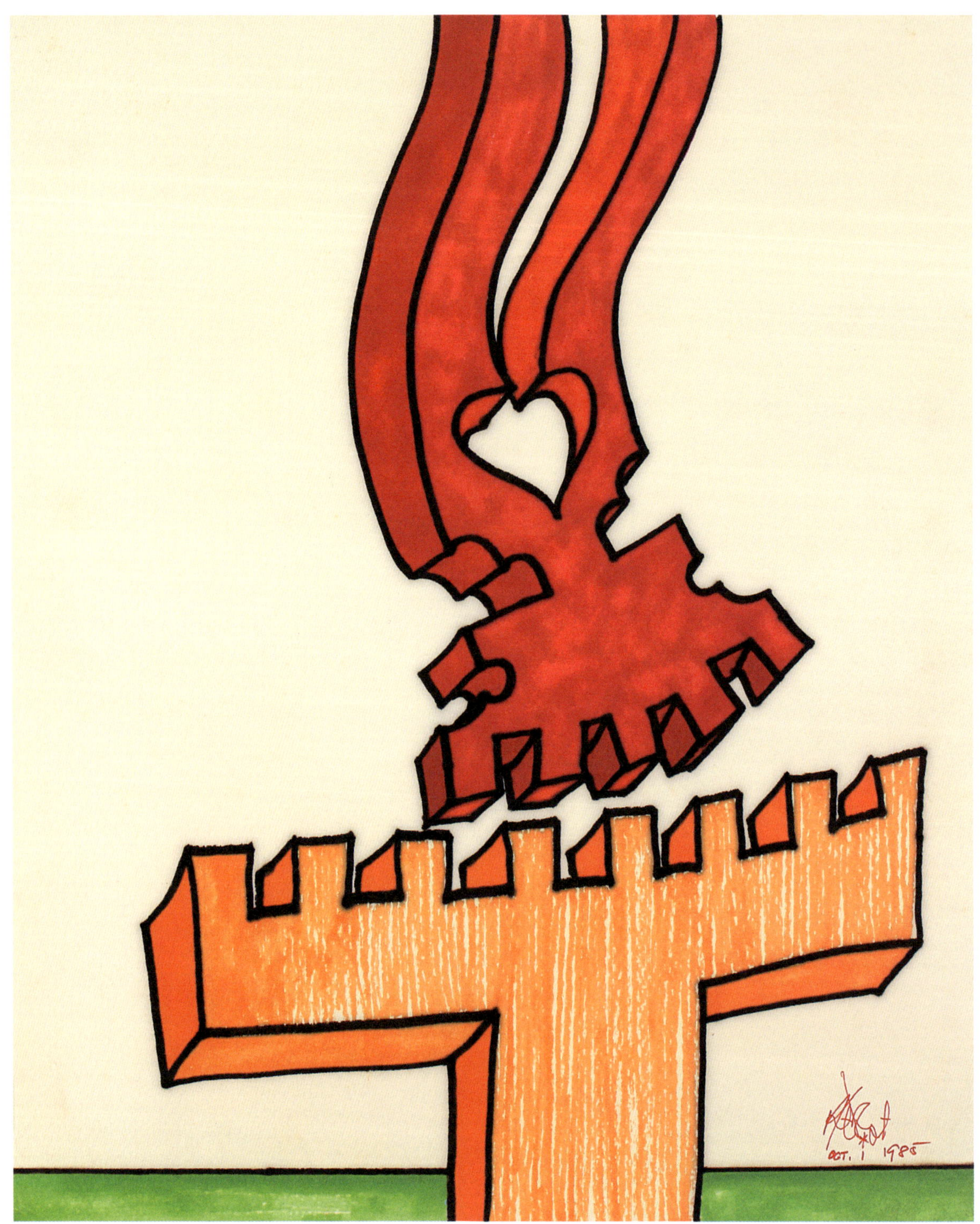

Untitled, October 7, 1985

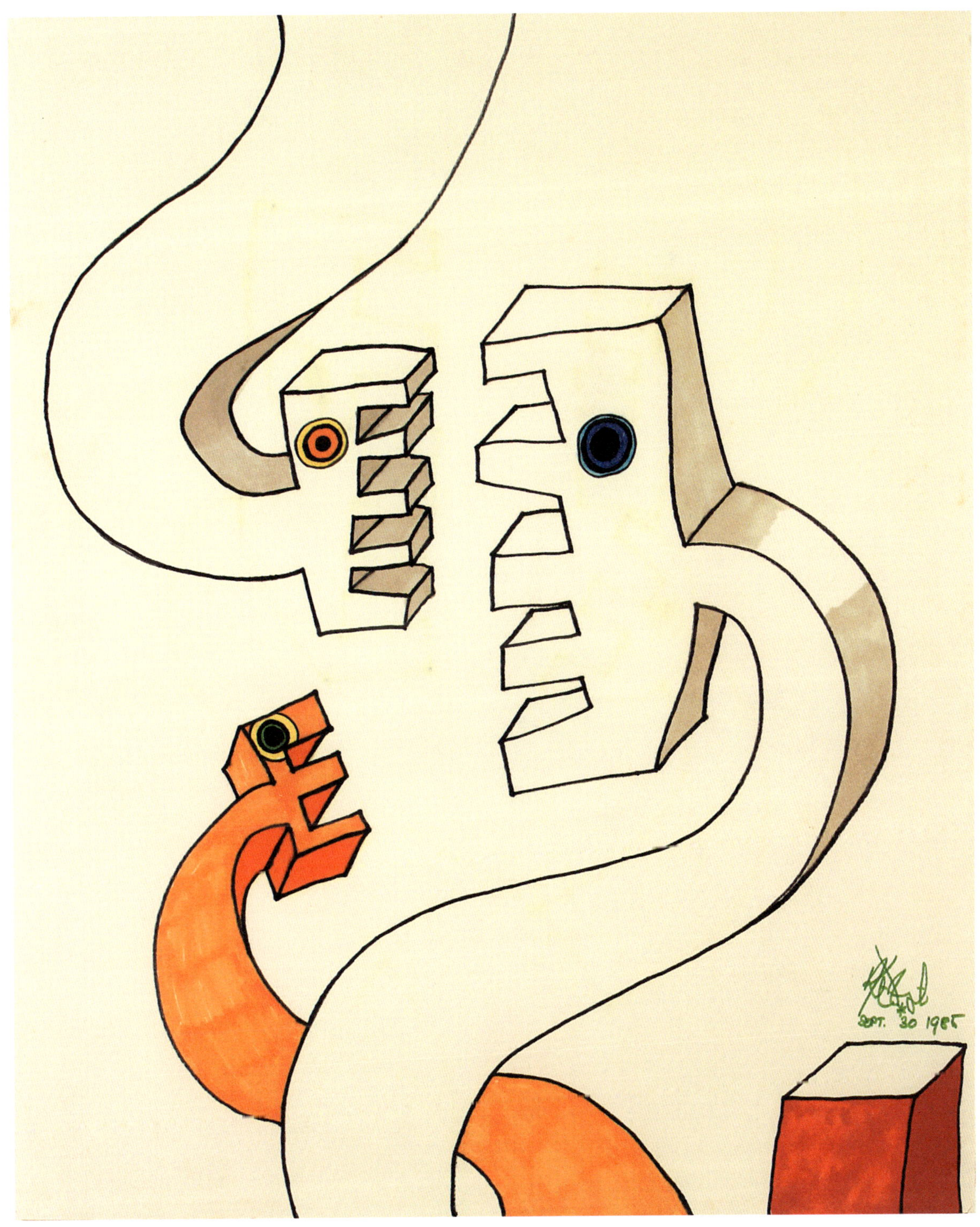

Untitled, September 30, 1985

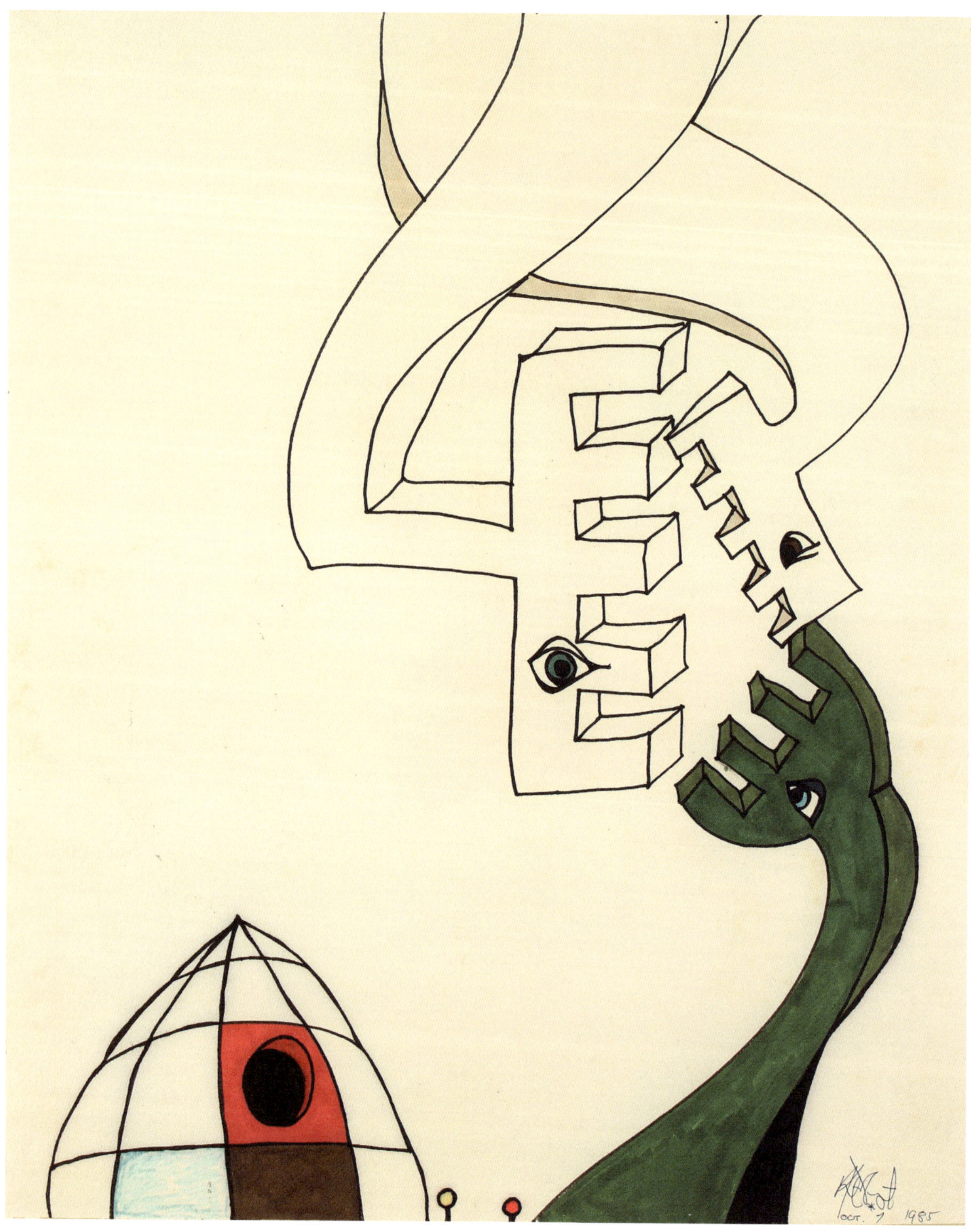

Untitled, October 7, 1985

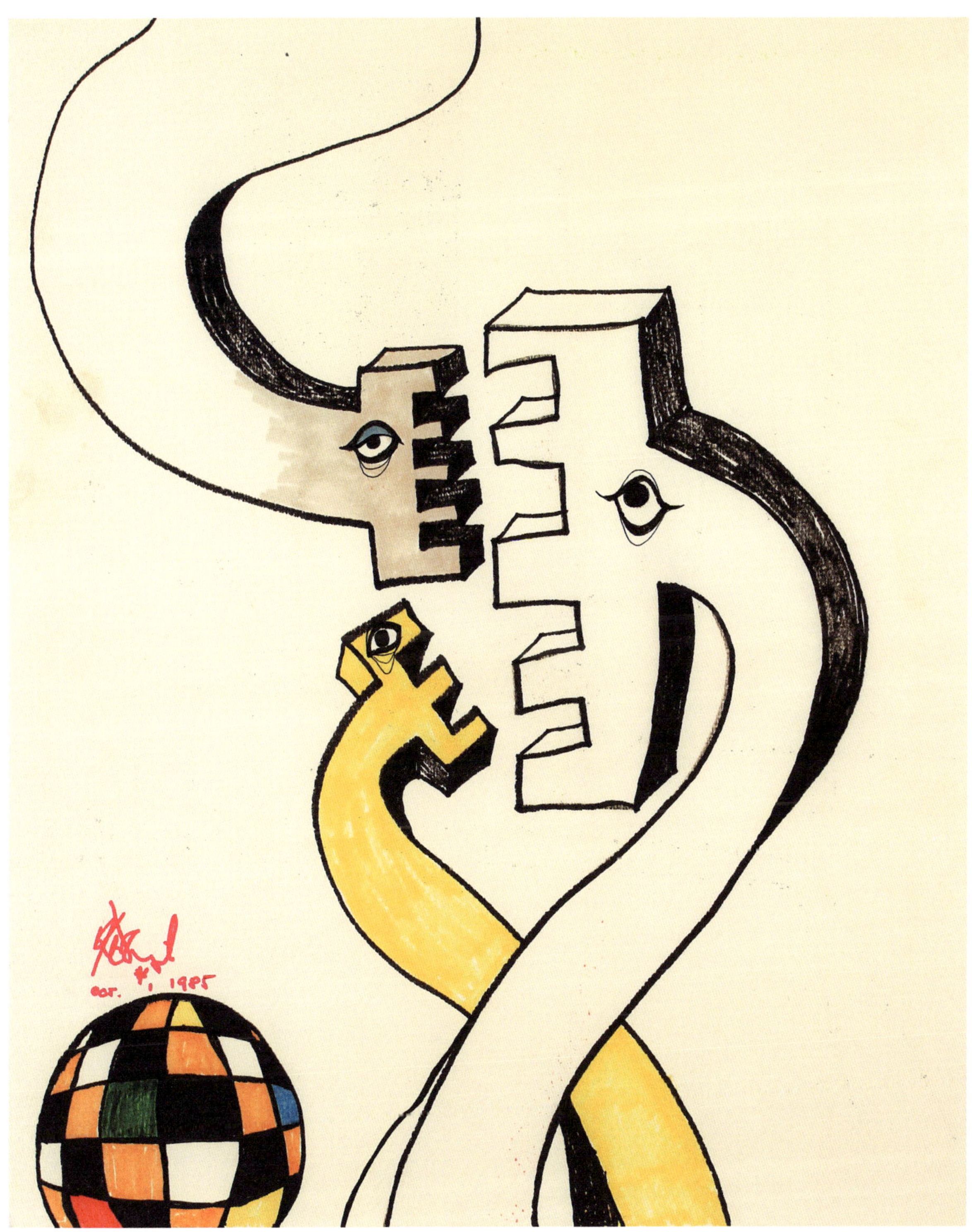

Untitled, October 1, 1985

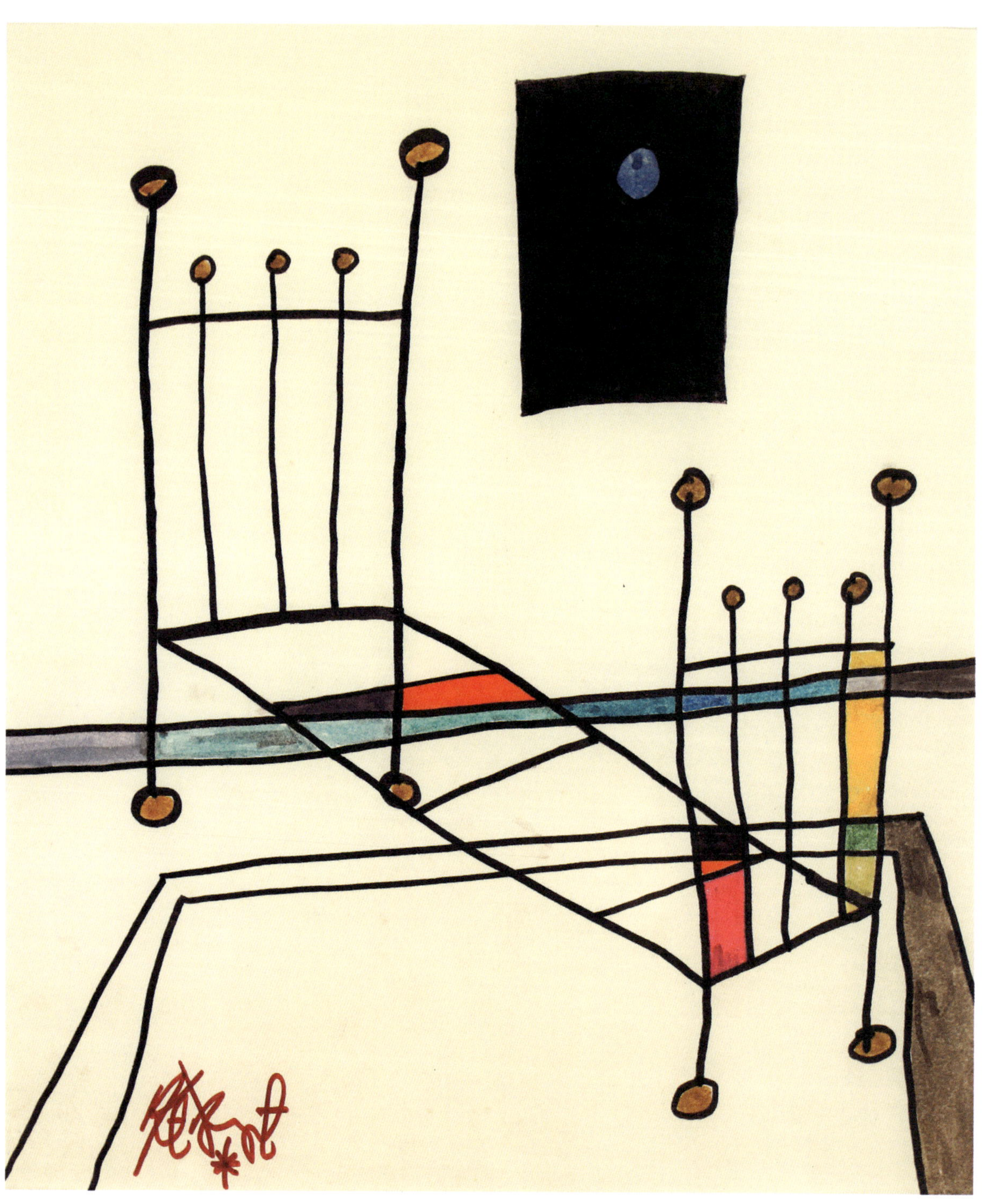

Untitled, n.d.

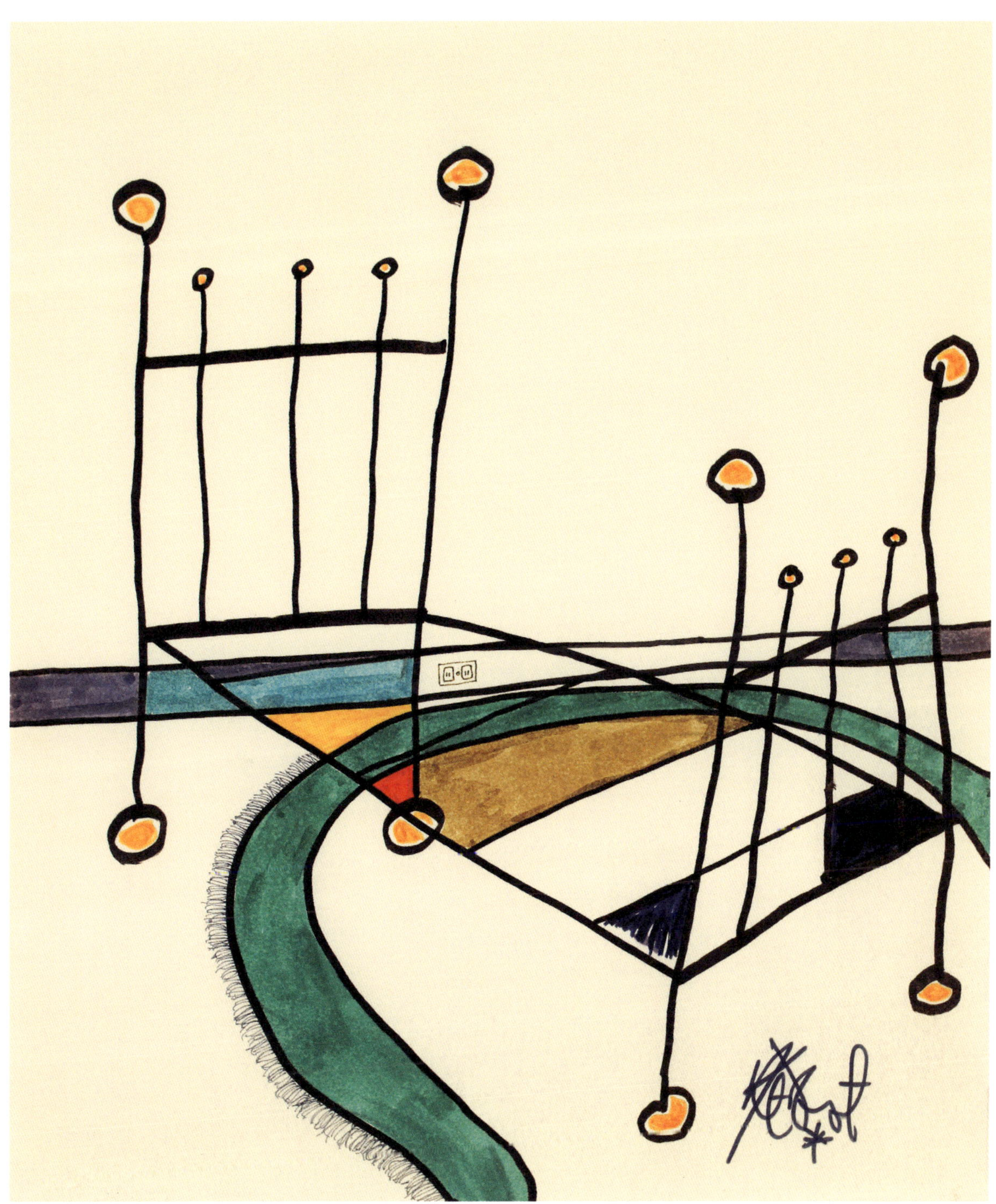

Untitled, n.d.

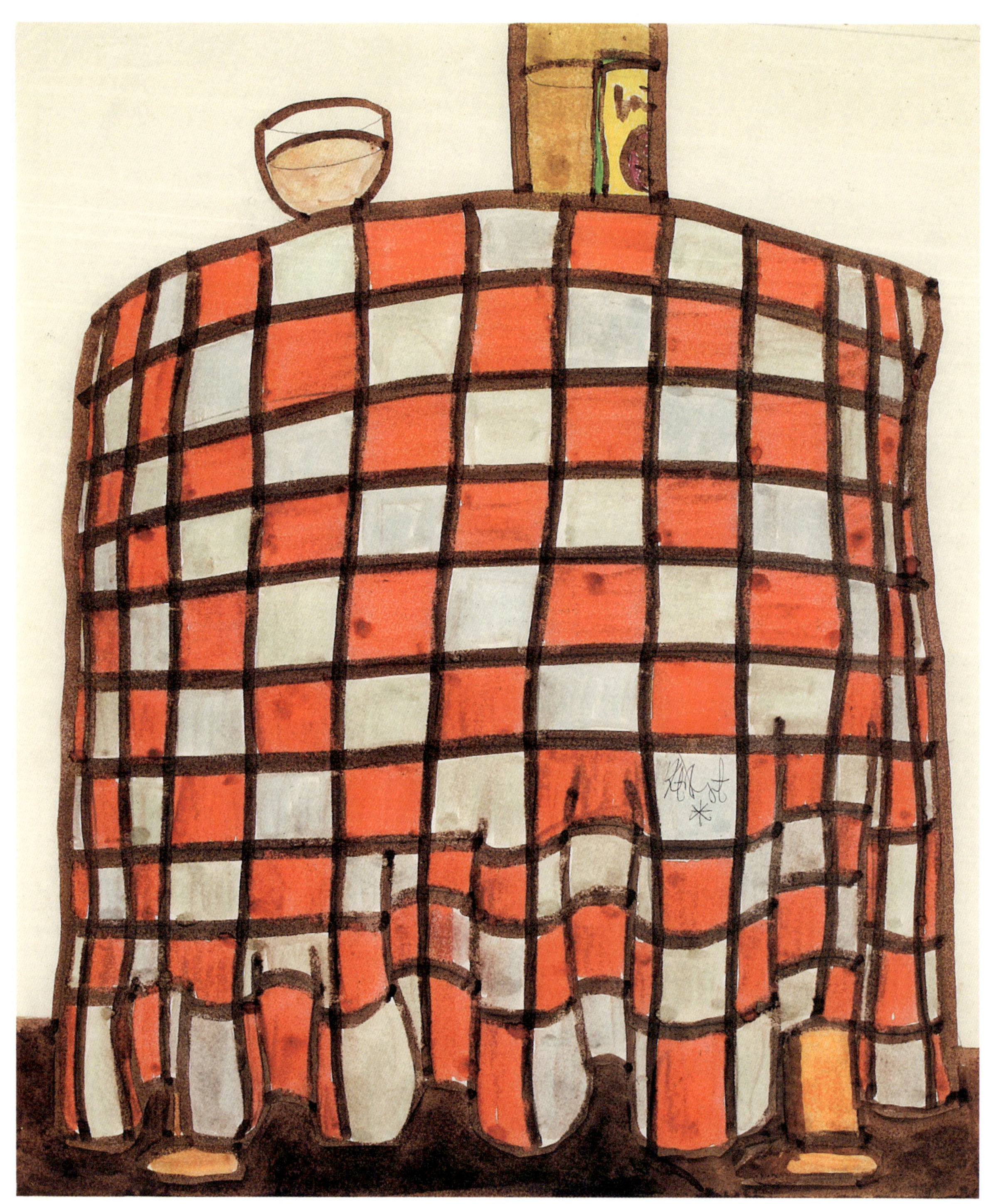

Untitled, n.d.

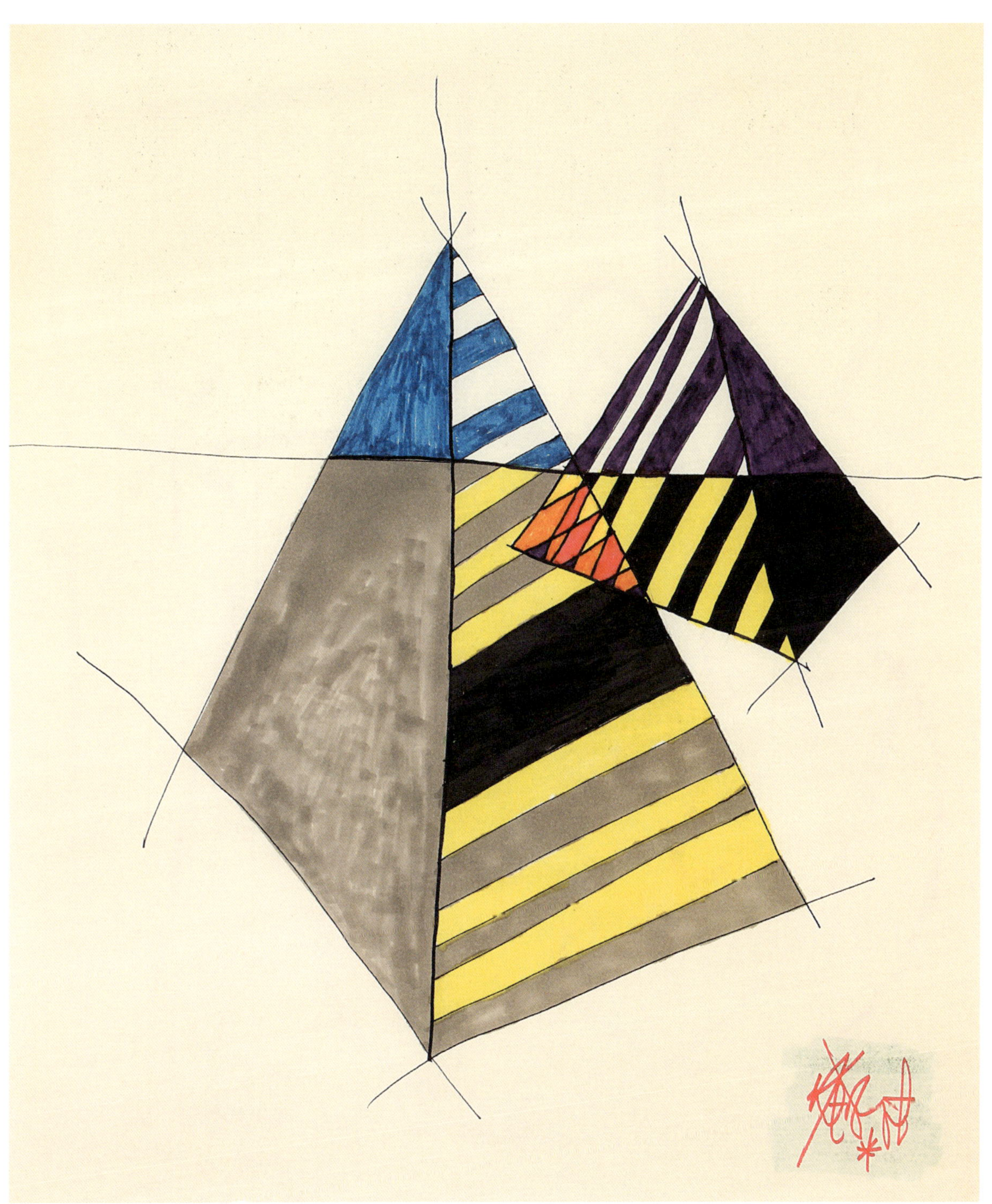

Untitled, n.d.

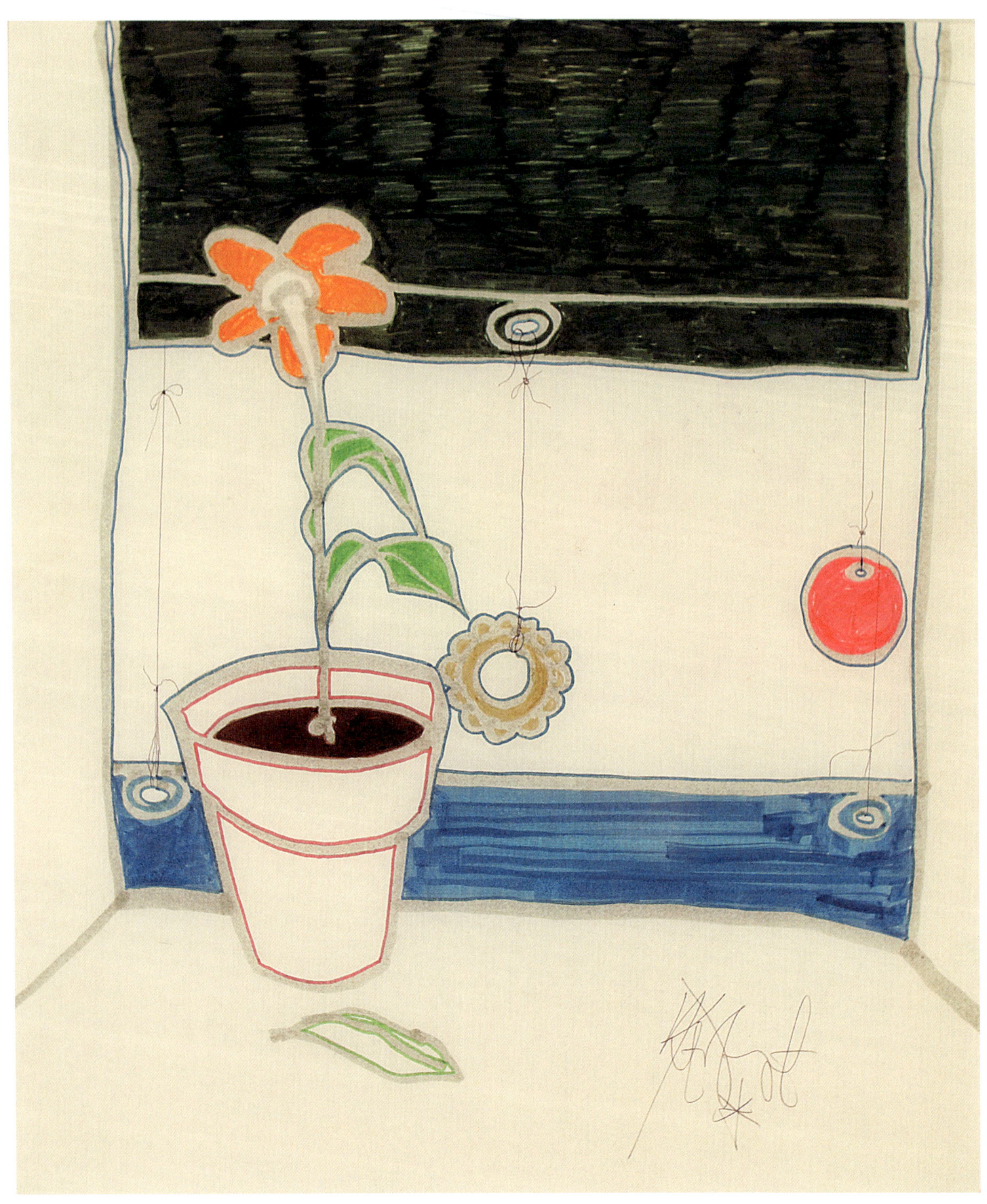

Untitled, n.d.

The most satisfied of all painters is the one who can become intoxicated for hours or days or weeks or years with what his or her hands and eyes can do with art materials, and let the rest of the world go hang.

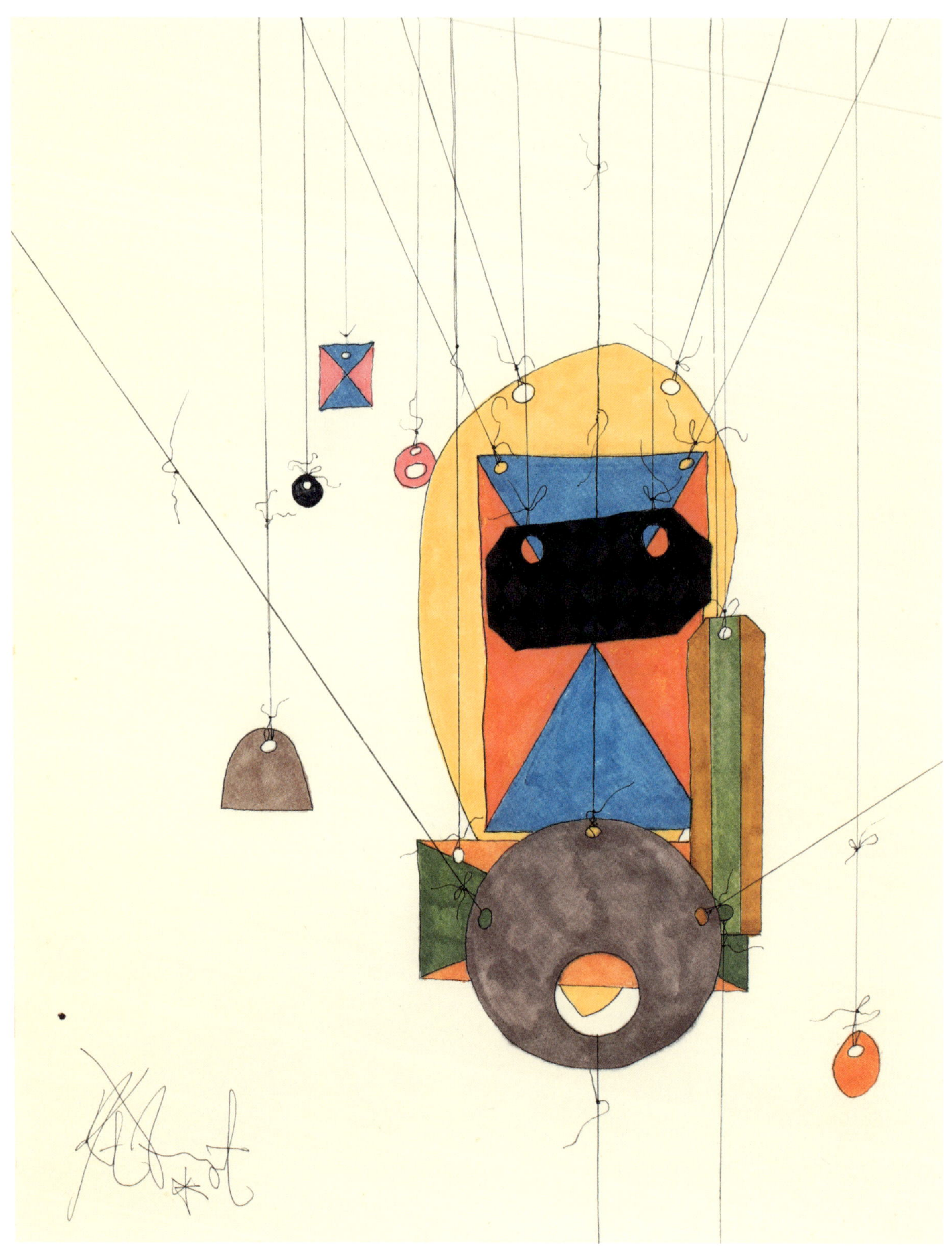

Untitled, n.d.

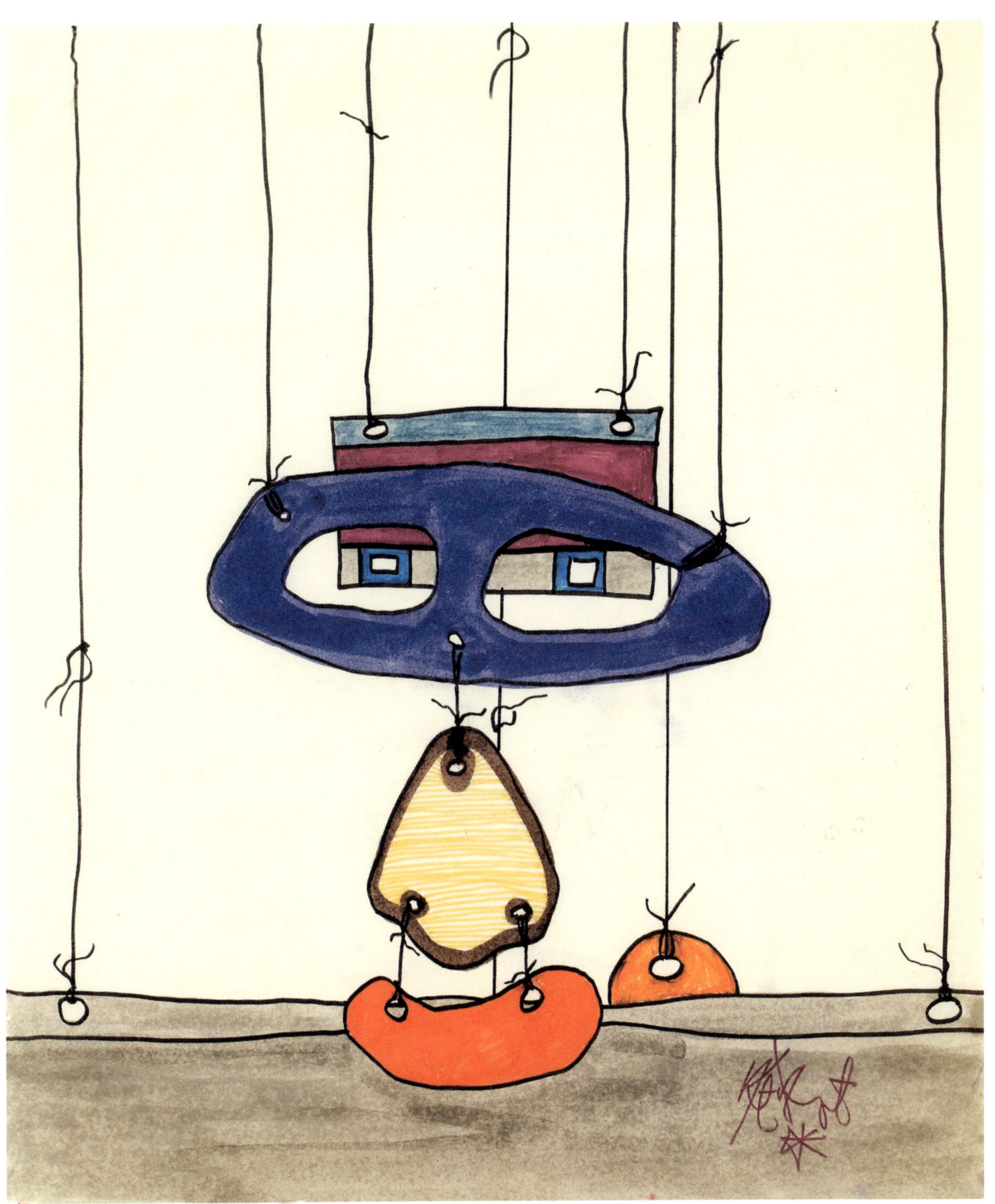

Untitled, n.d.

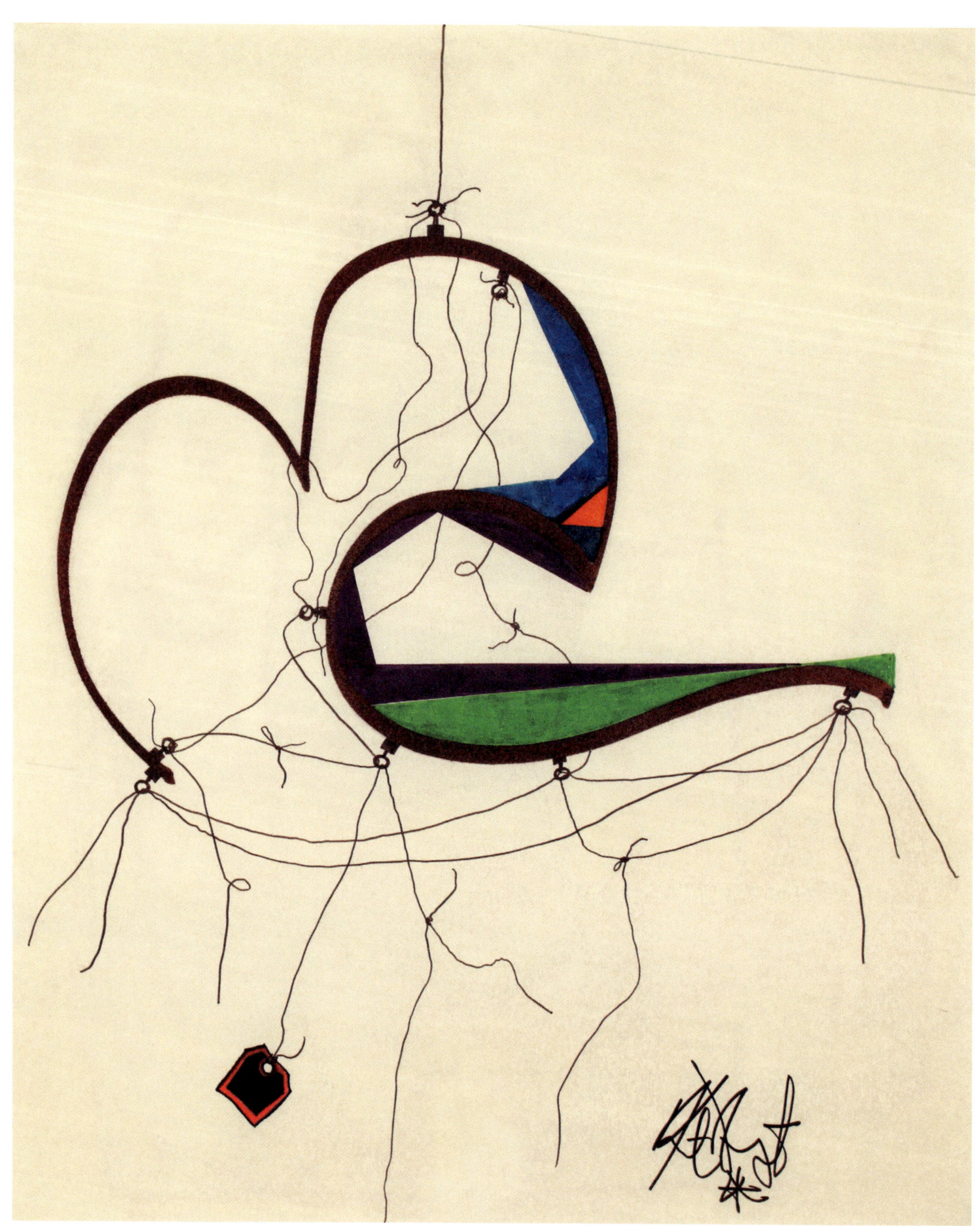

Untitled, n.d.

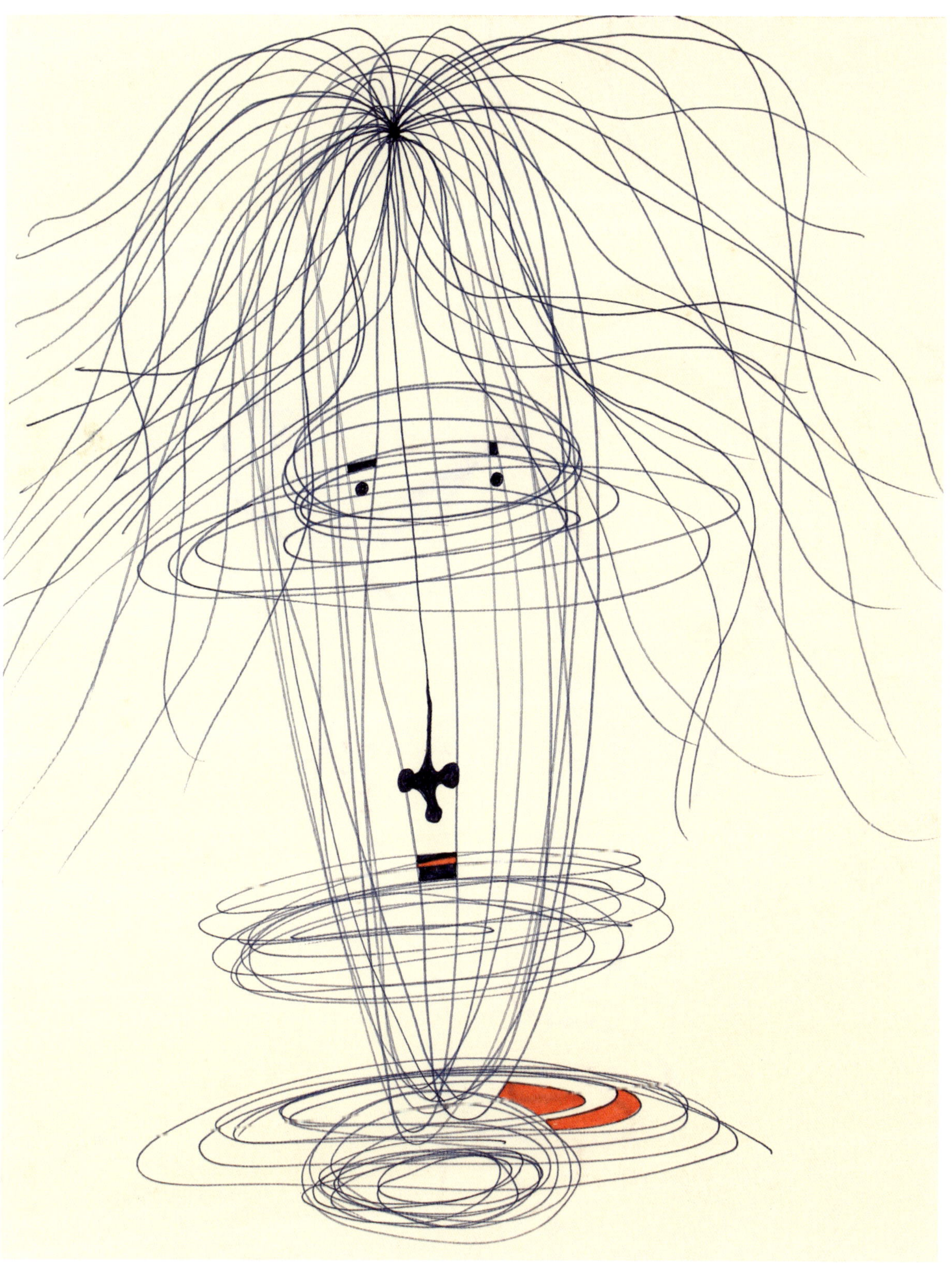

Untitled, n.d.

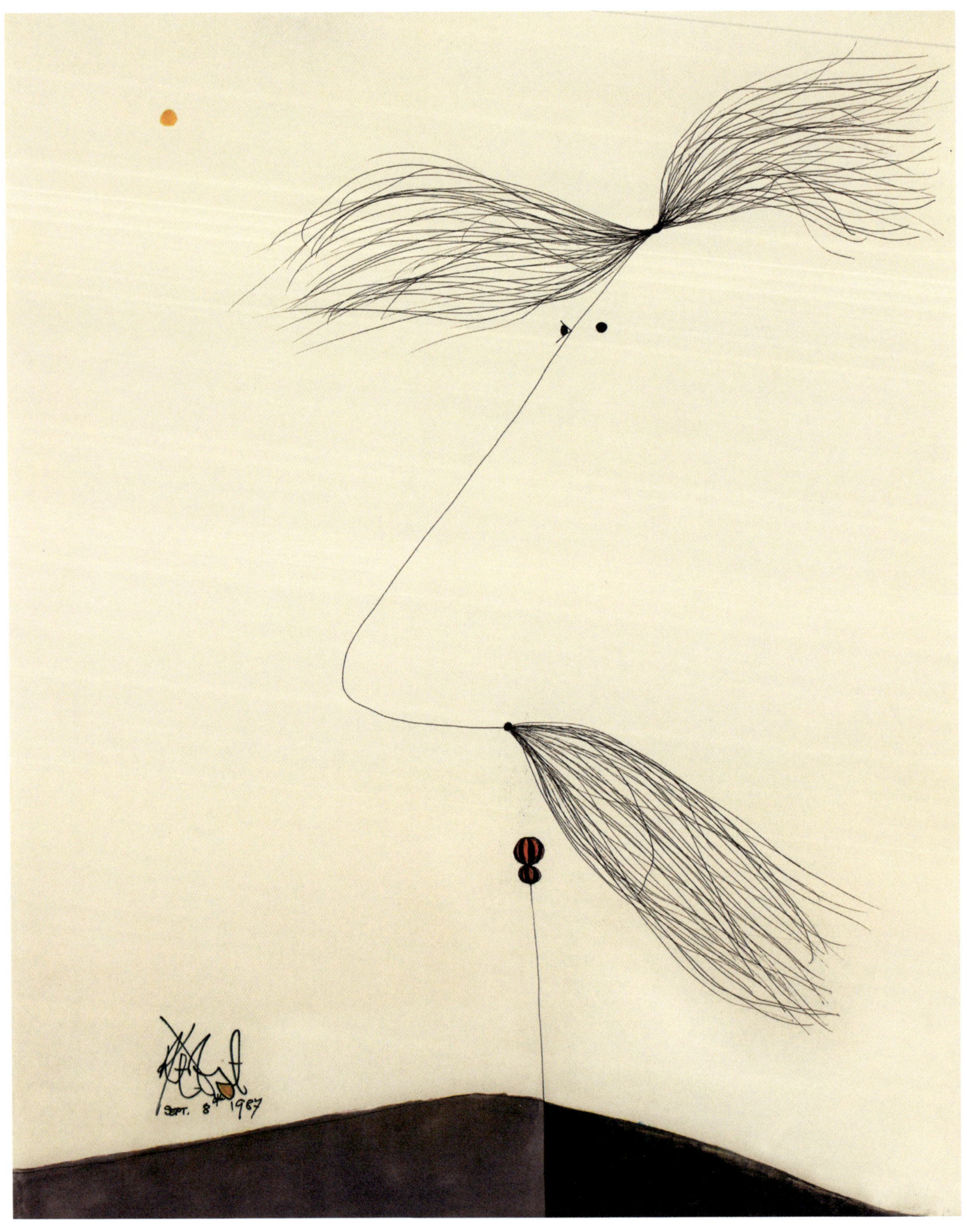

Untitled, September 8, 1987

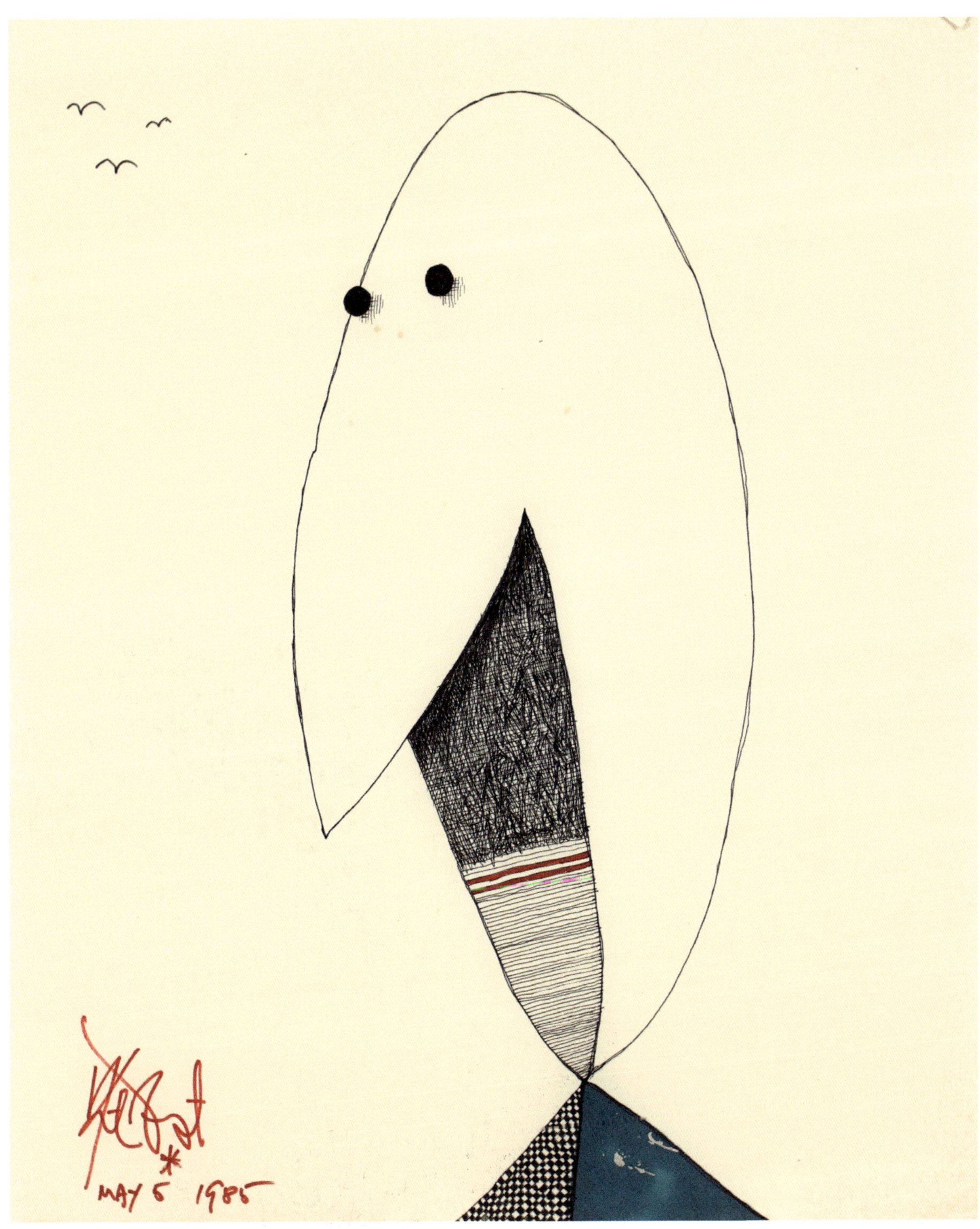

Untitled, May 5, 1985

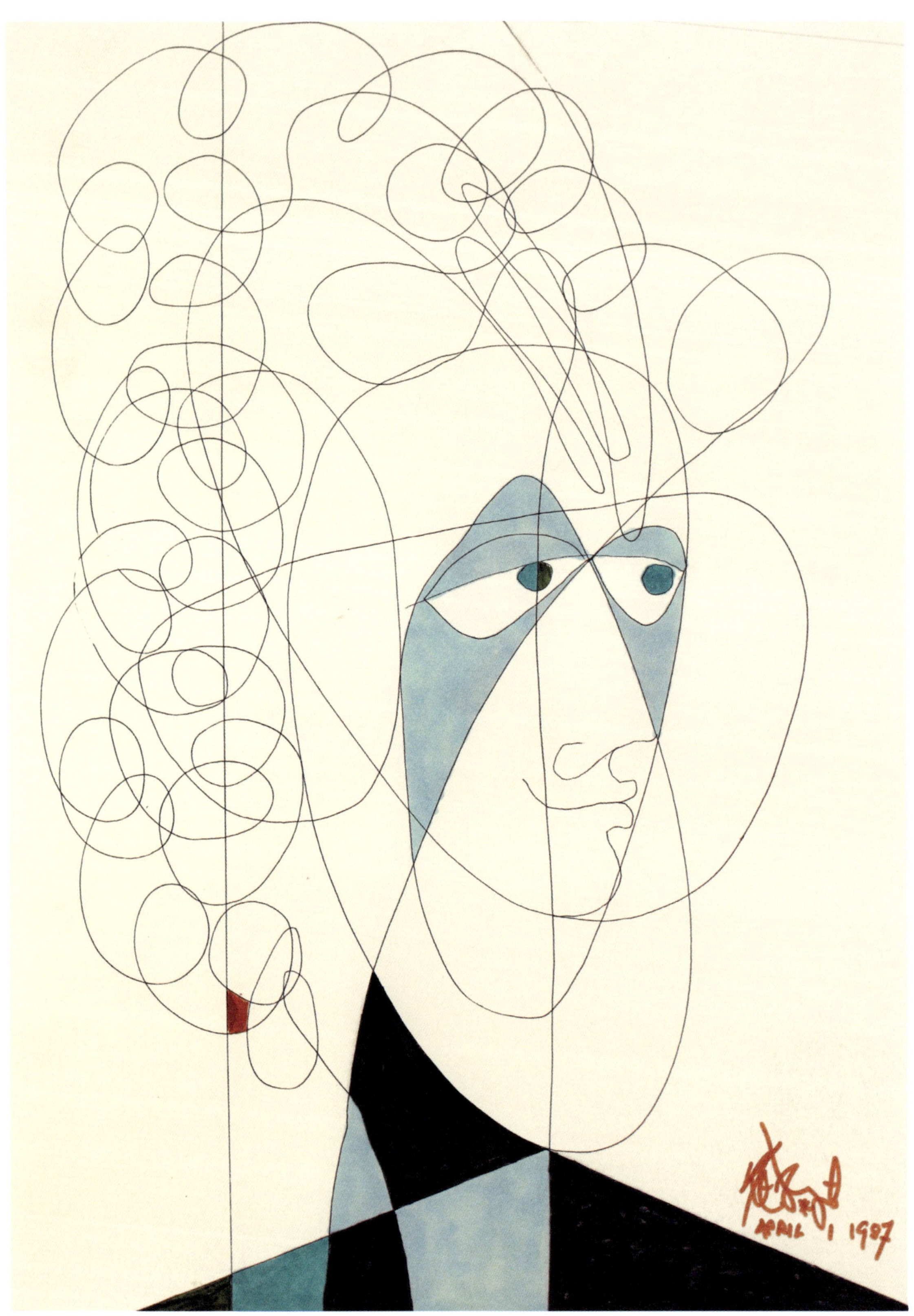

Untitled, April 1, 1987

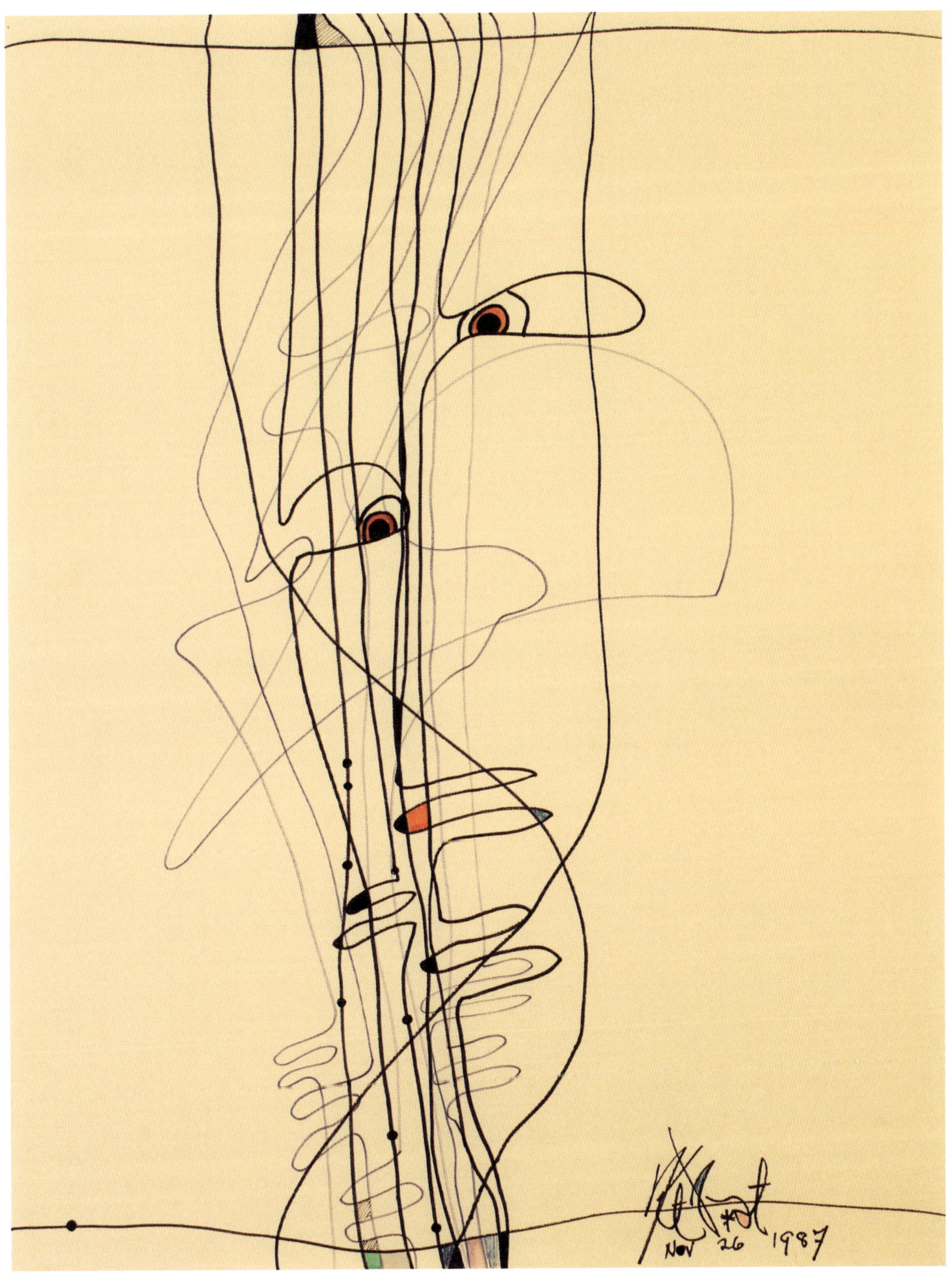

Untitled, November 26, 1987

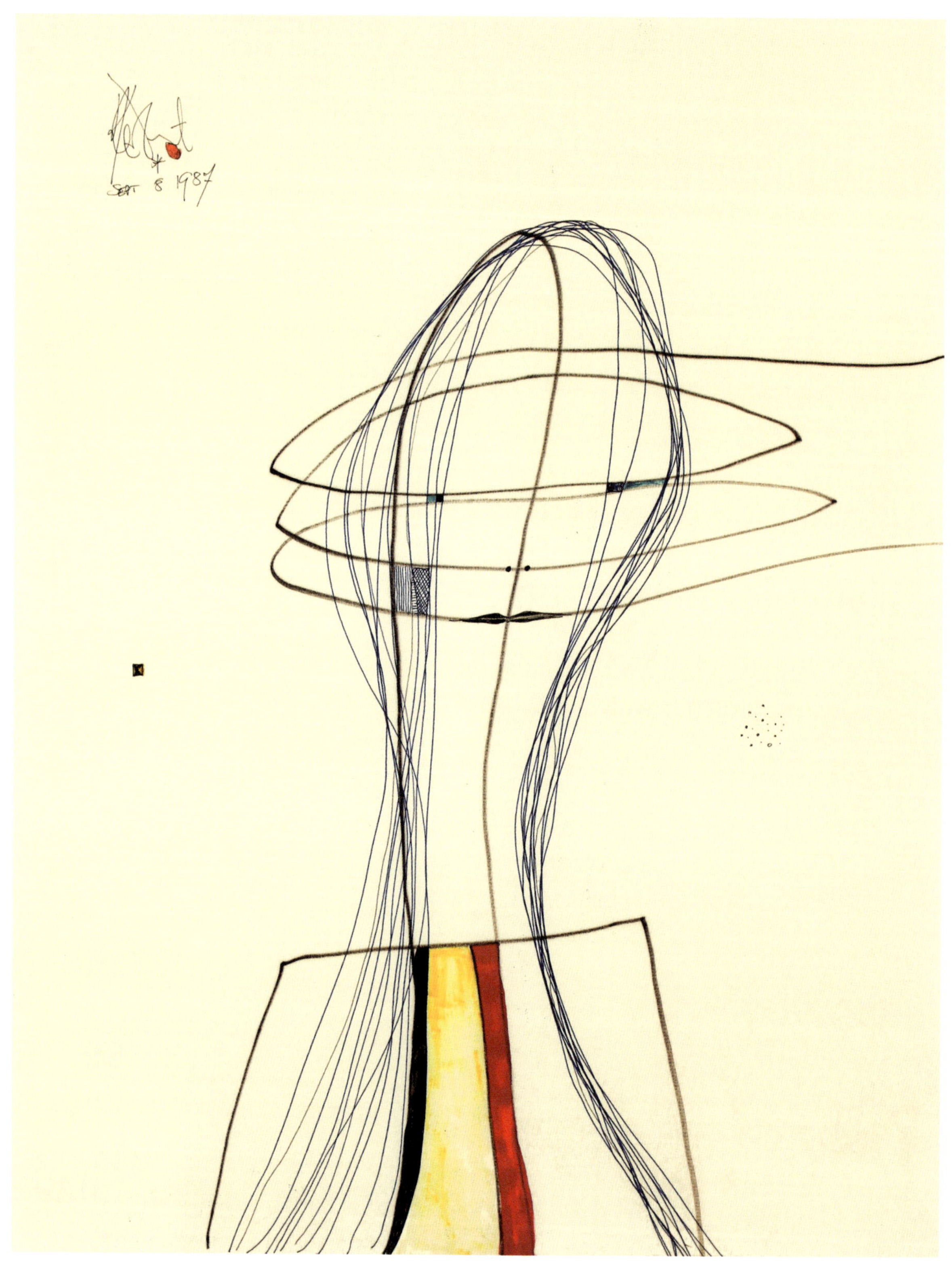

Untitled, September 8, 1987

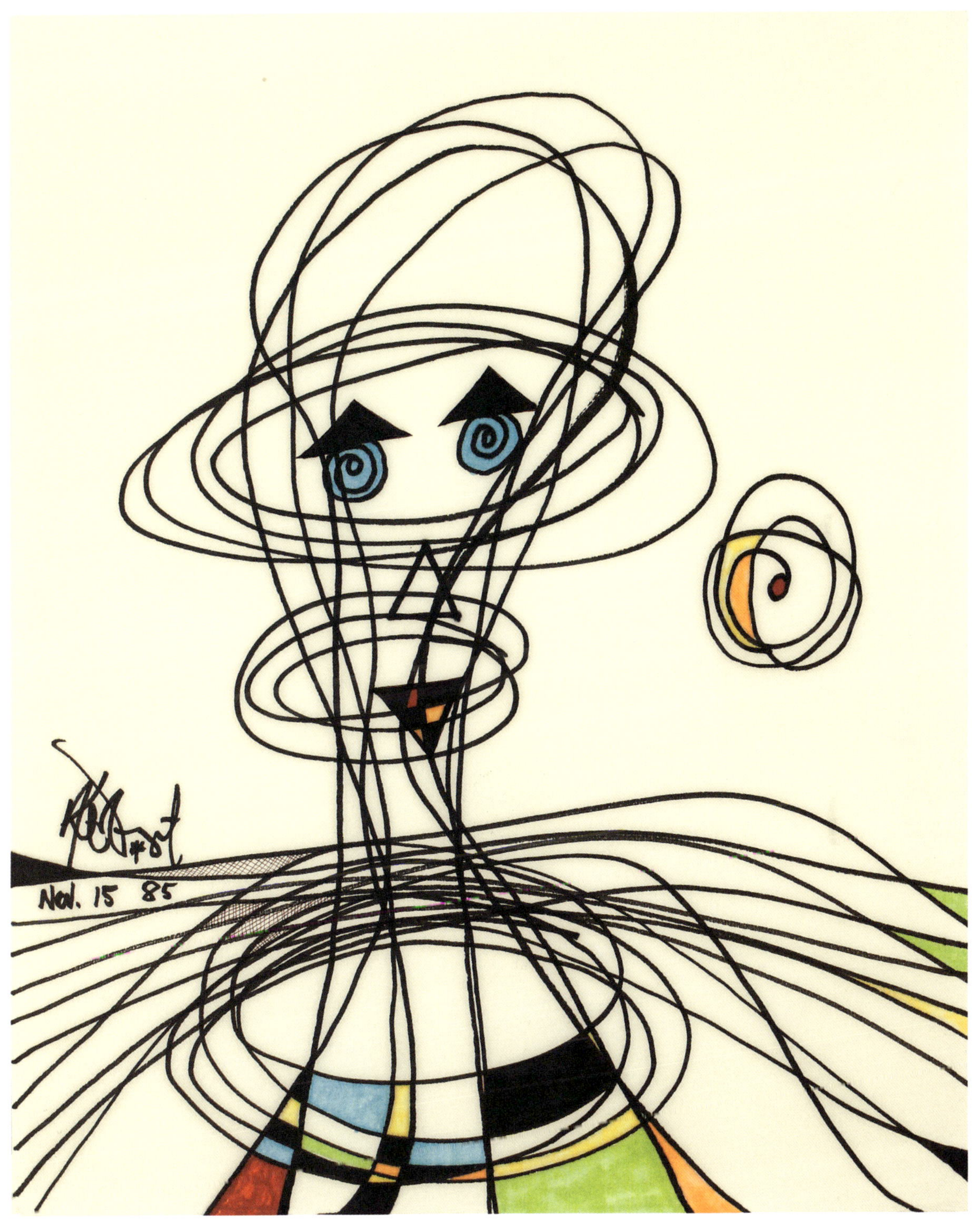

Untitled, November 15, 1985

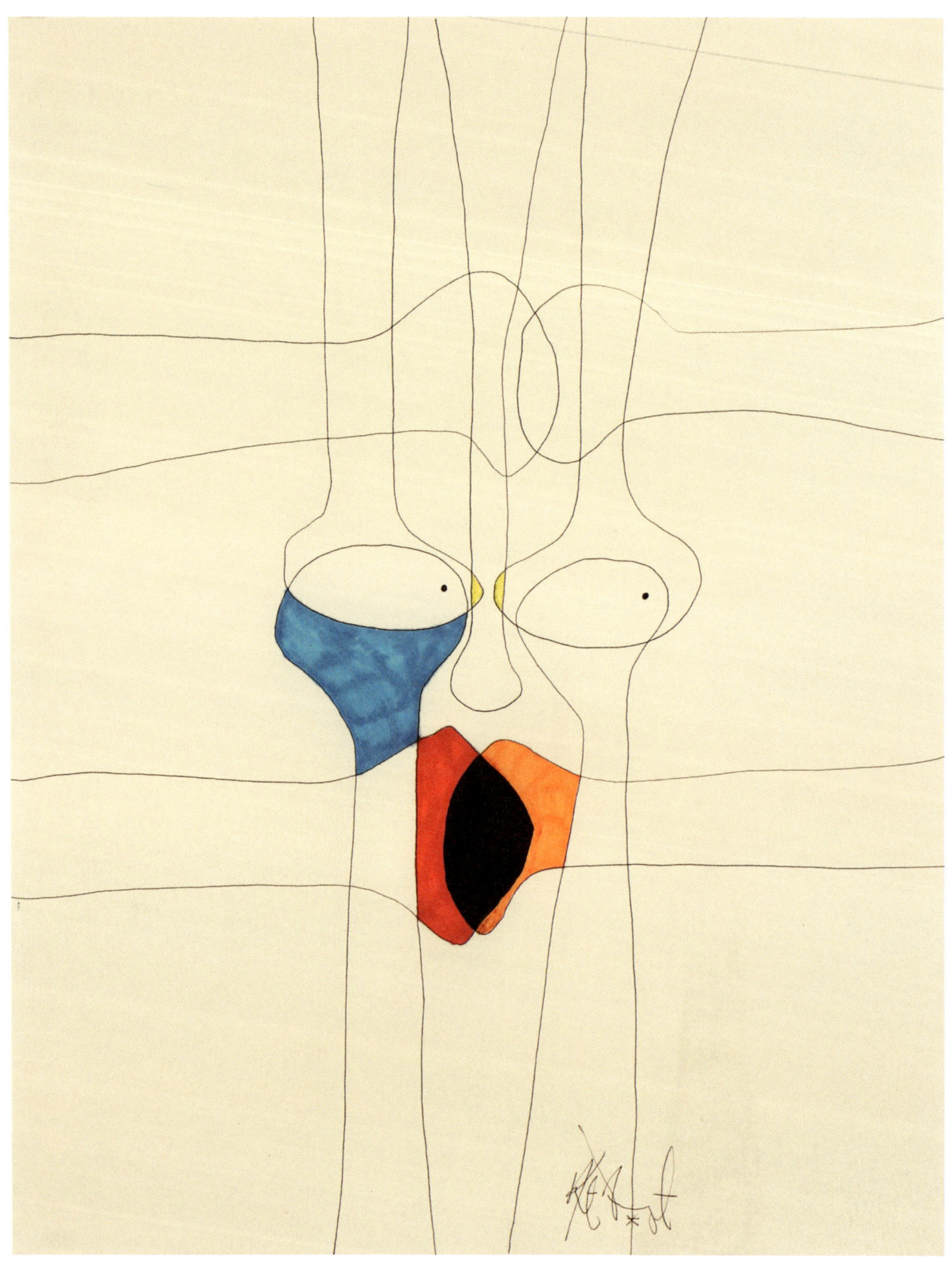

Untitled, n.d.

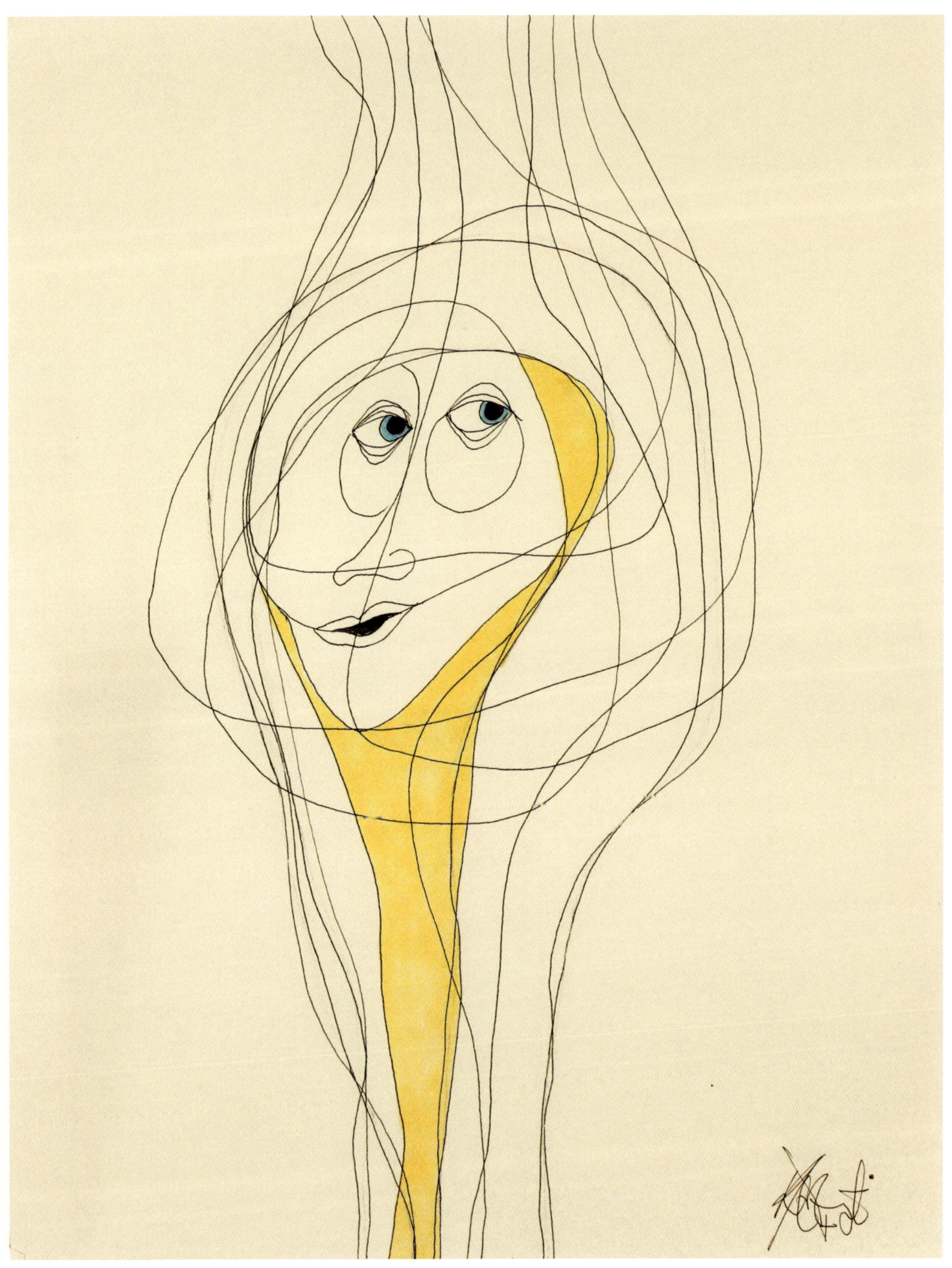

Untitled, n.d.

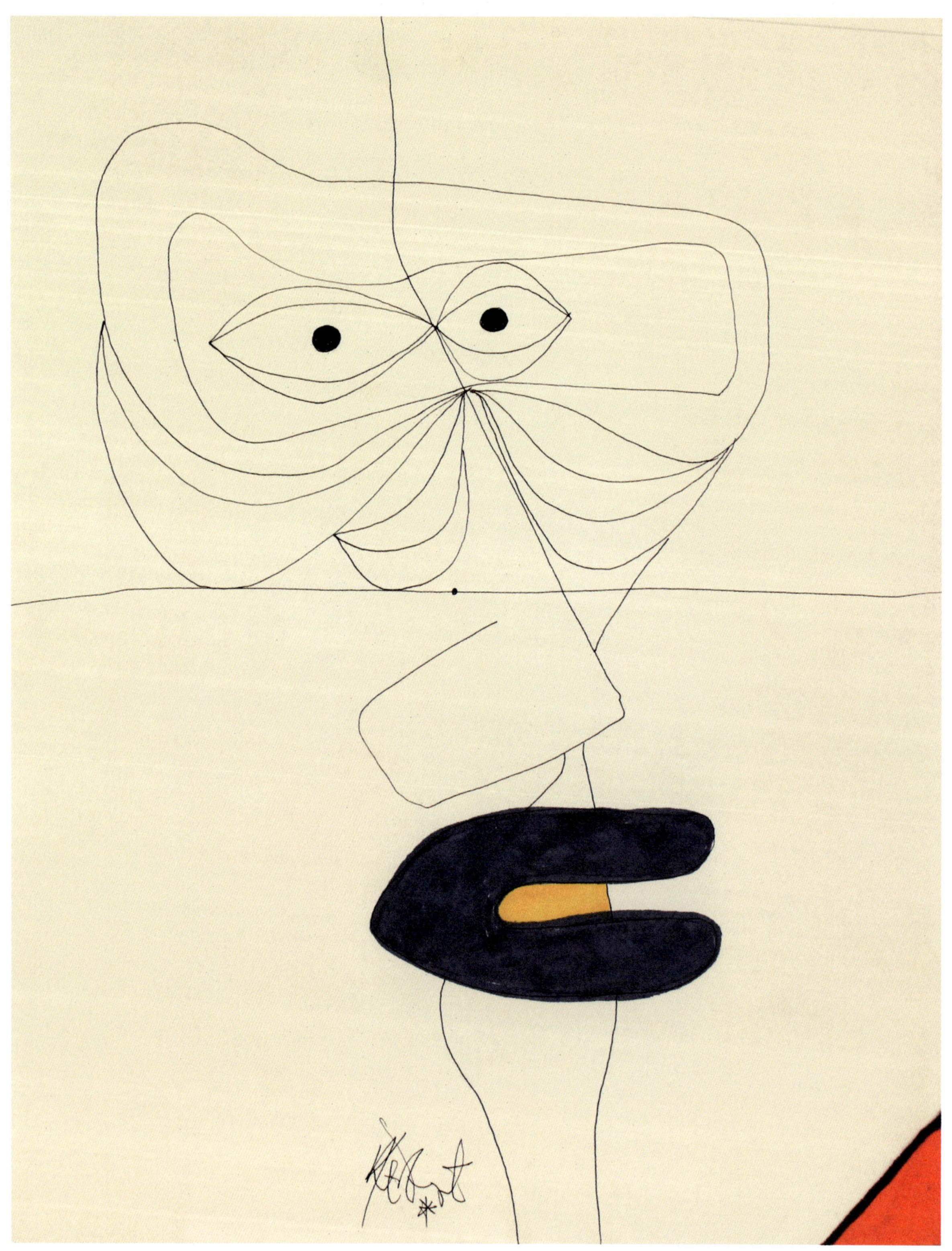

Untitled, n.d.

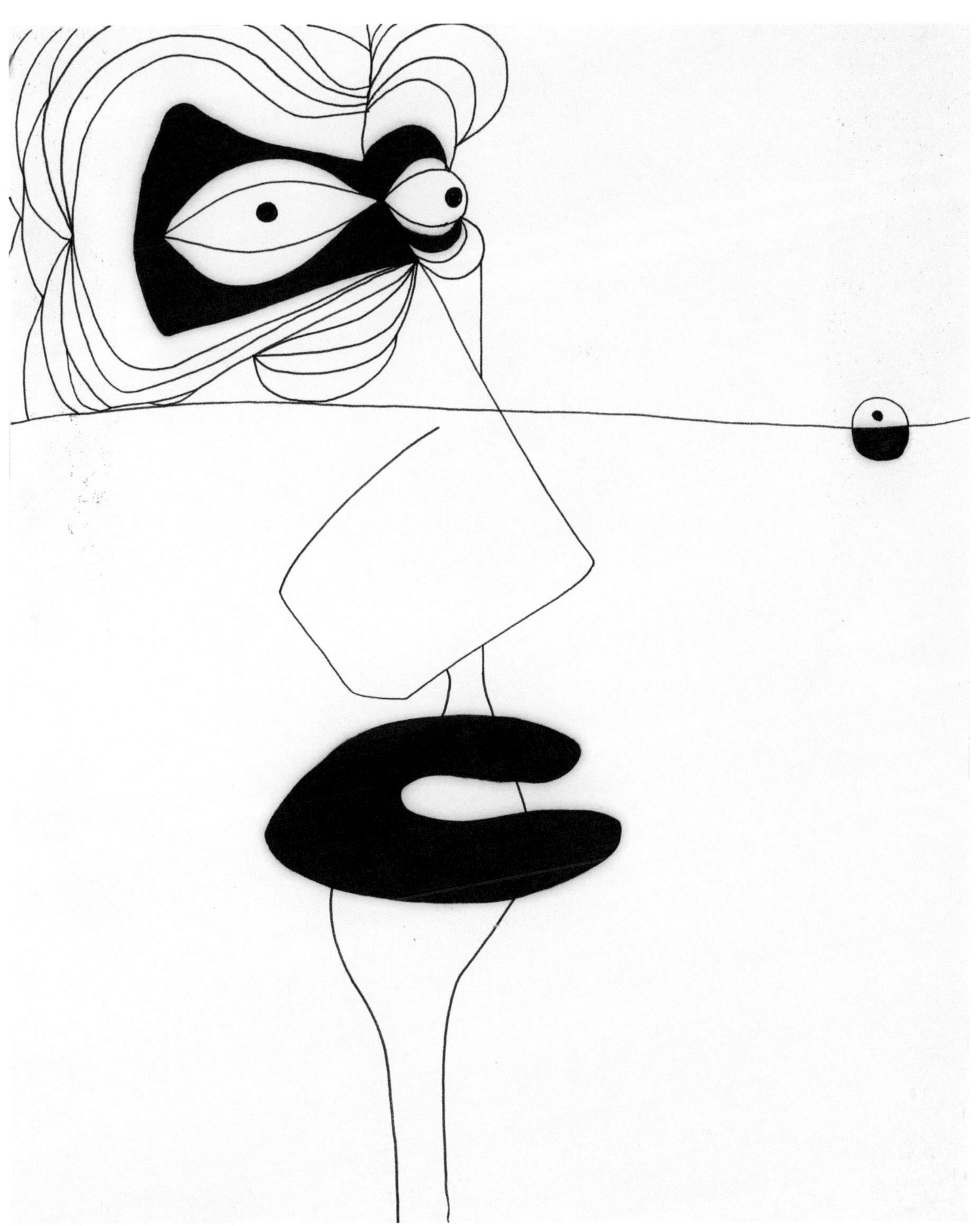

Untitled, n.d.

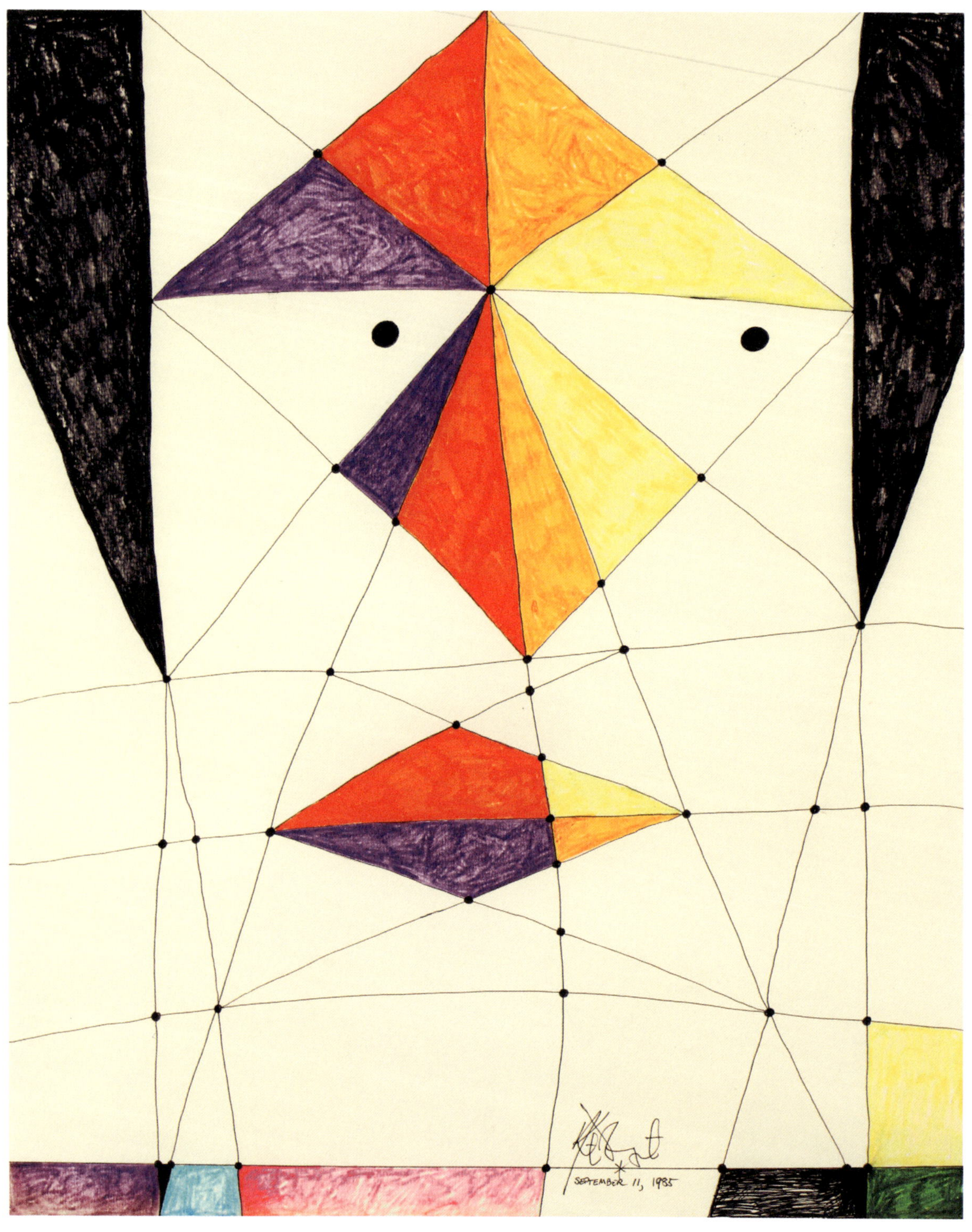

Untitled, September 11, 1985

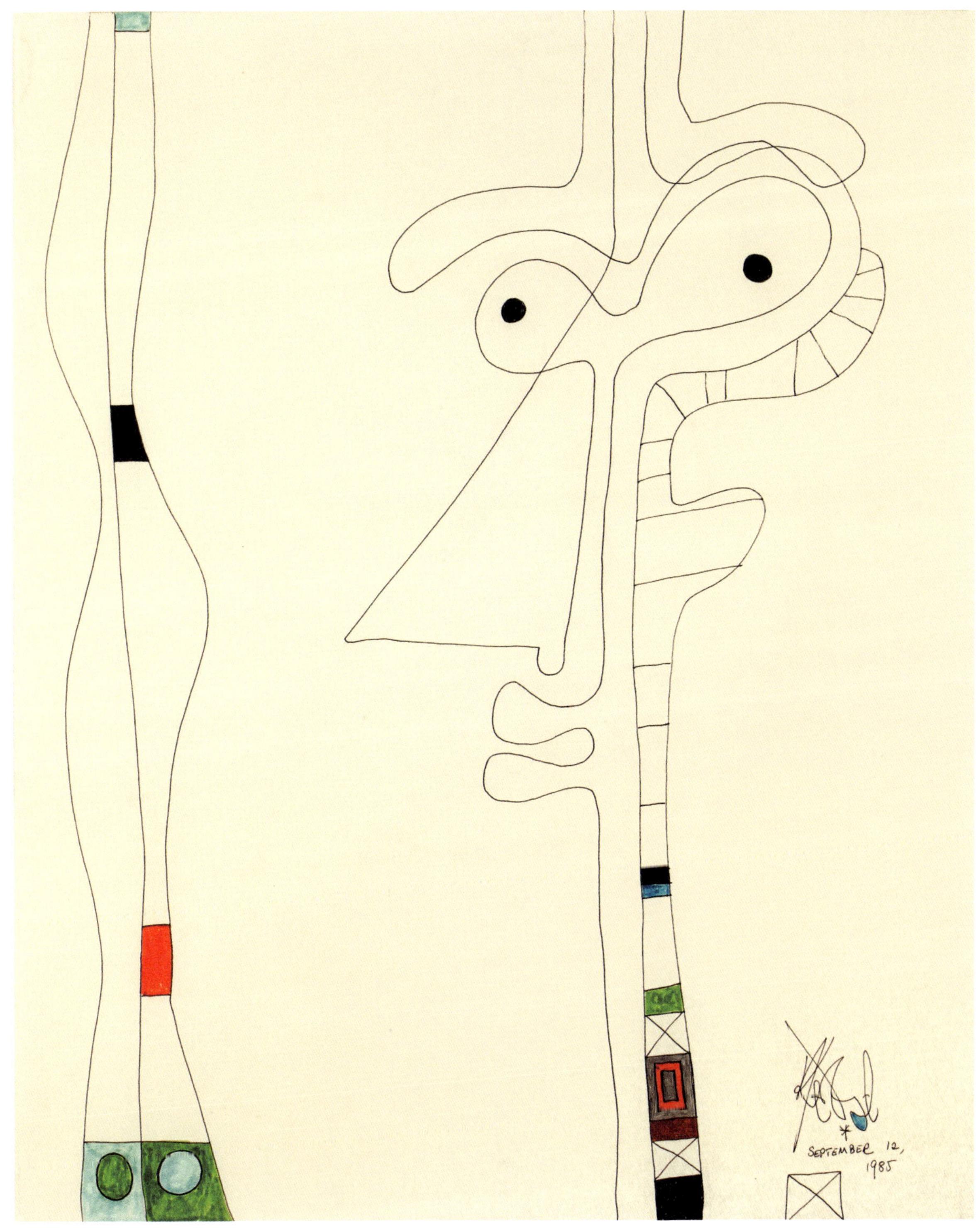

Untitled, September 12, 1985

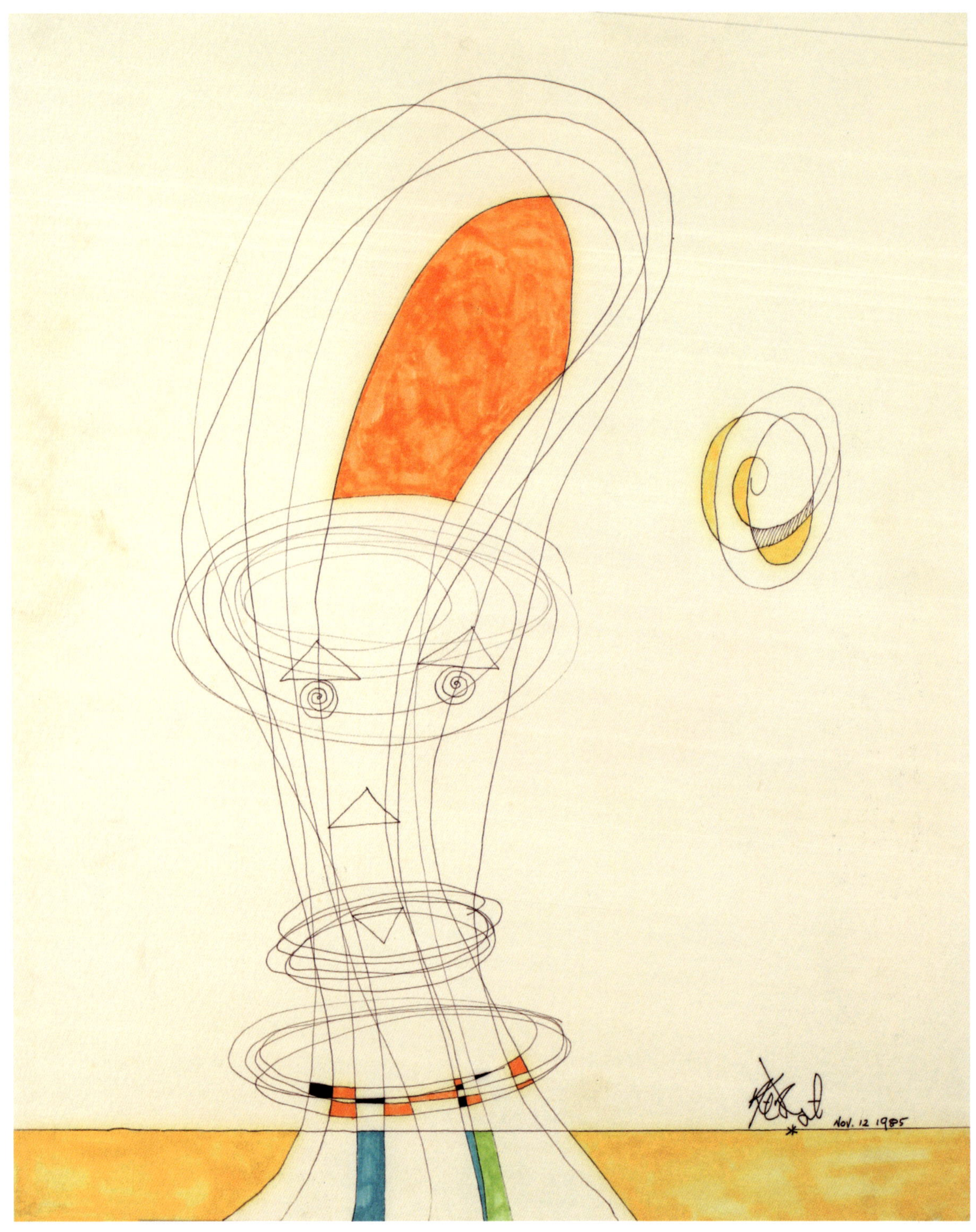

Untitled, November 12, 1985

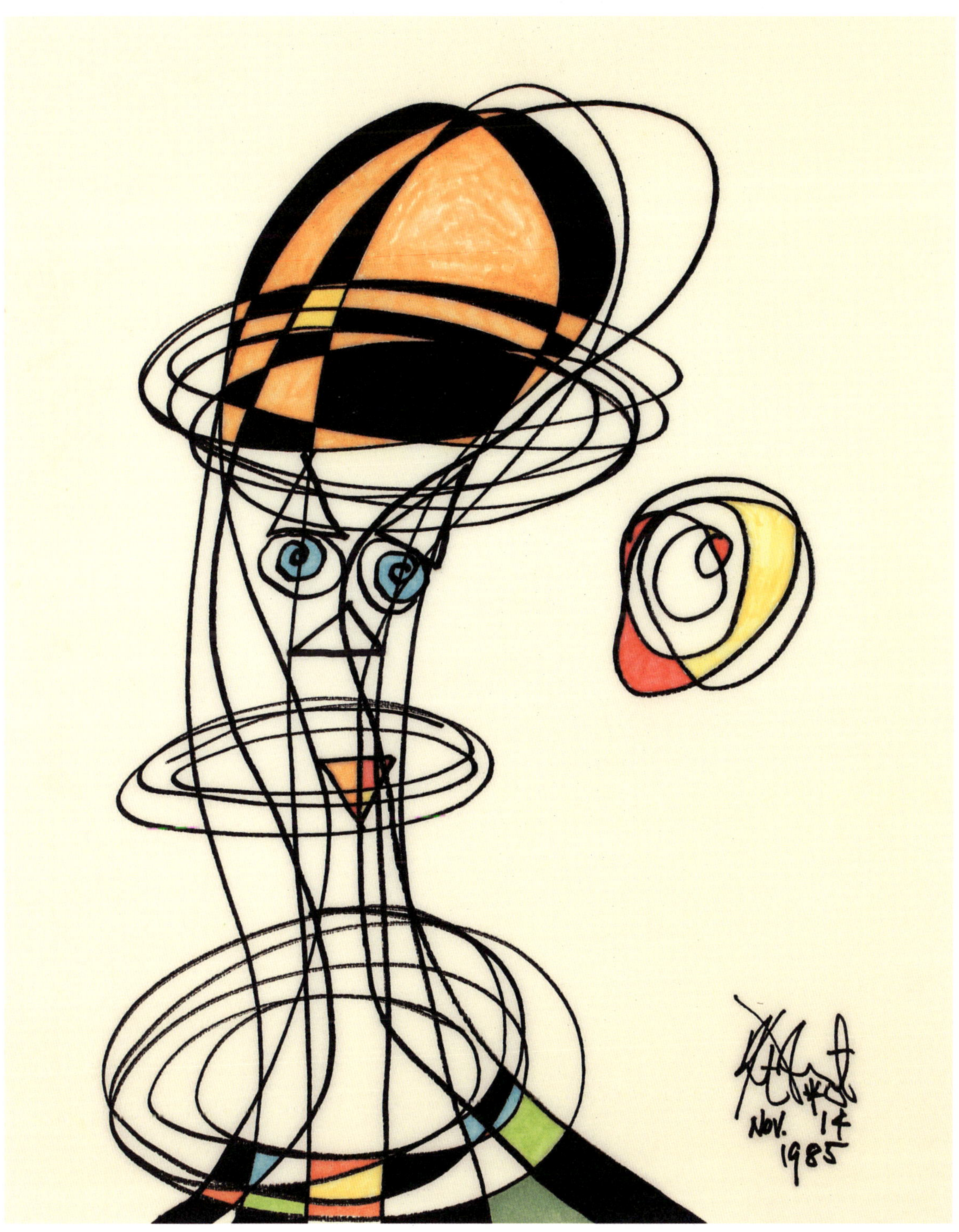

Untitled, November 14, 1985

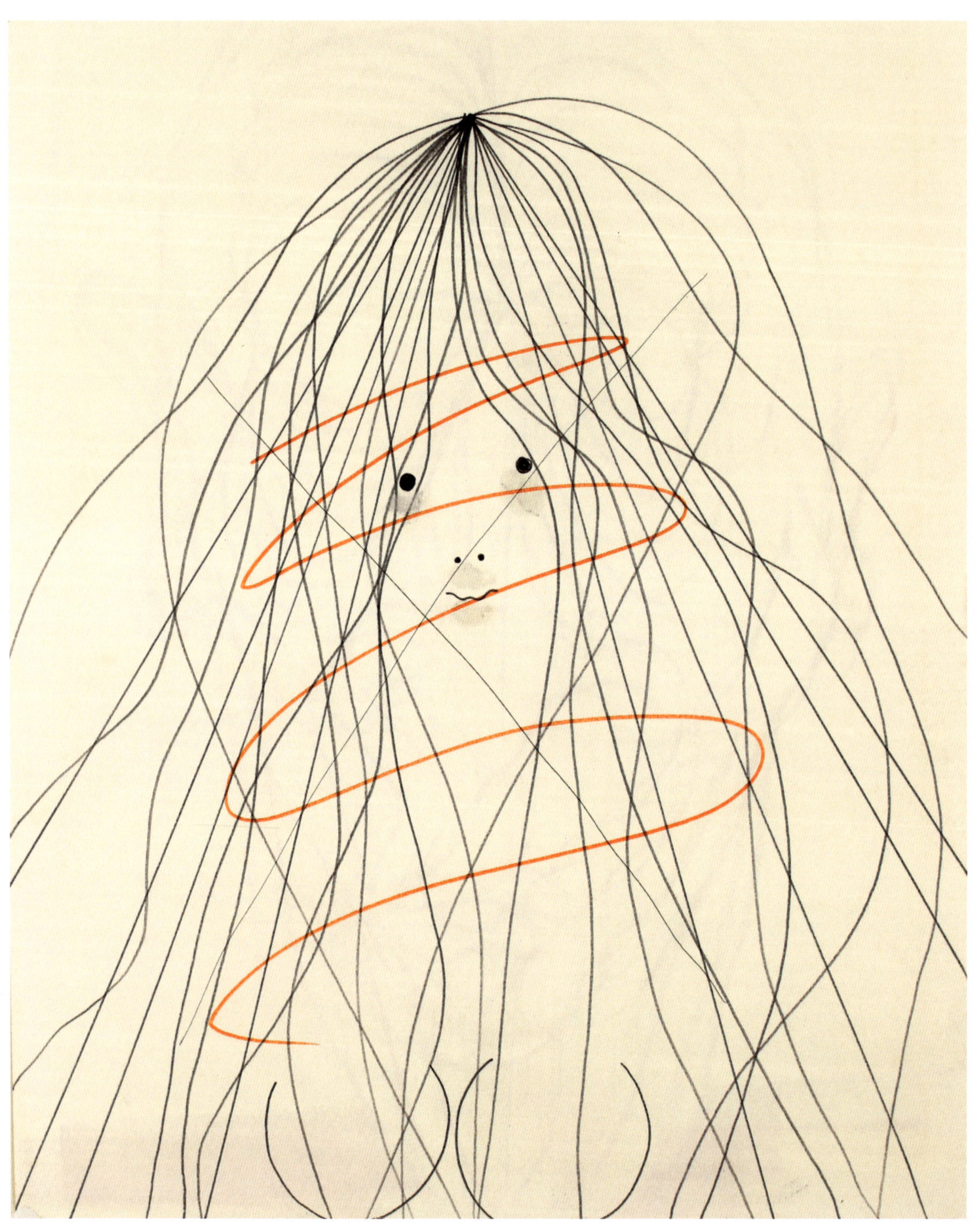

Untitled, 1985

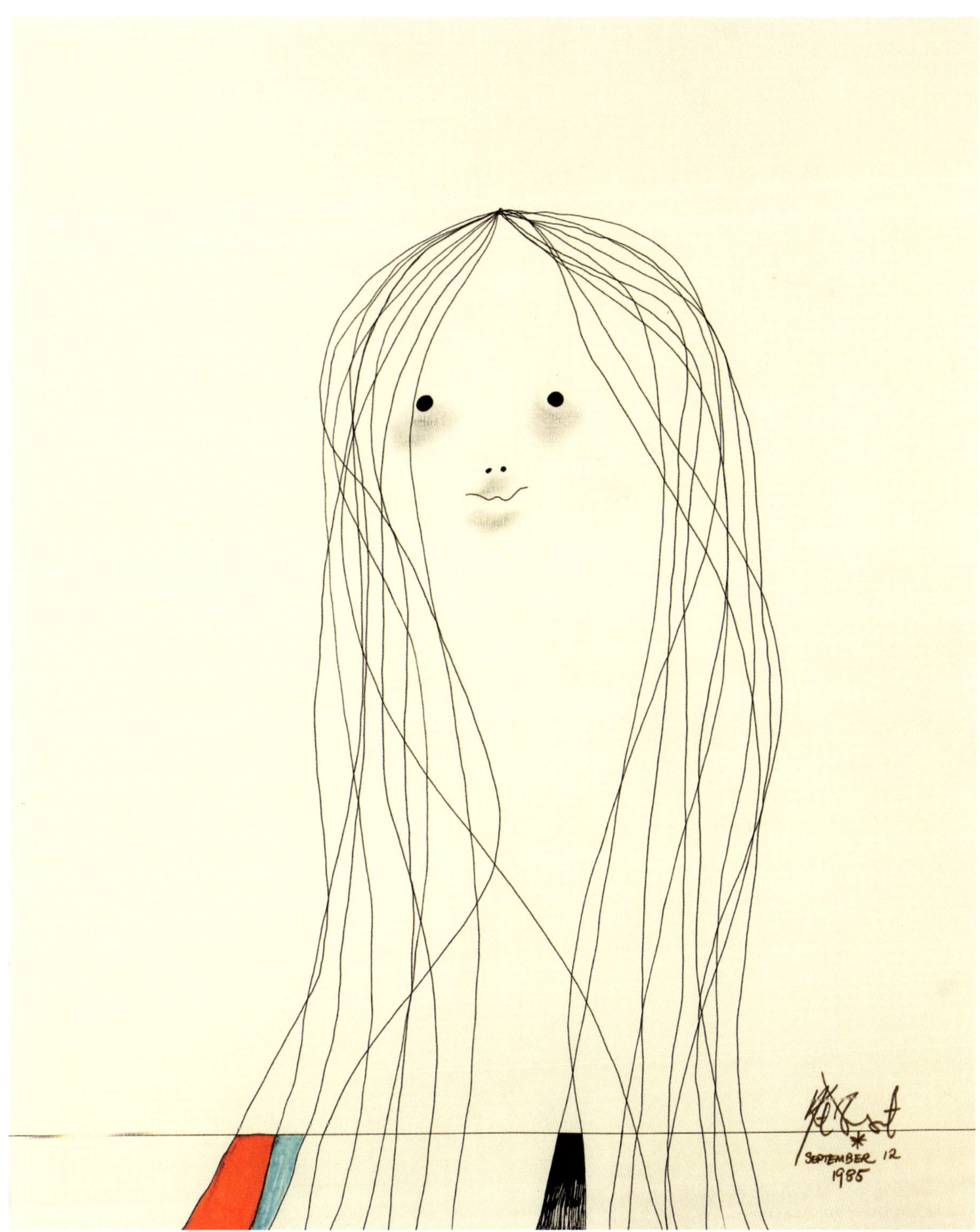

Untitled, September 12, 1985

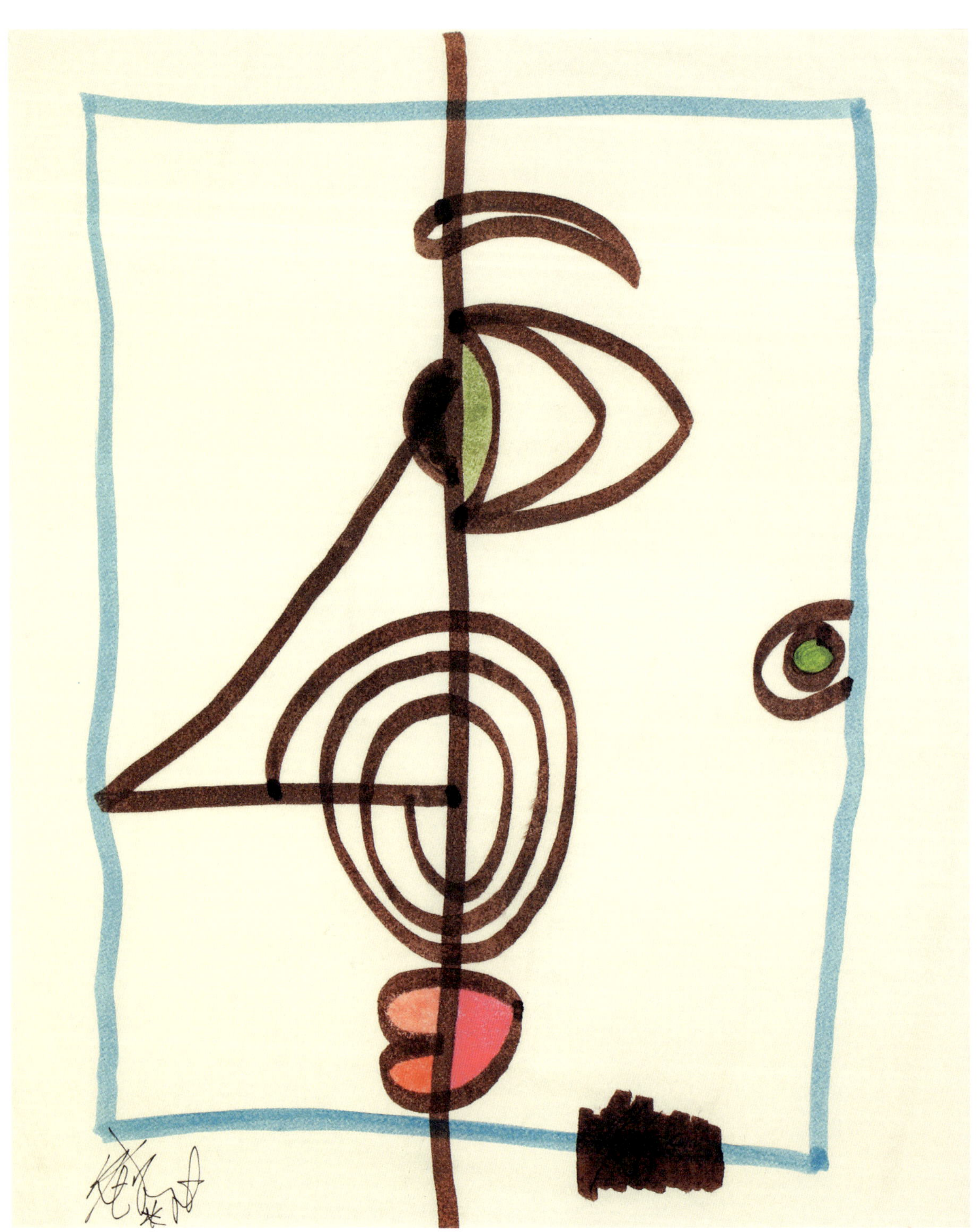

Untitled, n.d.

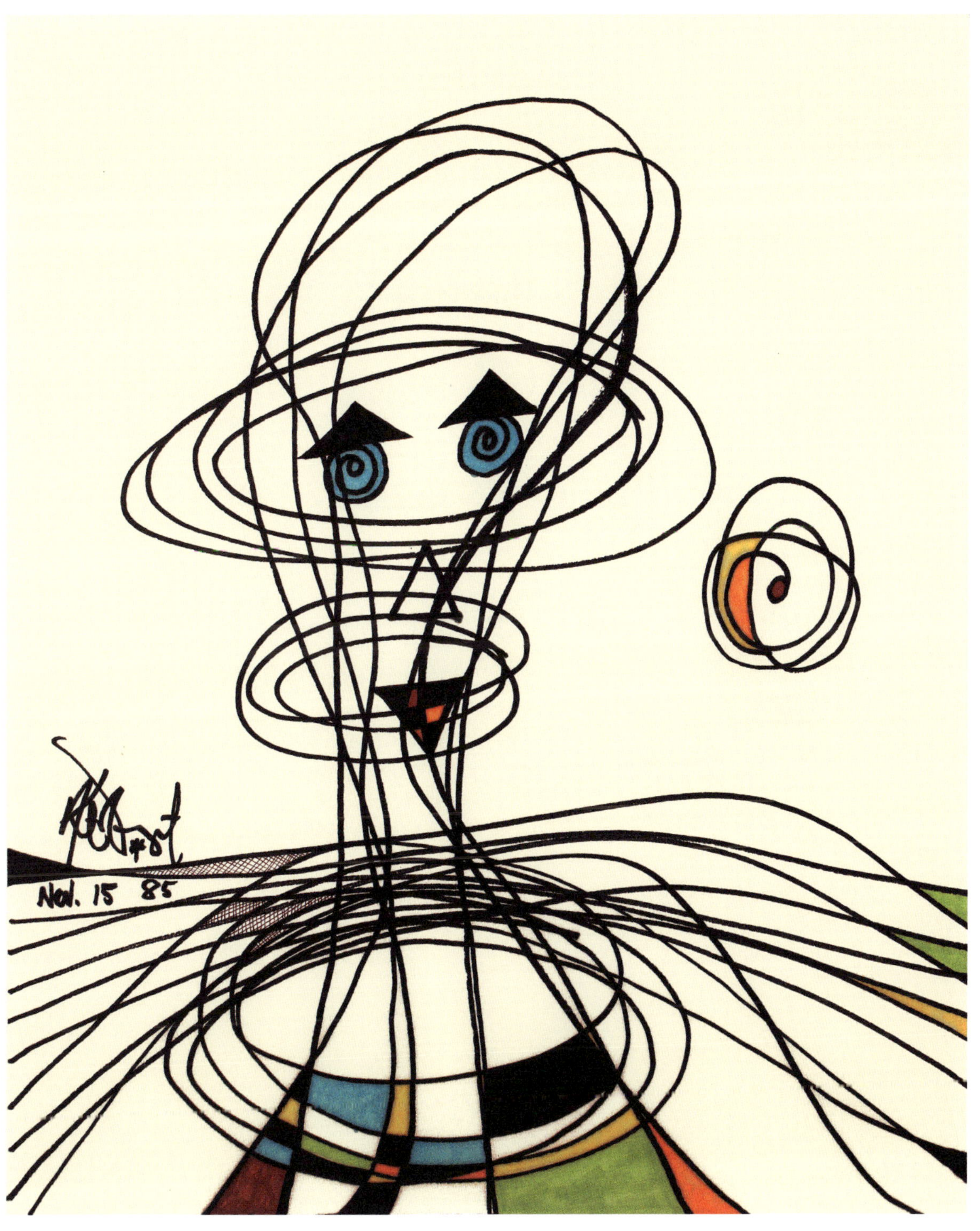

Untitled, November 15, 1985

Was there ever a more cunning experiment devised to make the unconscious reveal itself? Has any psychological experiment yielded a more delightful suggestion than this one: that there is a part of the mind without ambition or information, which nonetheless is expert on what is beautiful?

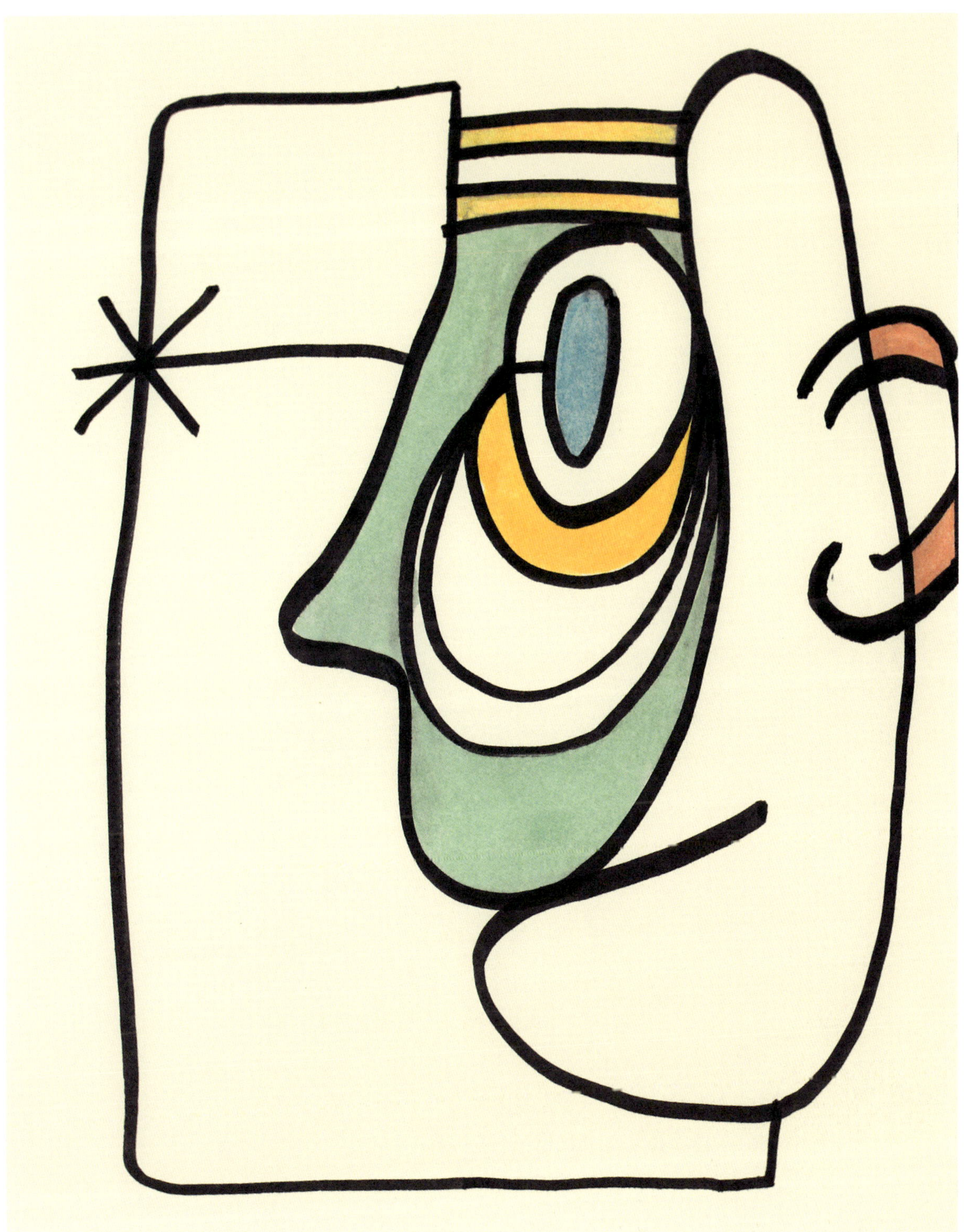

Untitled, n.d.

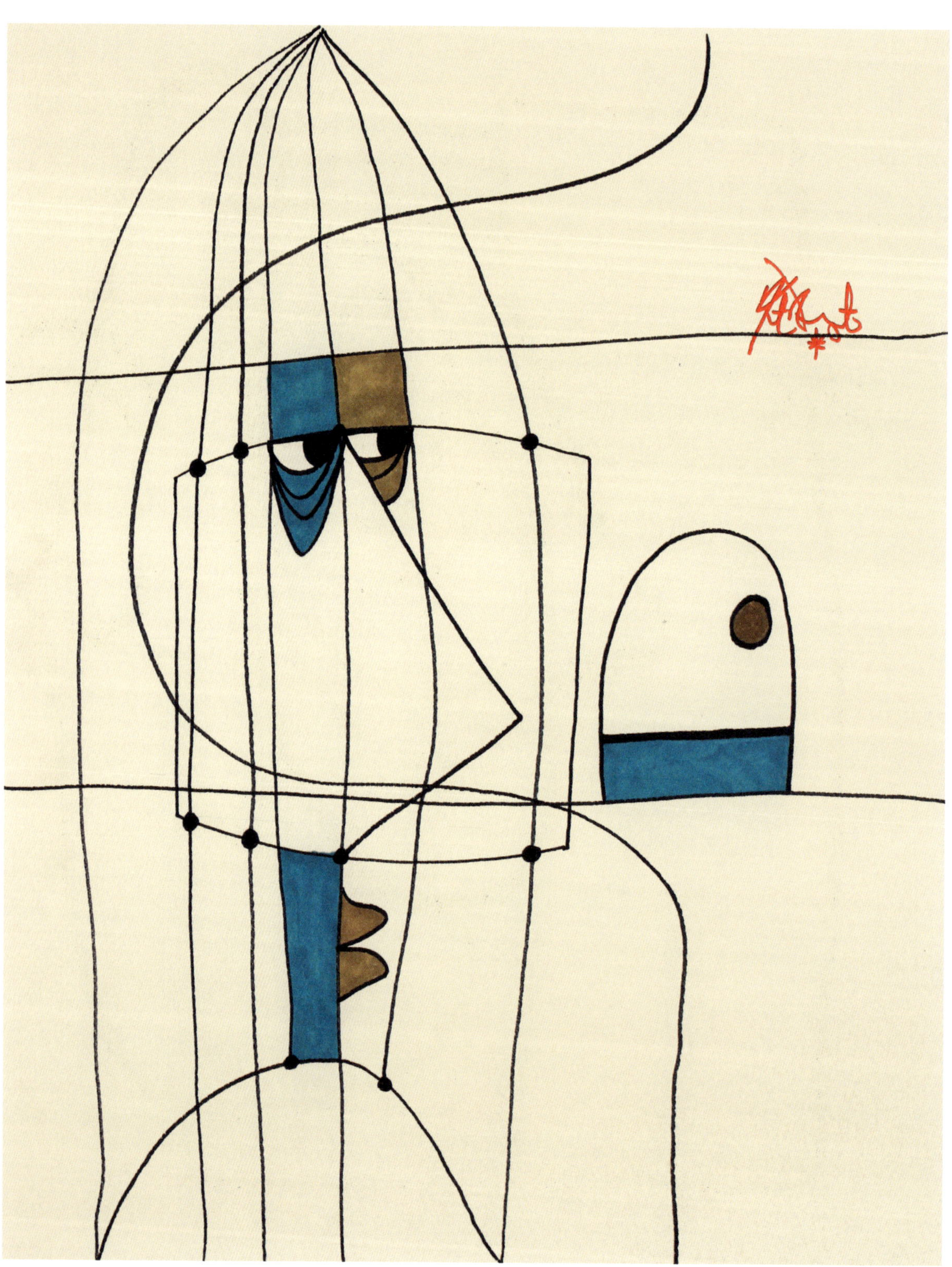

Untitled, n.d.

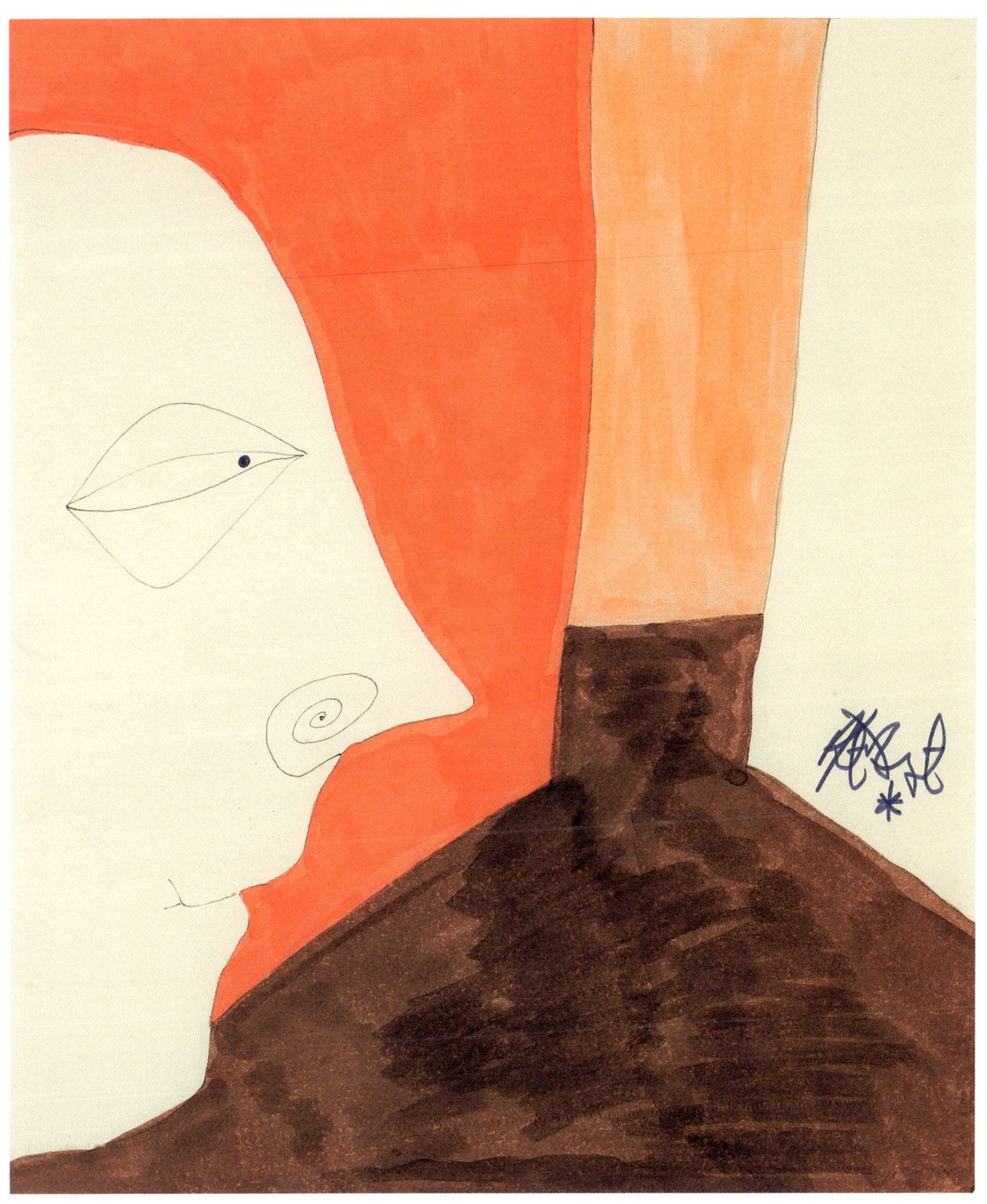

Untitled, n.d.

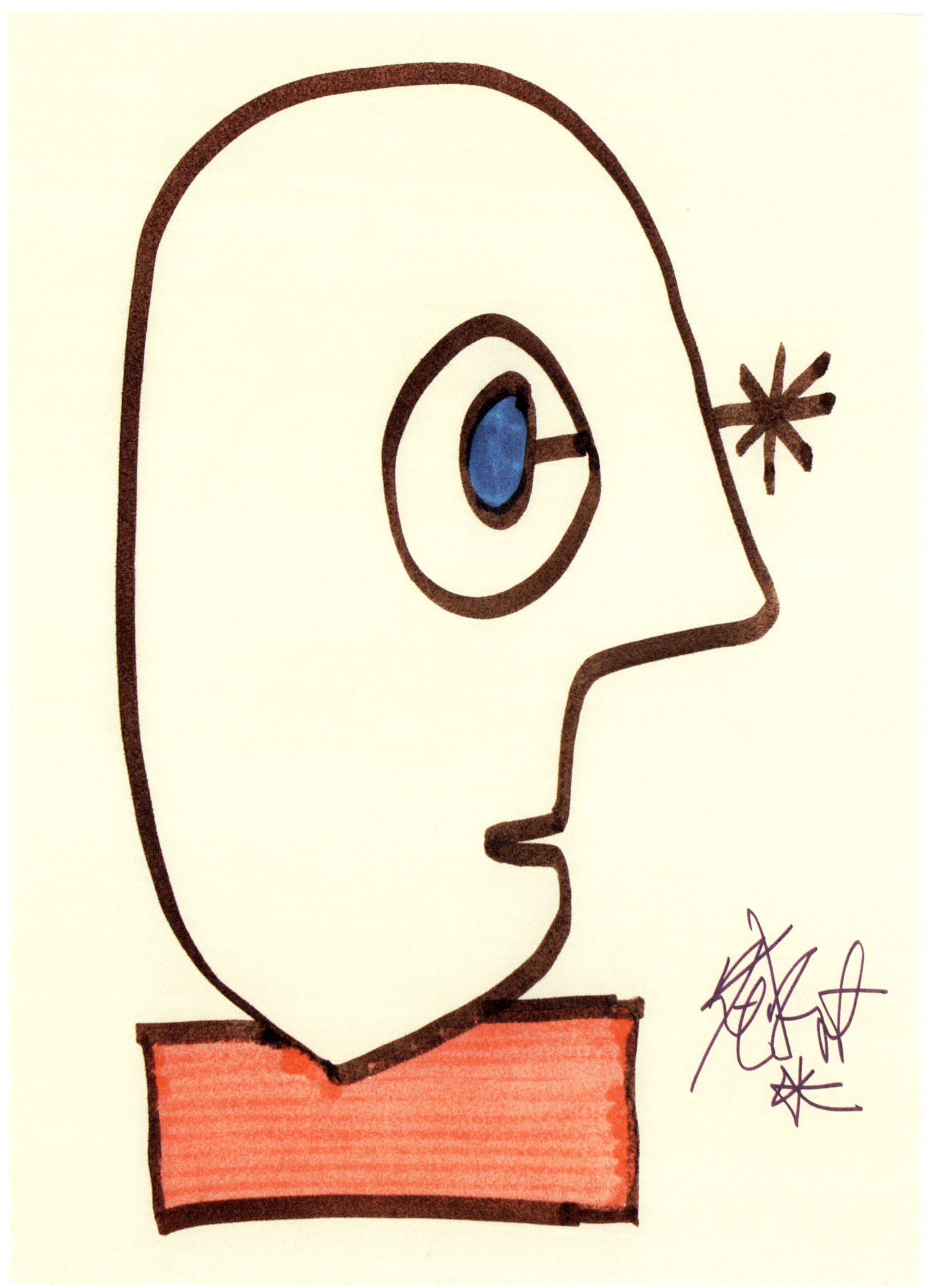

Untitled, n.d.

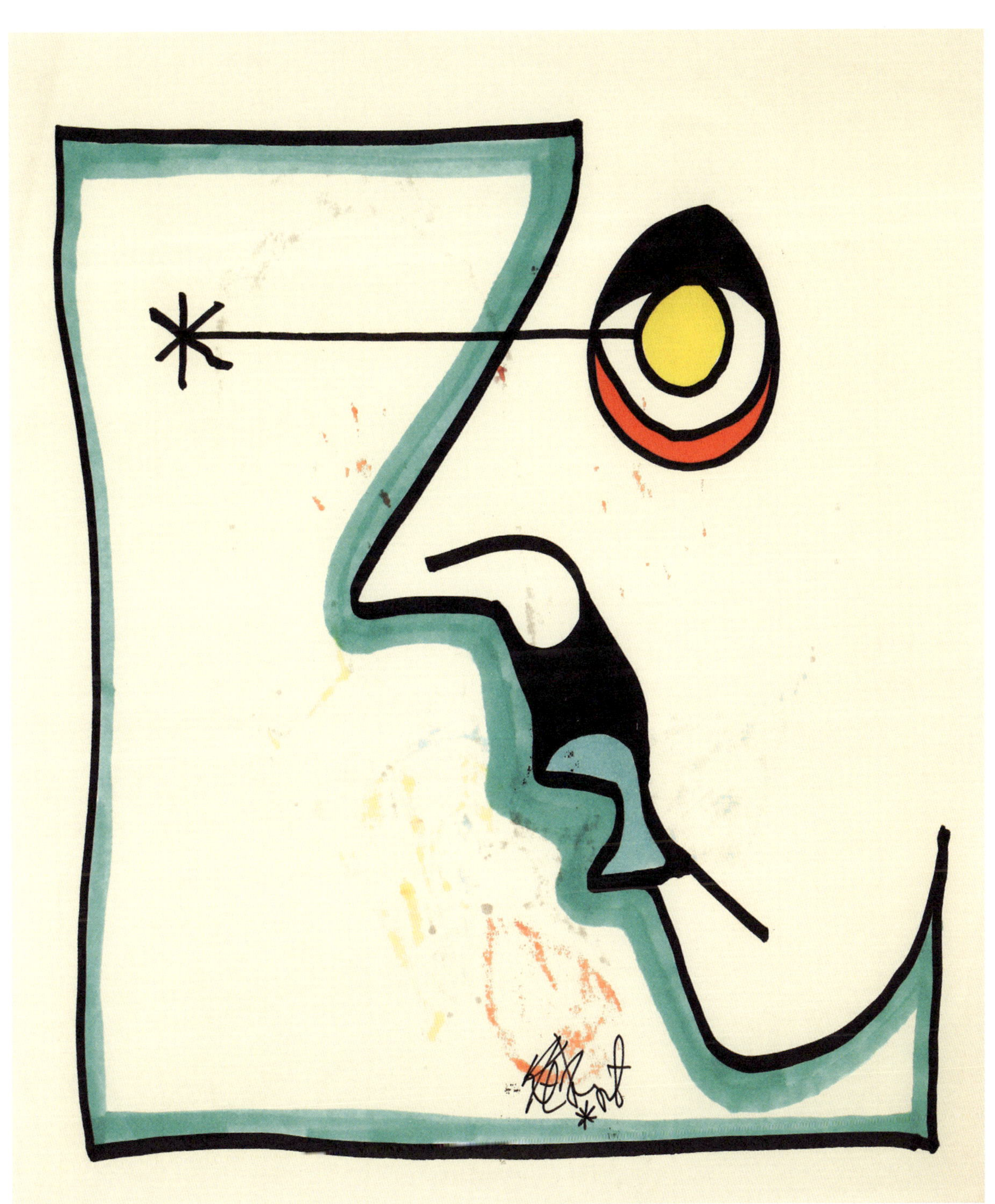

Untitled, n.d.

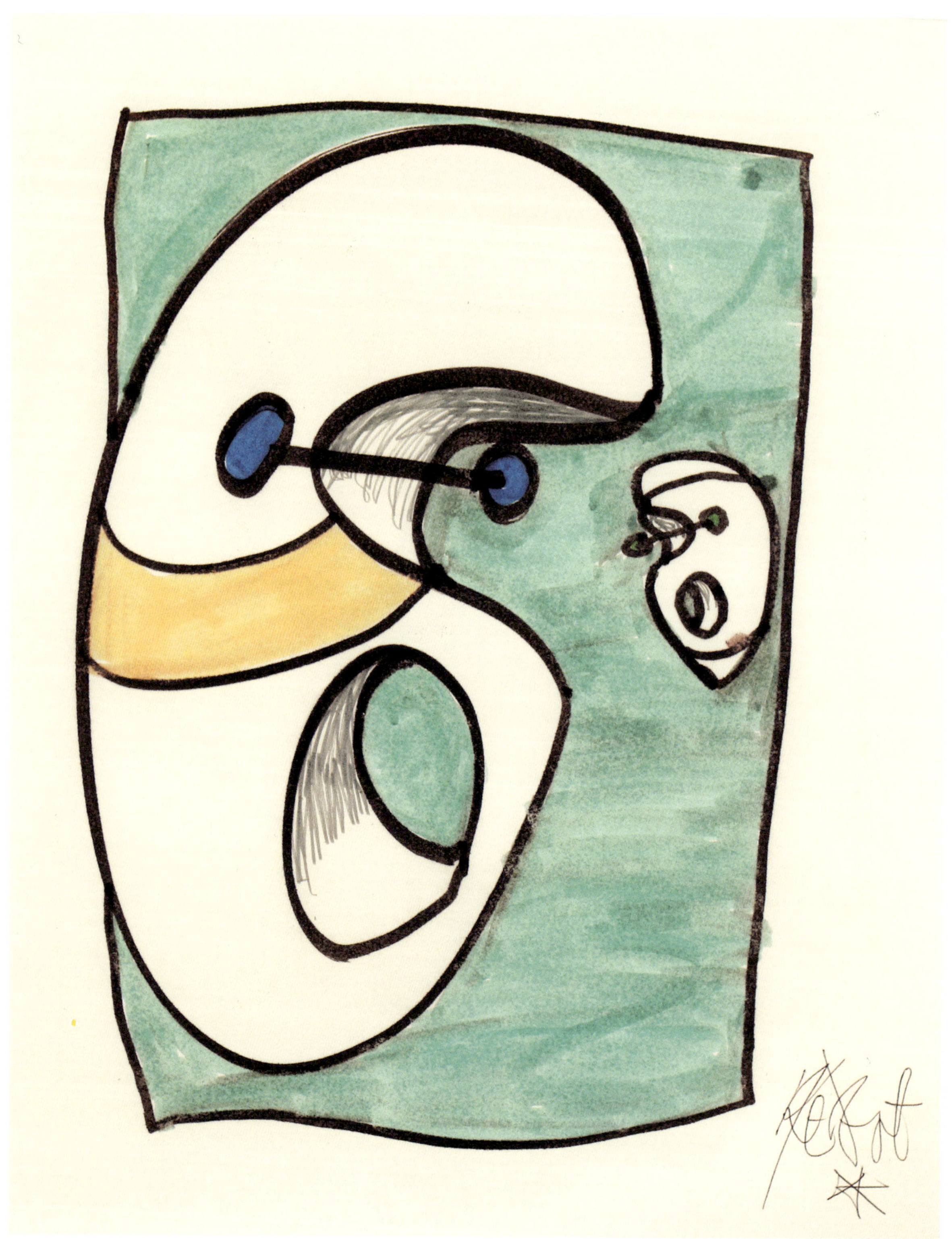

Untitled, n.d.

Good examples of harmless toots are some of the things children do. They get smashed for hours on some strictly limited aspect of the Great Big Everything, the Universe, such as water or snow or mud or colors or rocks (throwing little ones, looking under big ones) . . . Only two people are involved: the child and the Universe. The child does a little something to the Universe, and the Great Big Everything does something funny or beautiful or sometimes disappointing or scary or even painful in return.

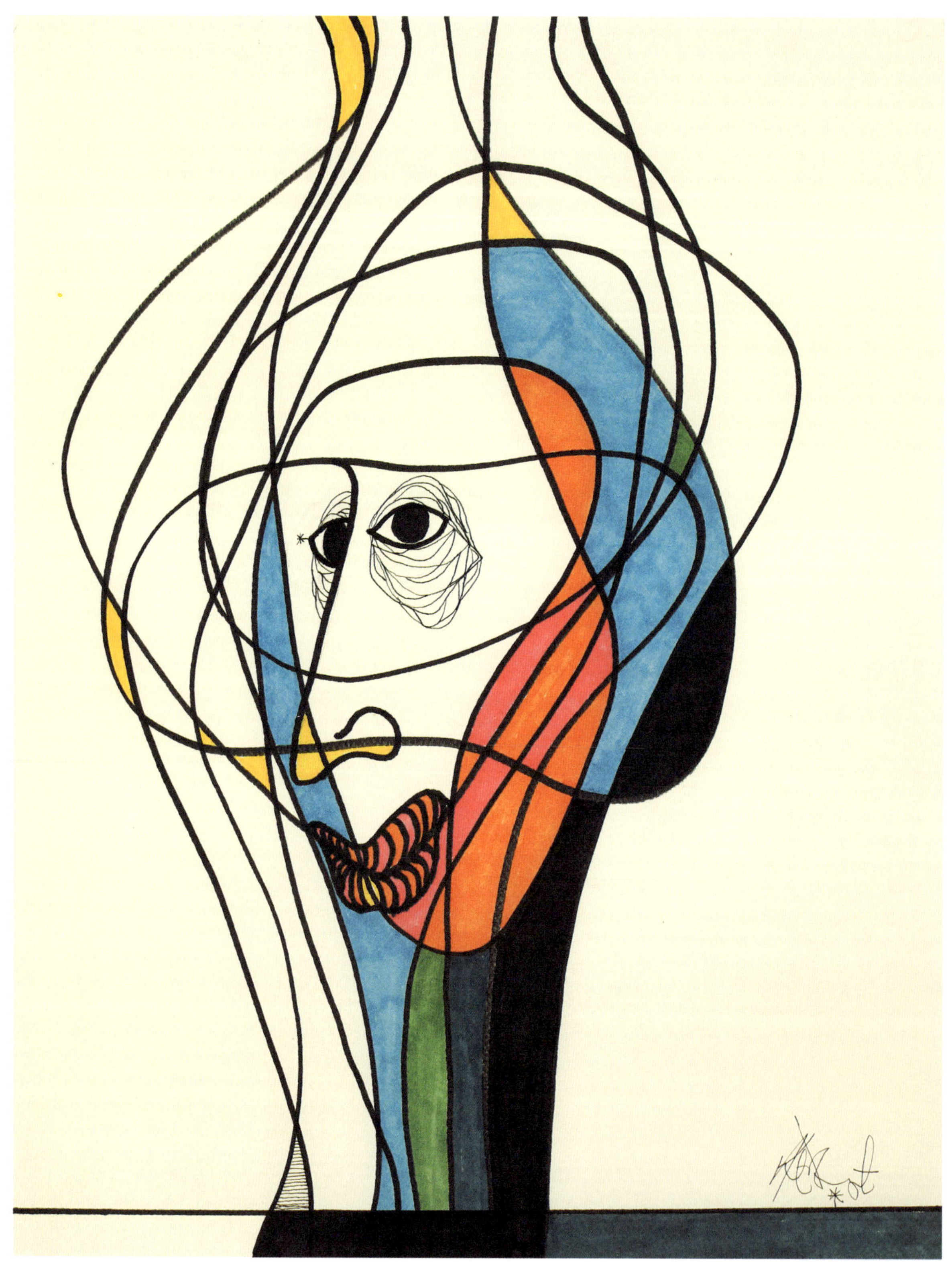

Untitled, n.d.

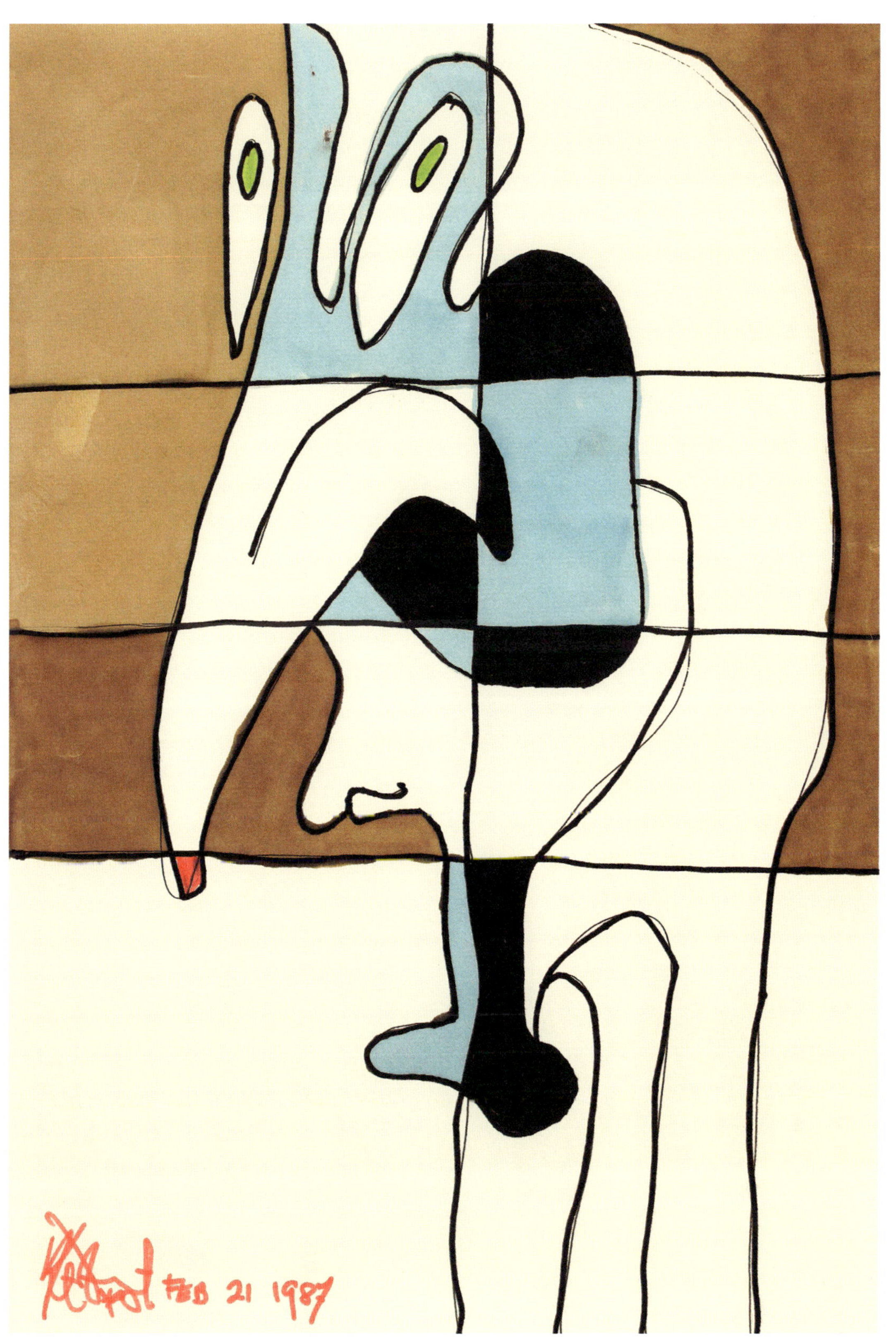

Untitled, February 21, 1987

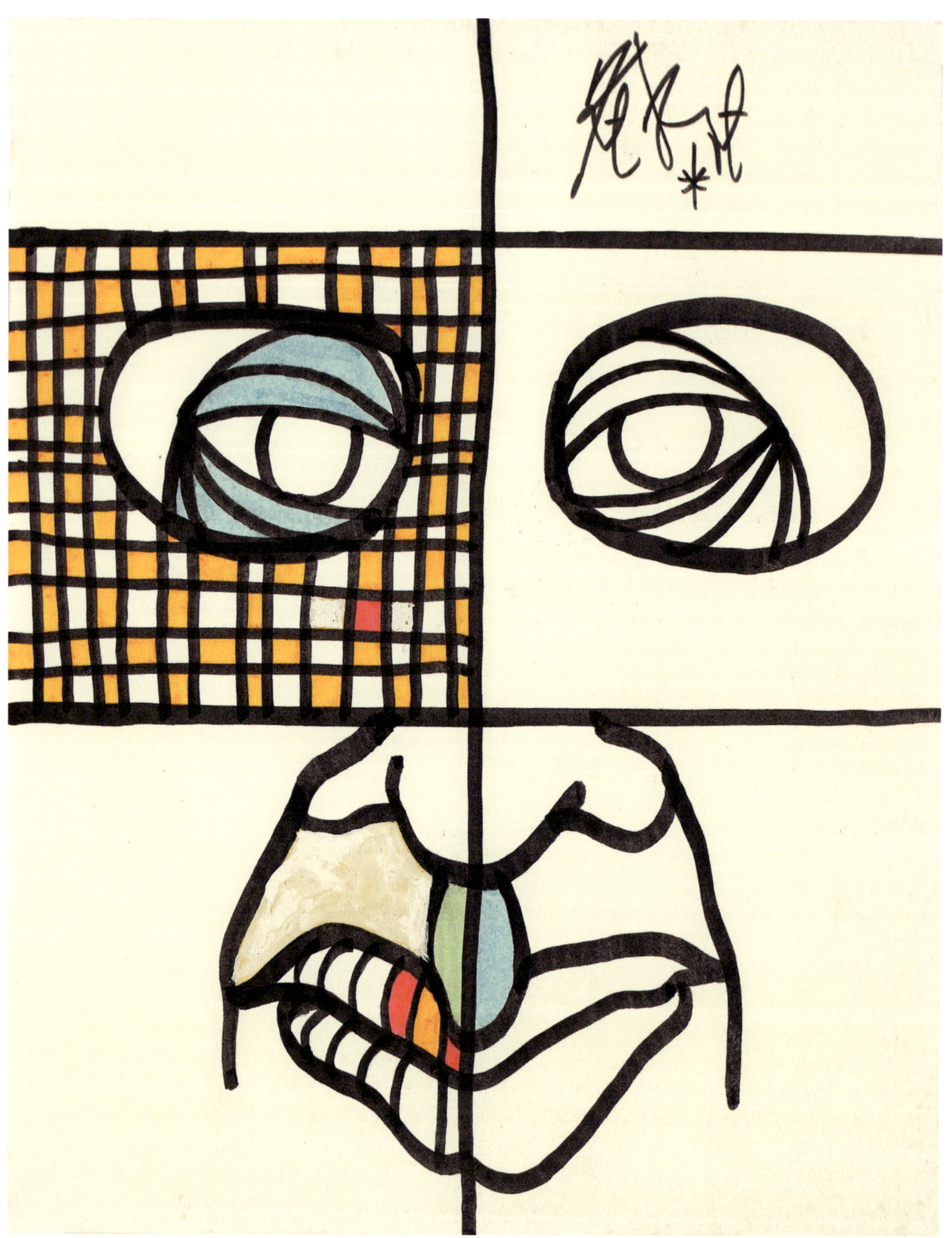

Untitled, n.d.

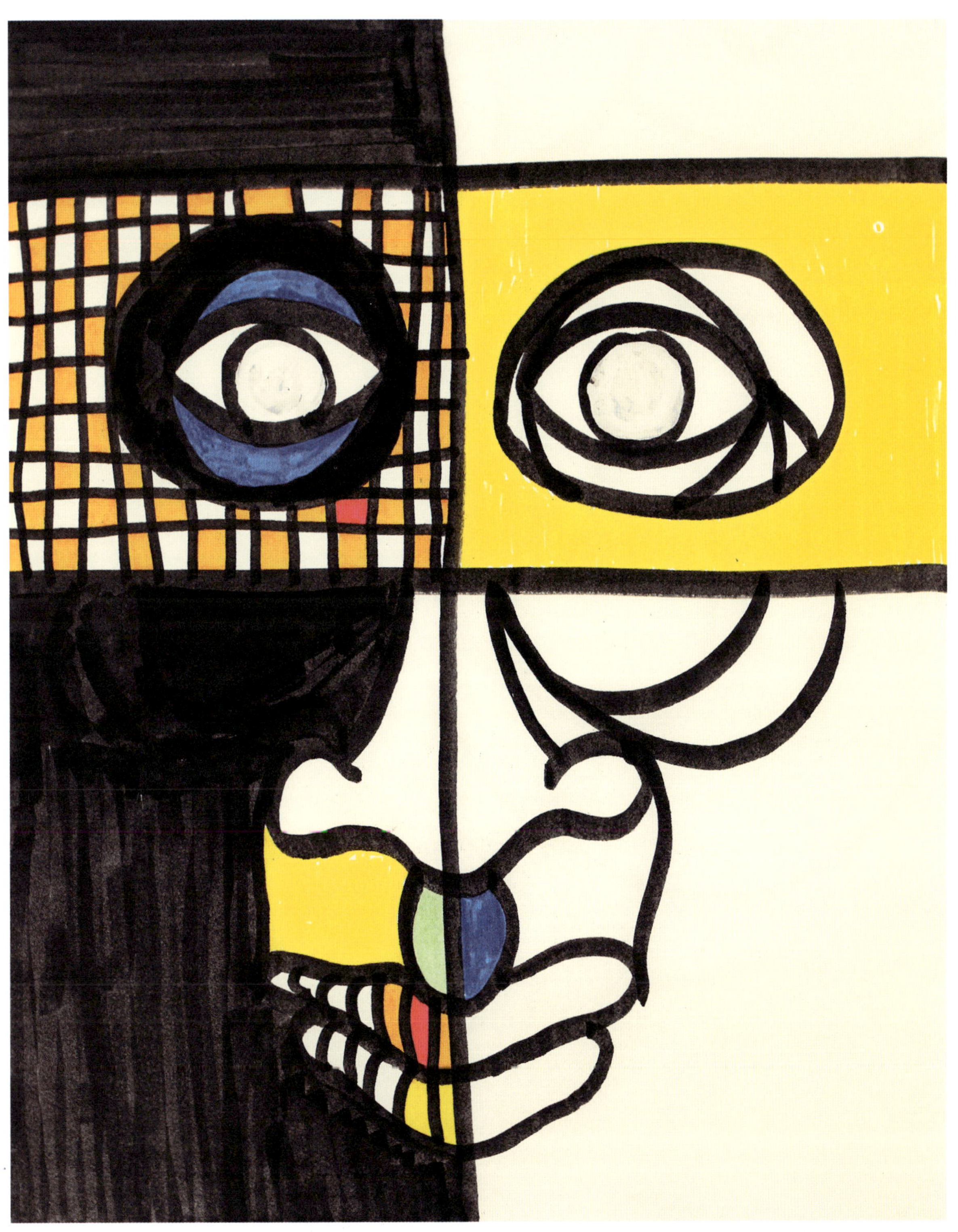

Untitled, n.d.

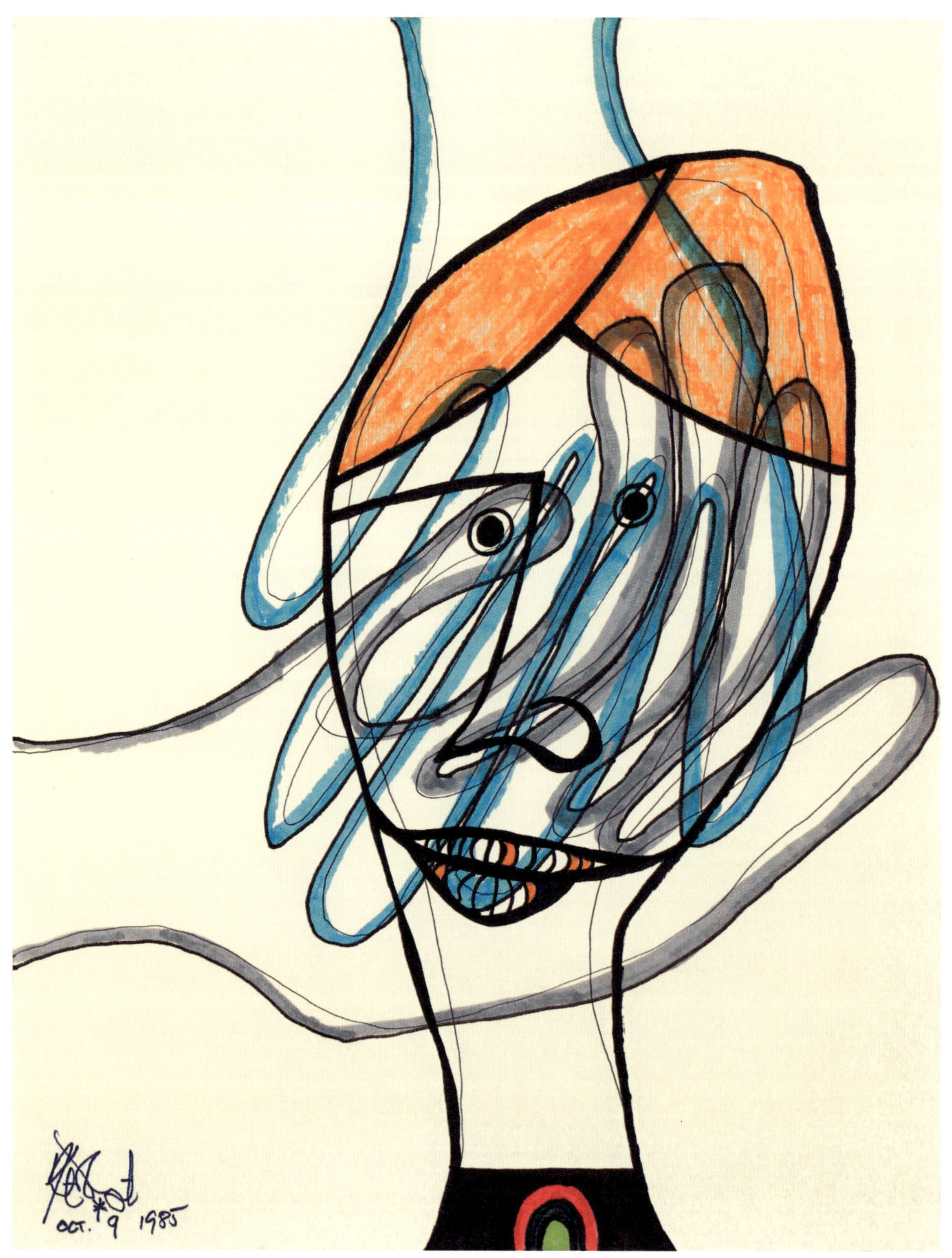

Untitled, October 9, 1985

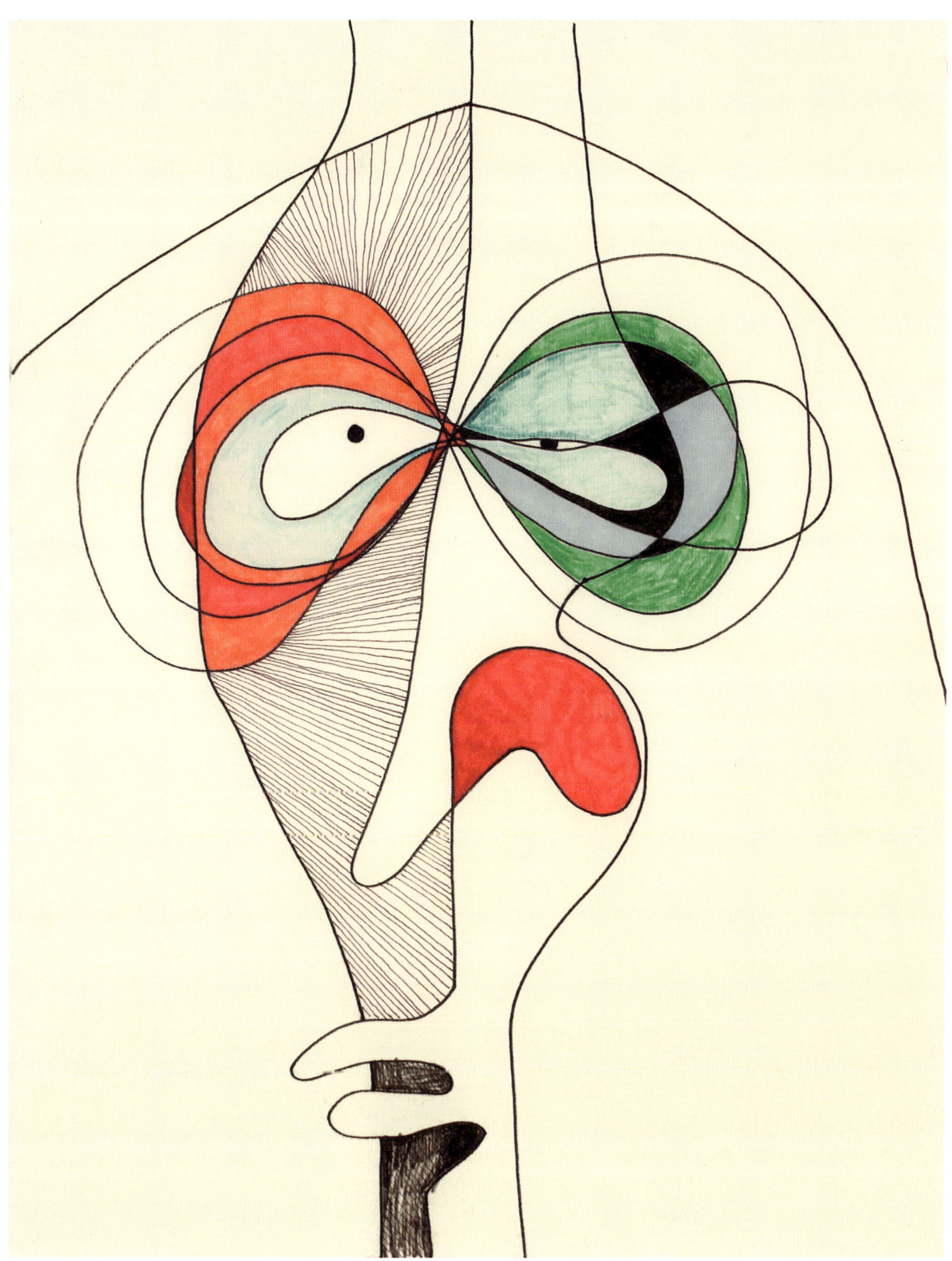

Untitled, n.d.

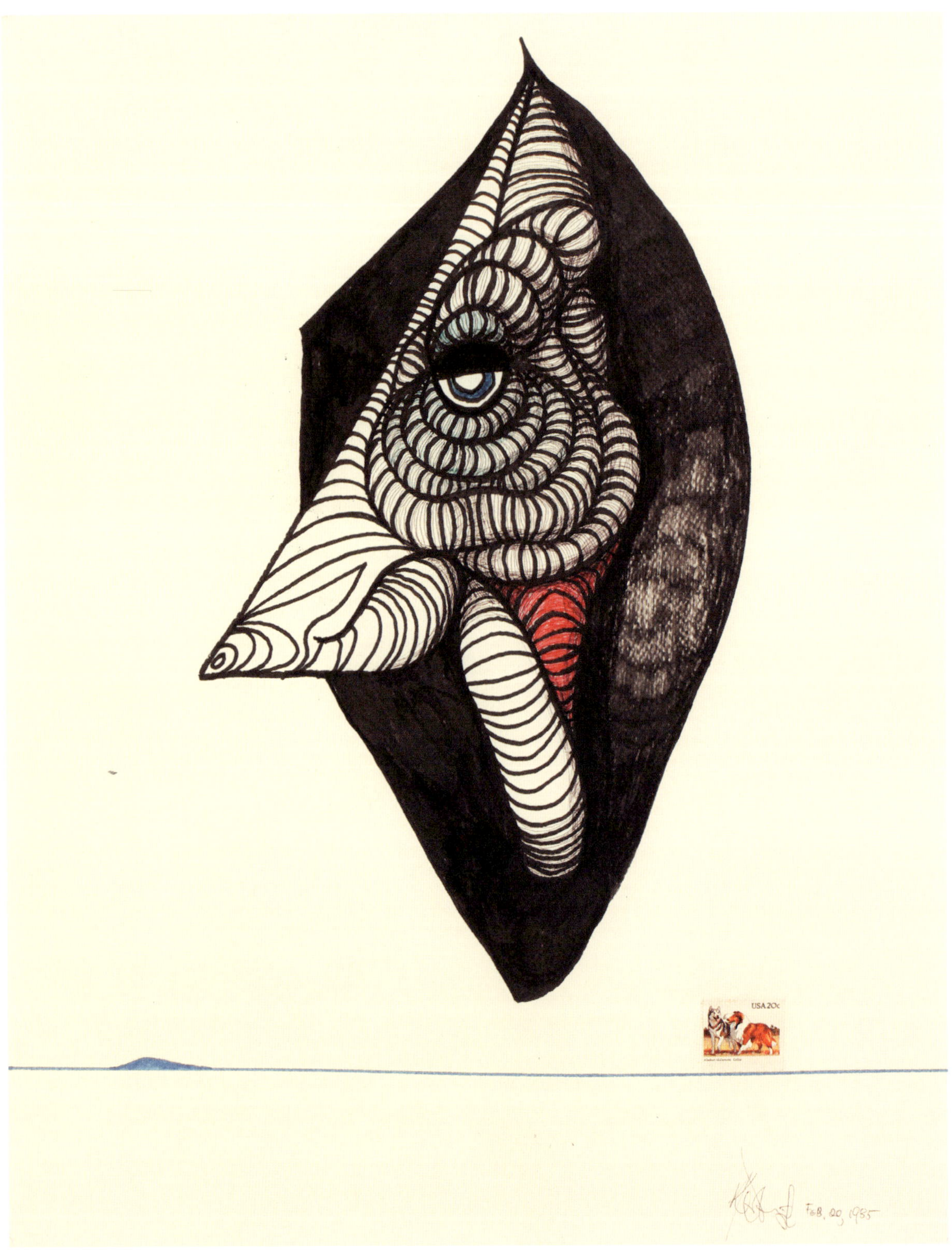

Untitled, February 20, 1985

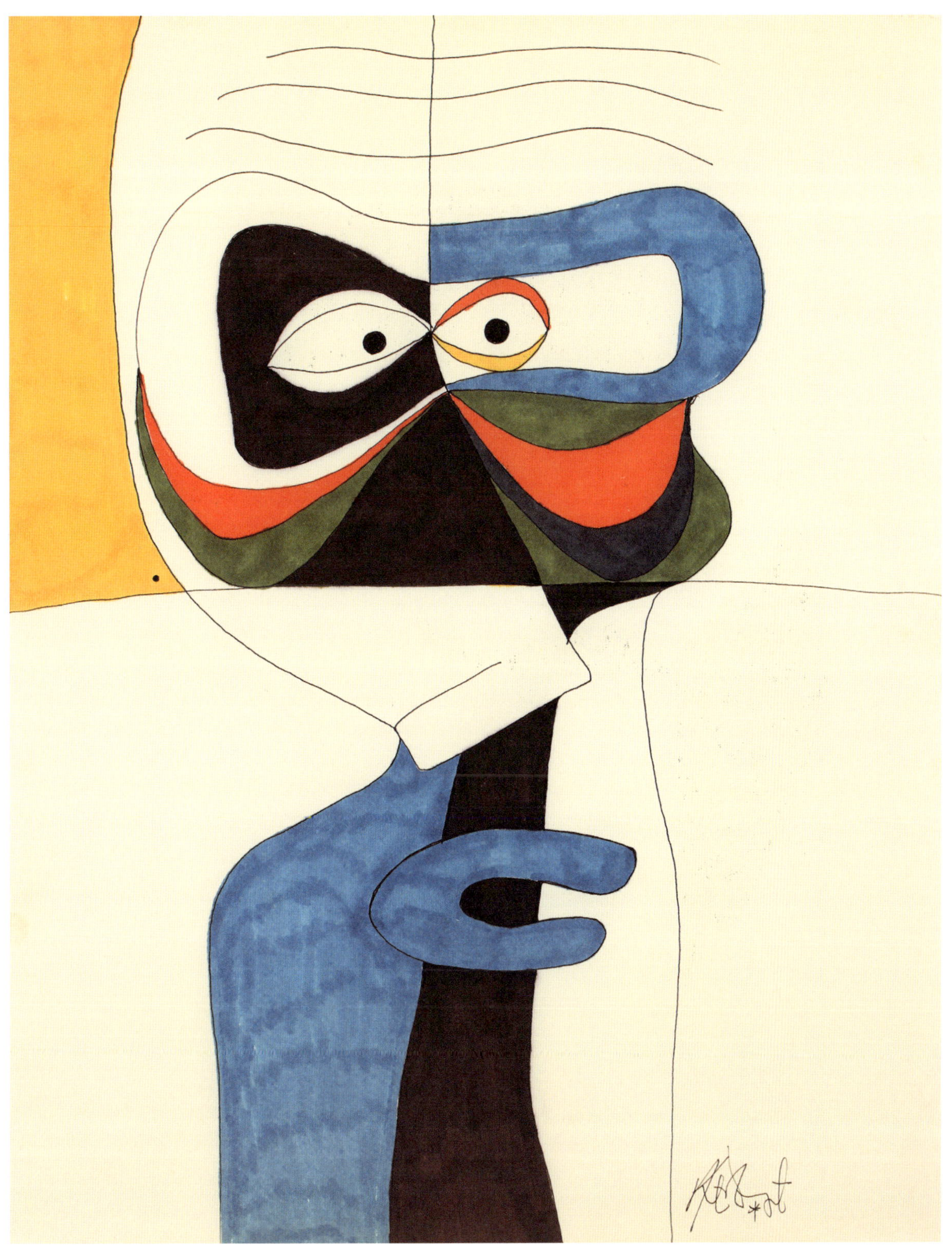

Untitled, n.d.

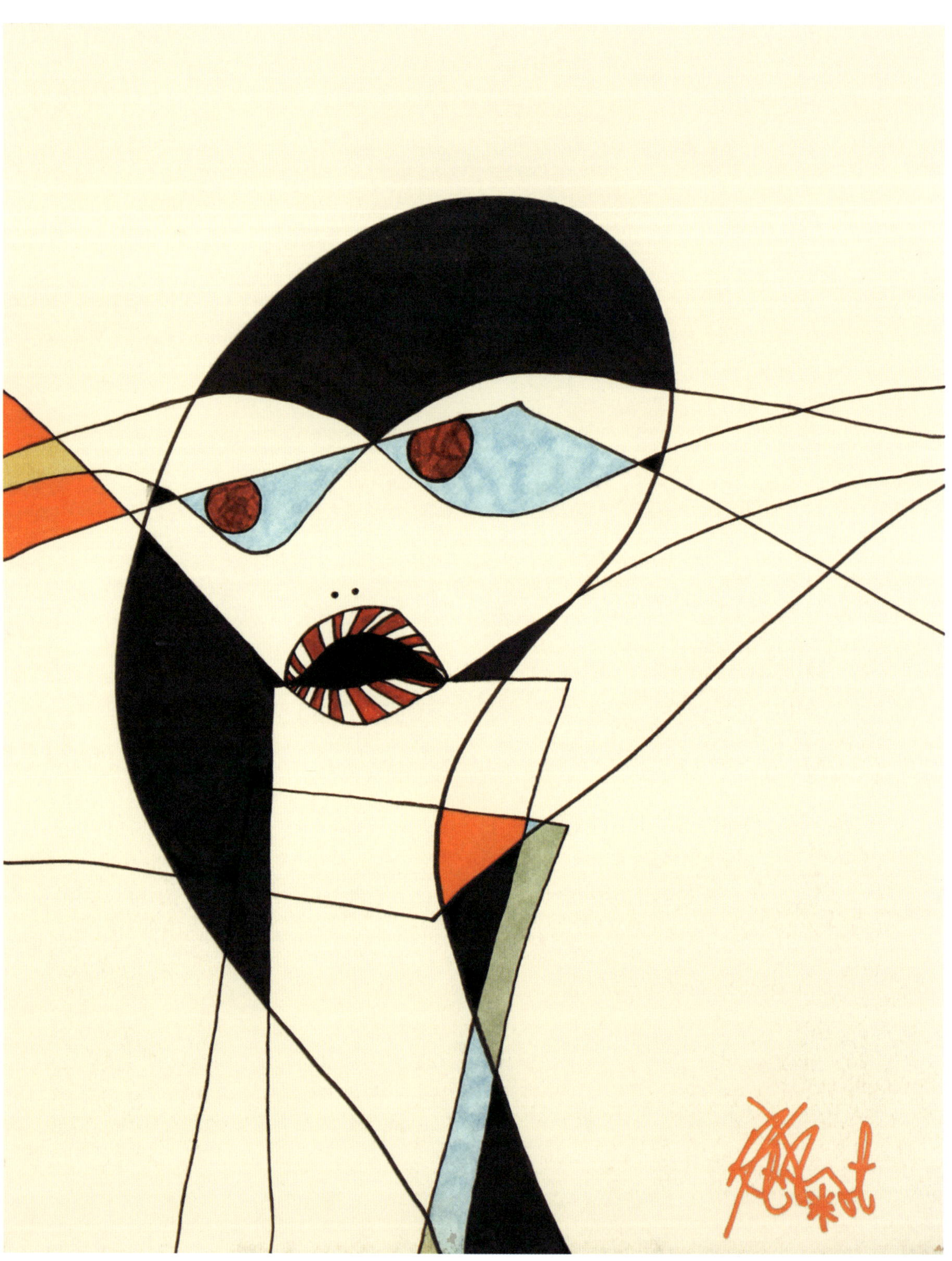

Untitled, n.d.

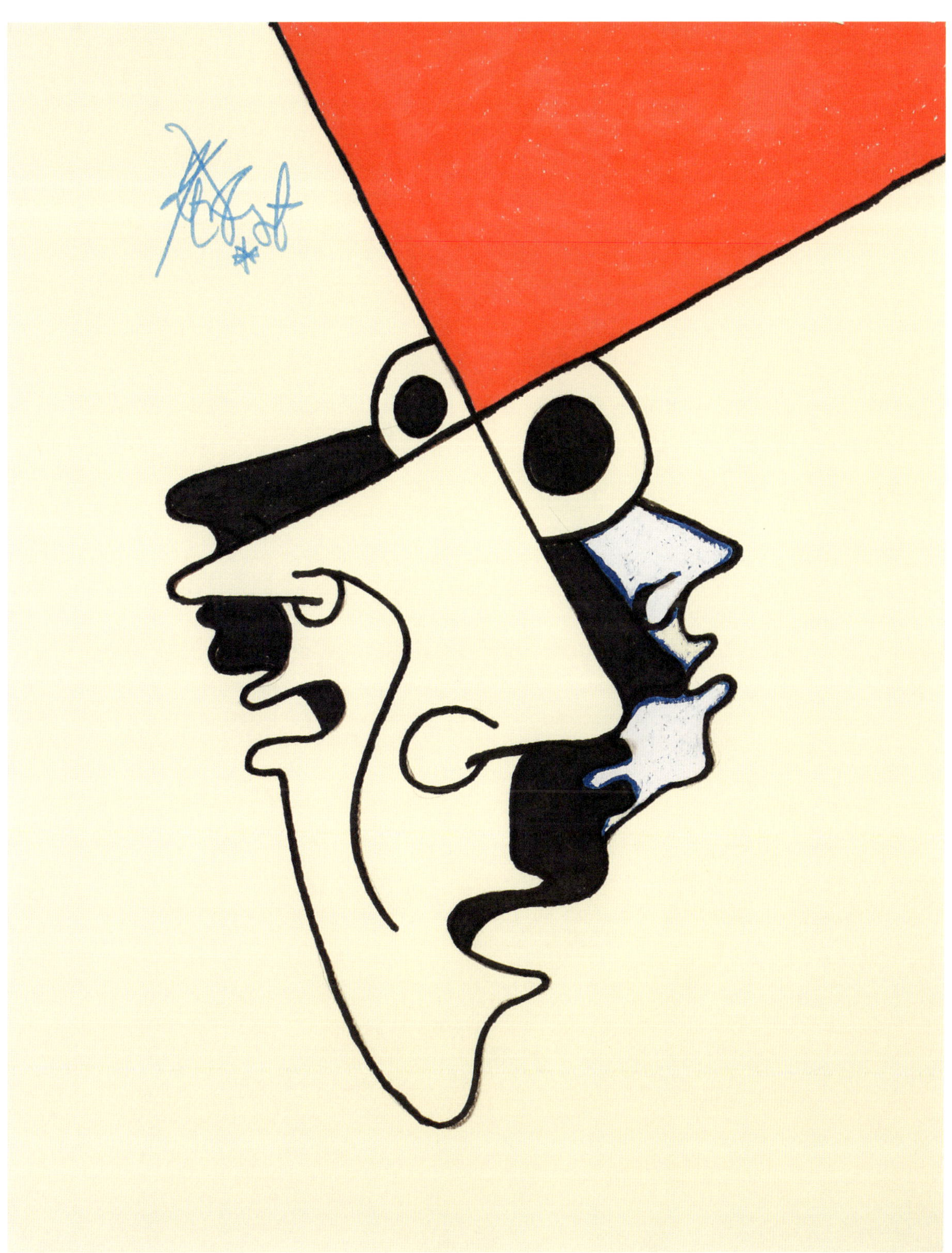

Untitled, n.d.

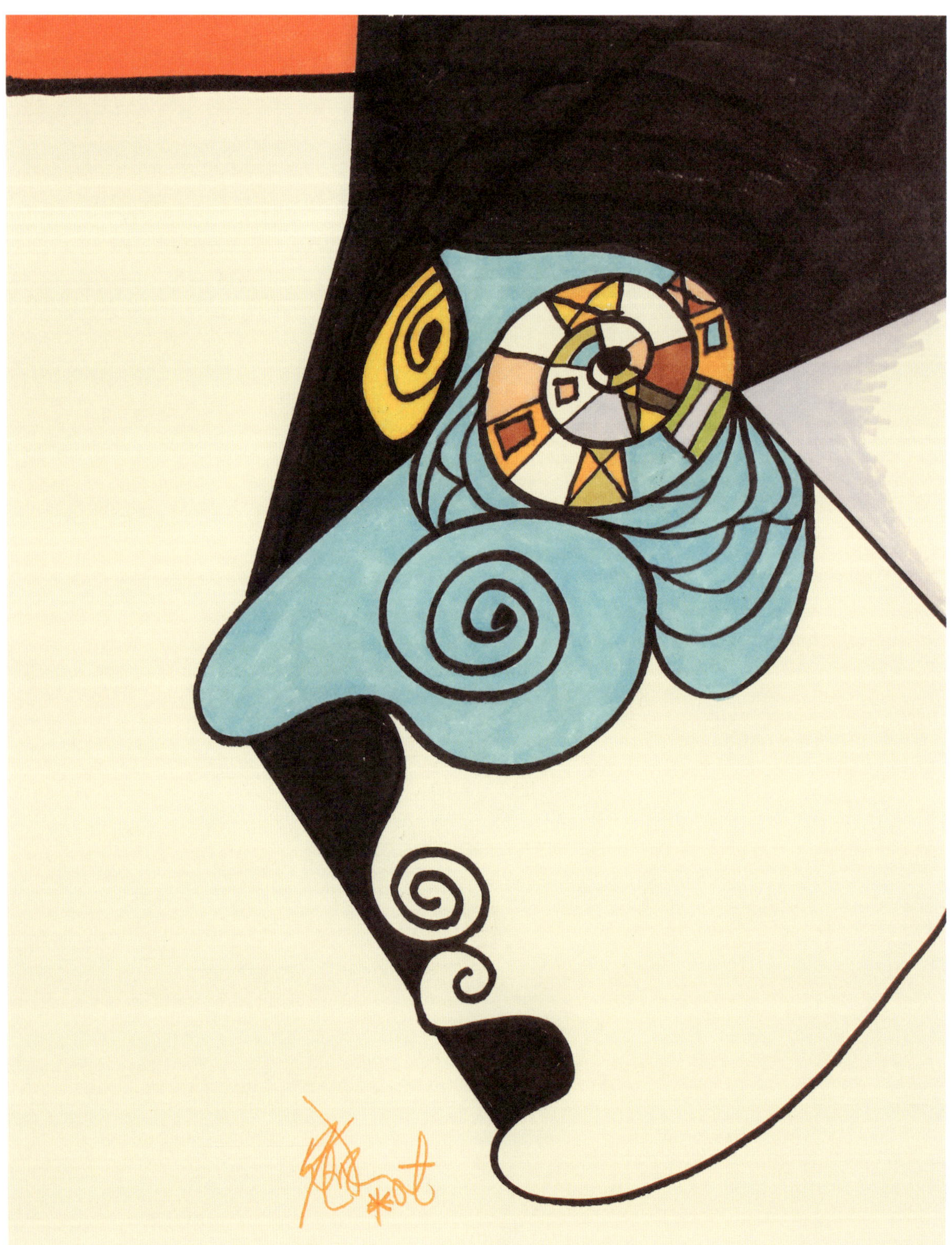

Untitled, n.d.

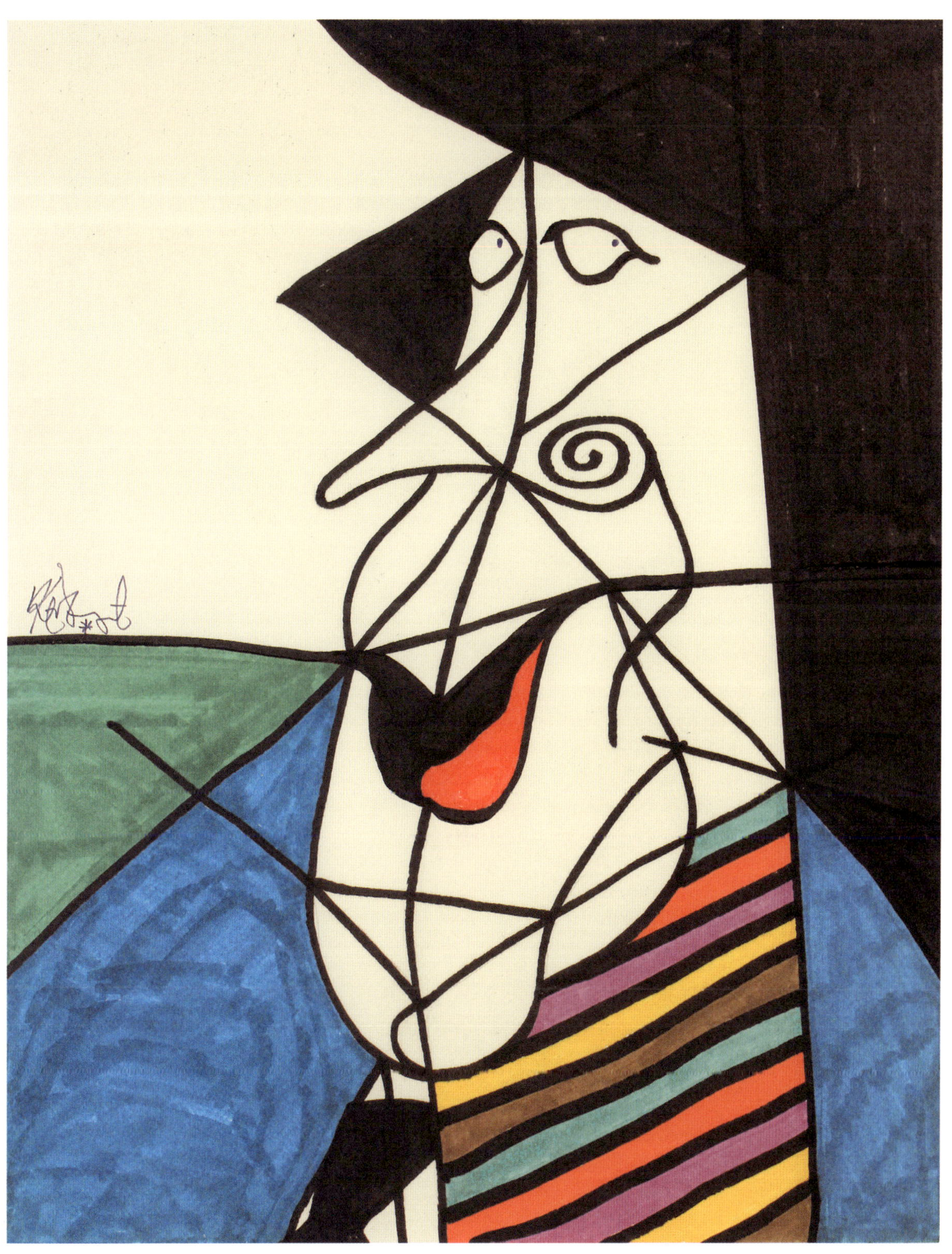

Untitled, n.d.

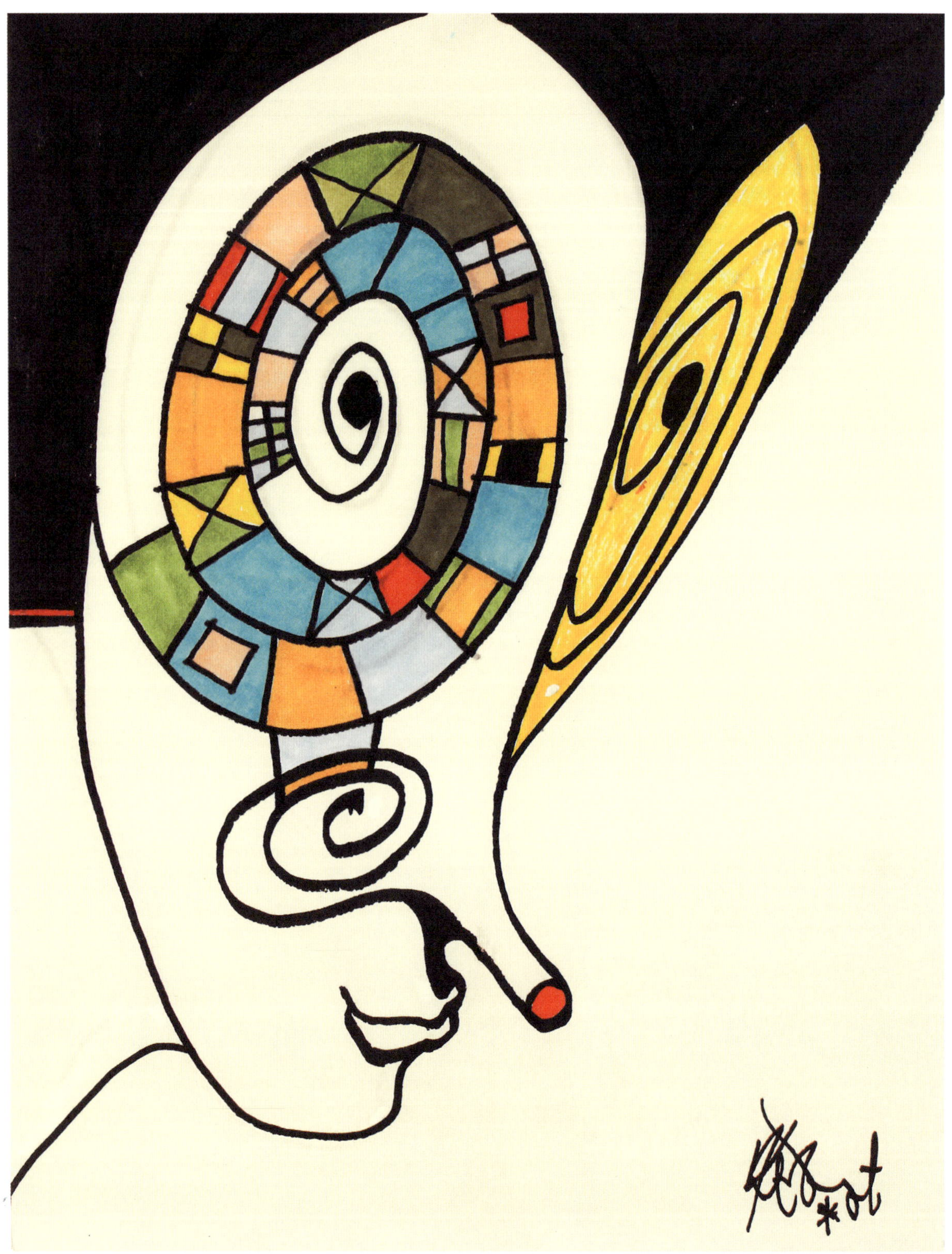

Untitled, n.d.

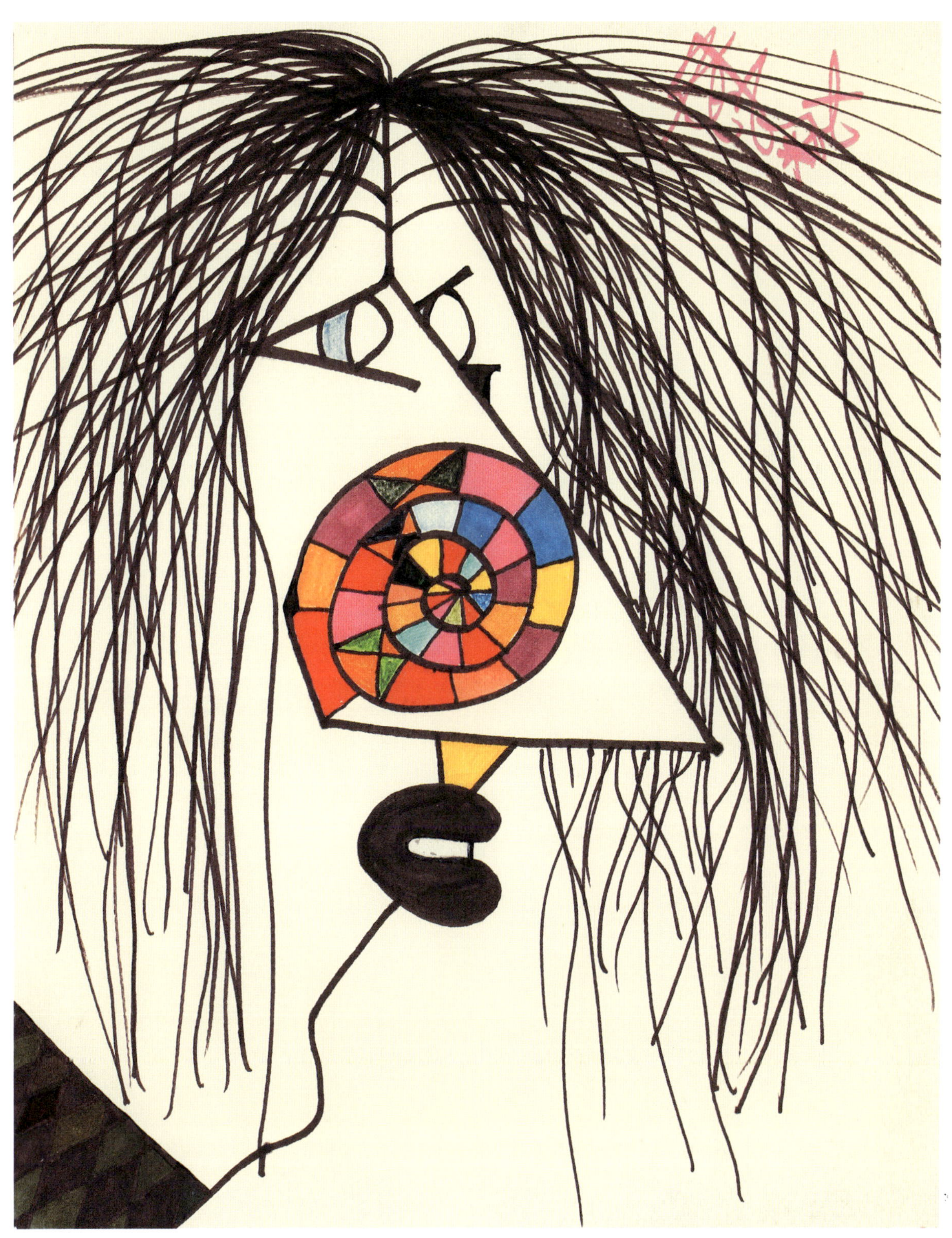

Untitled, n.d.

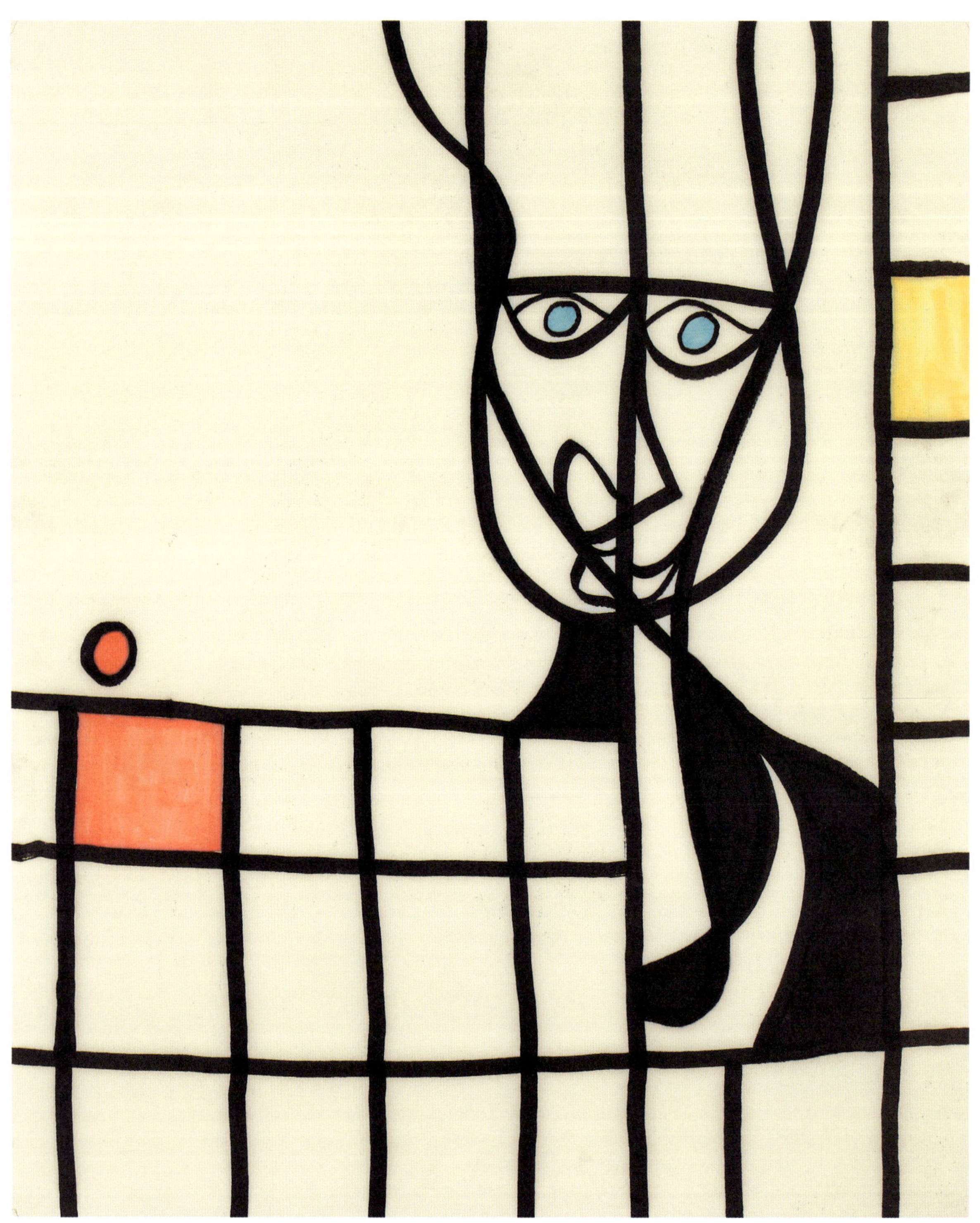

Untitled, 1985

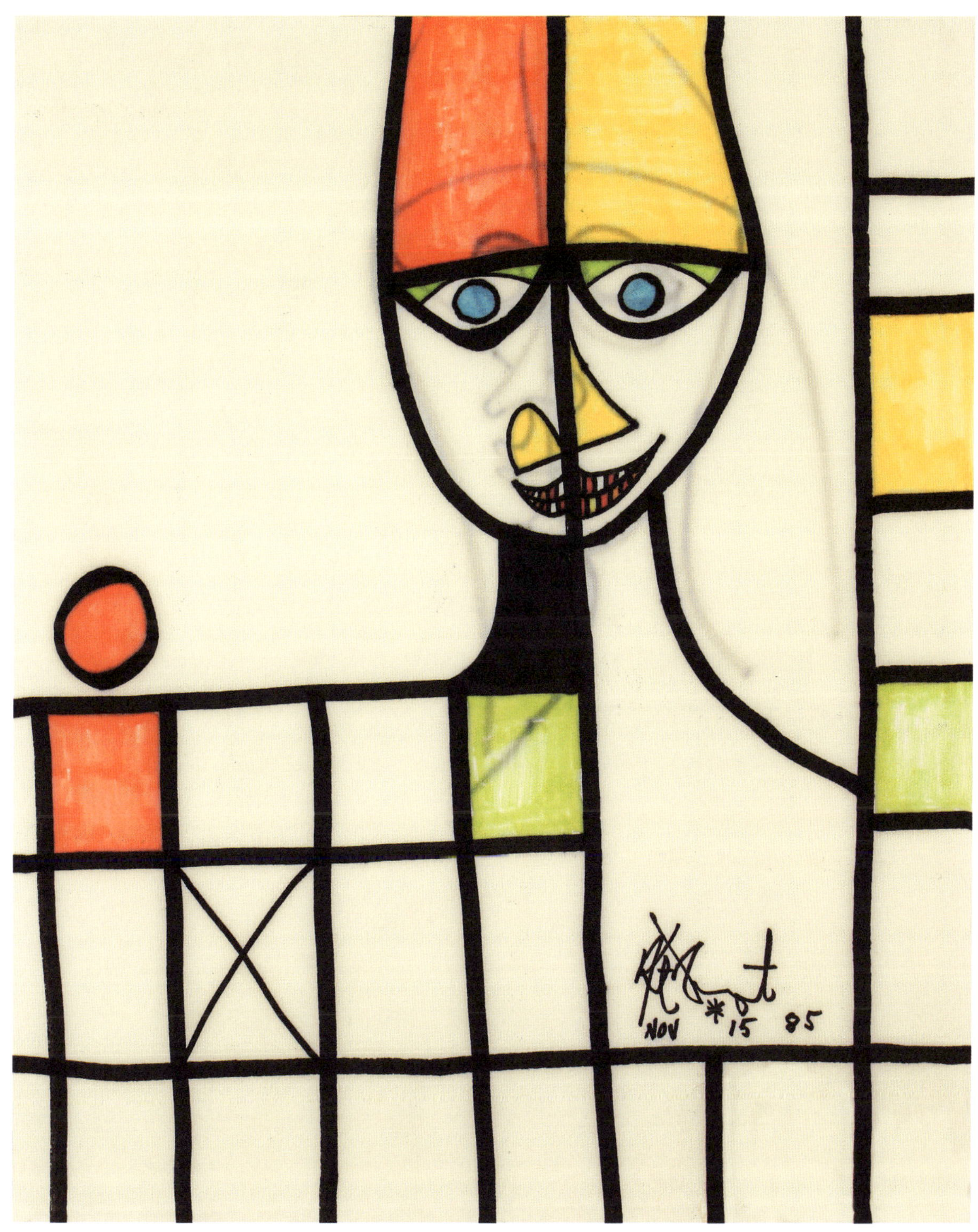

Untitled, November 15, 1985

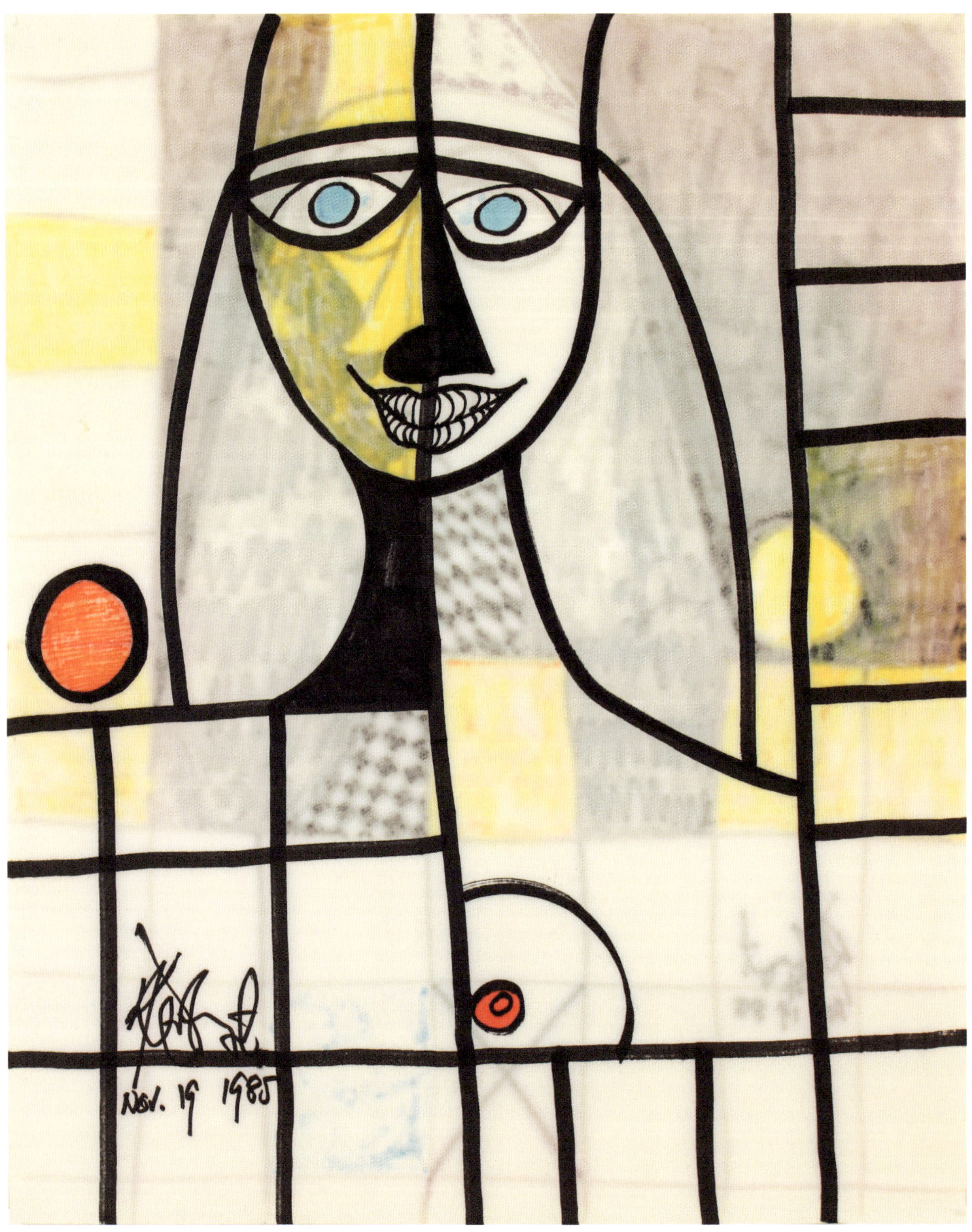

Untitled, November 19, 1985

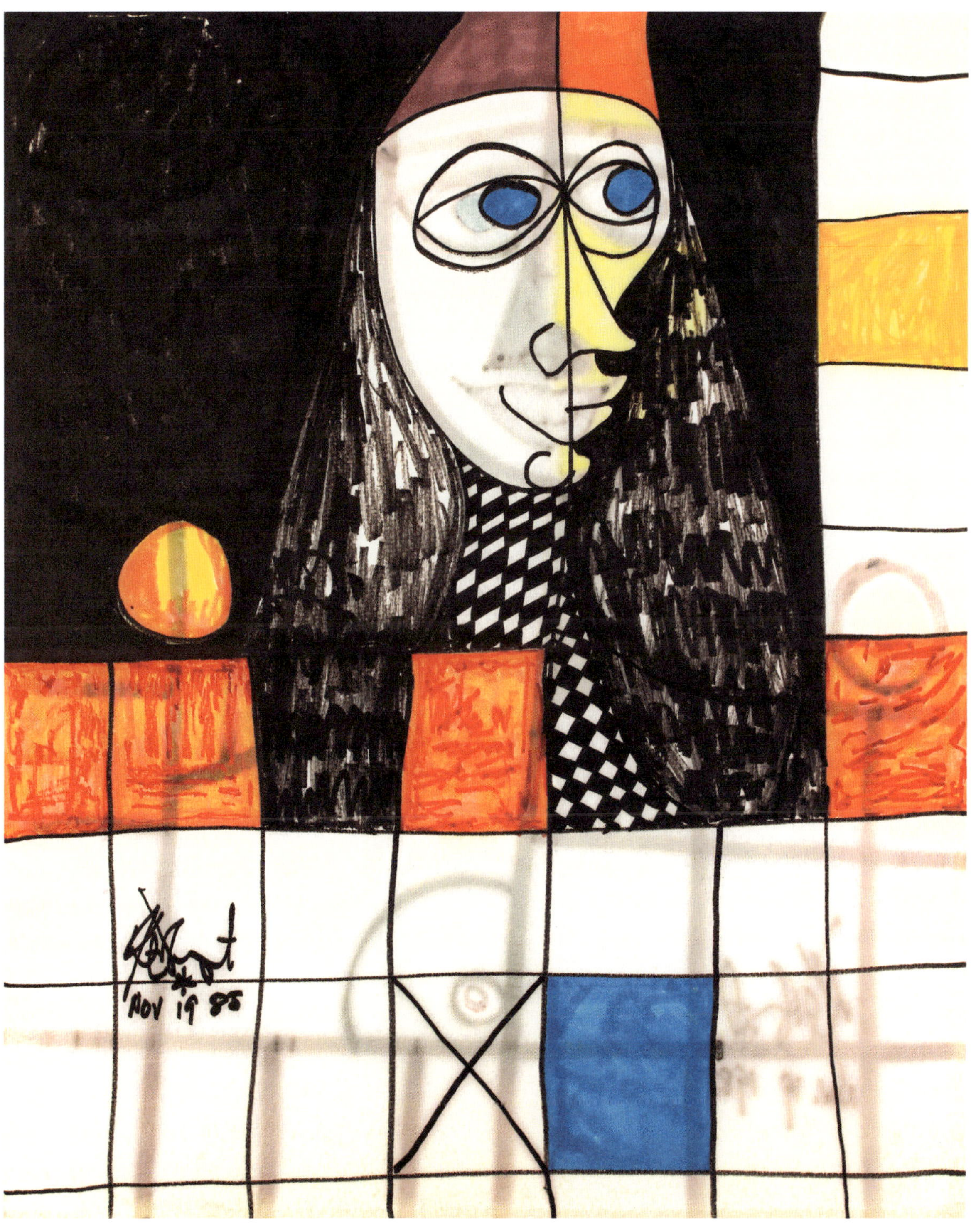

Untitled, November 19, 1985

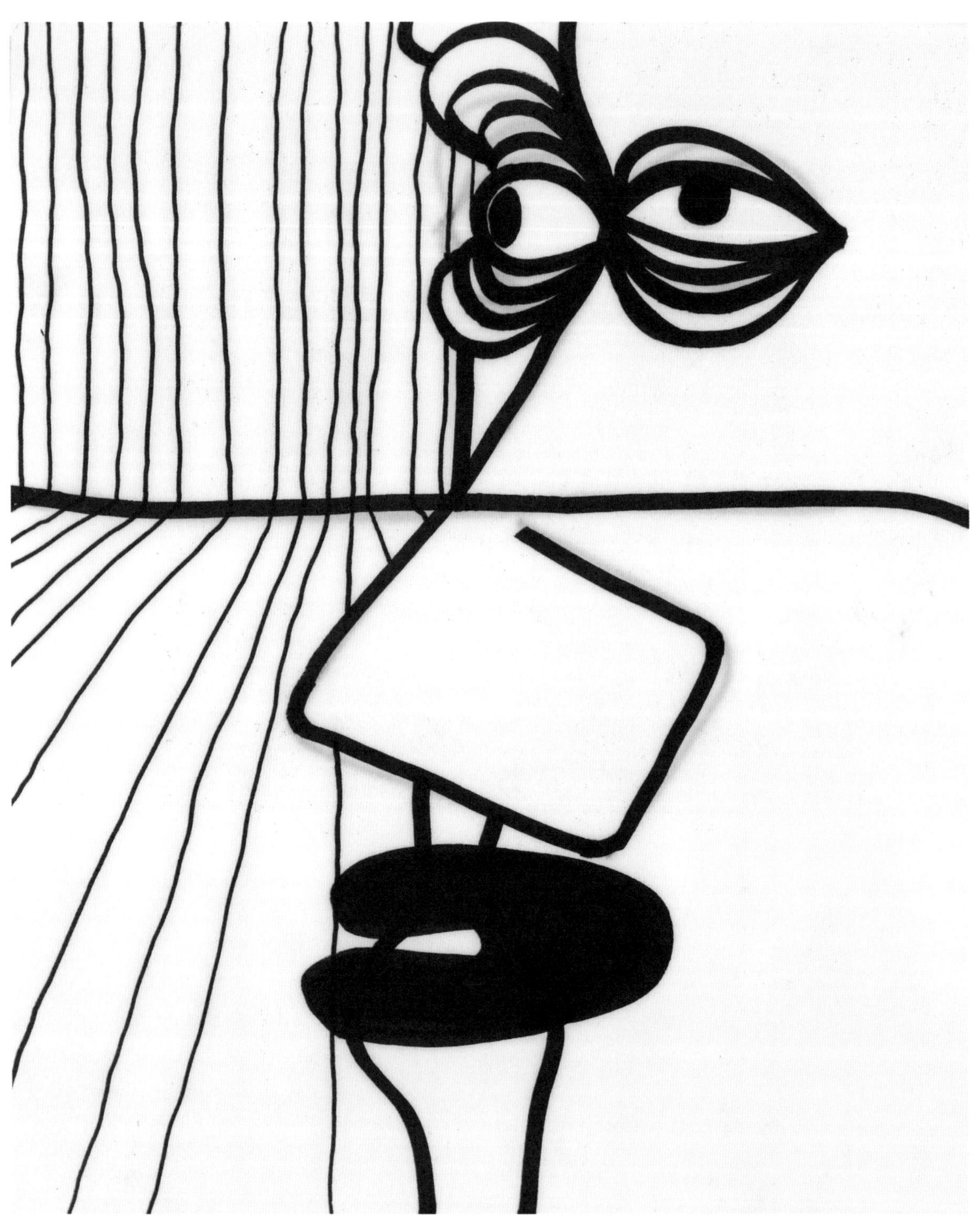

Untitled, n.d.

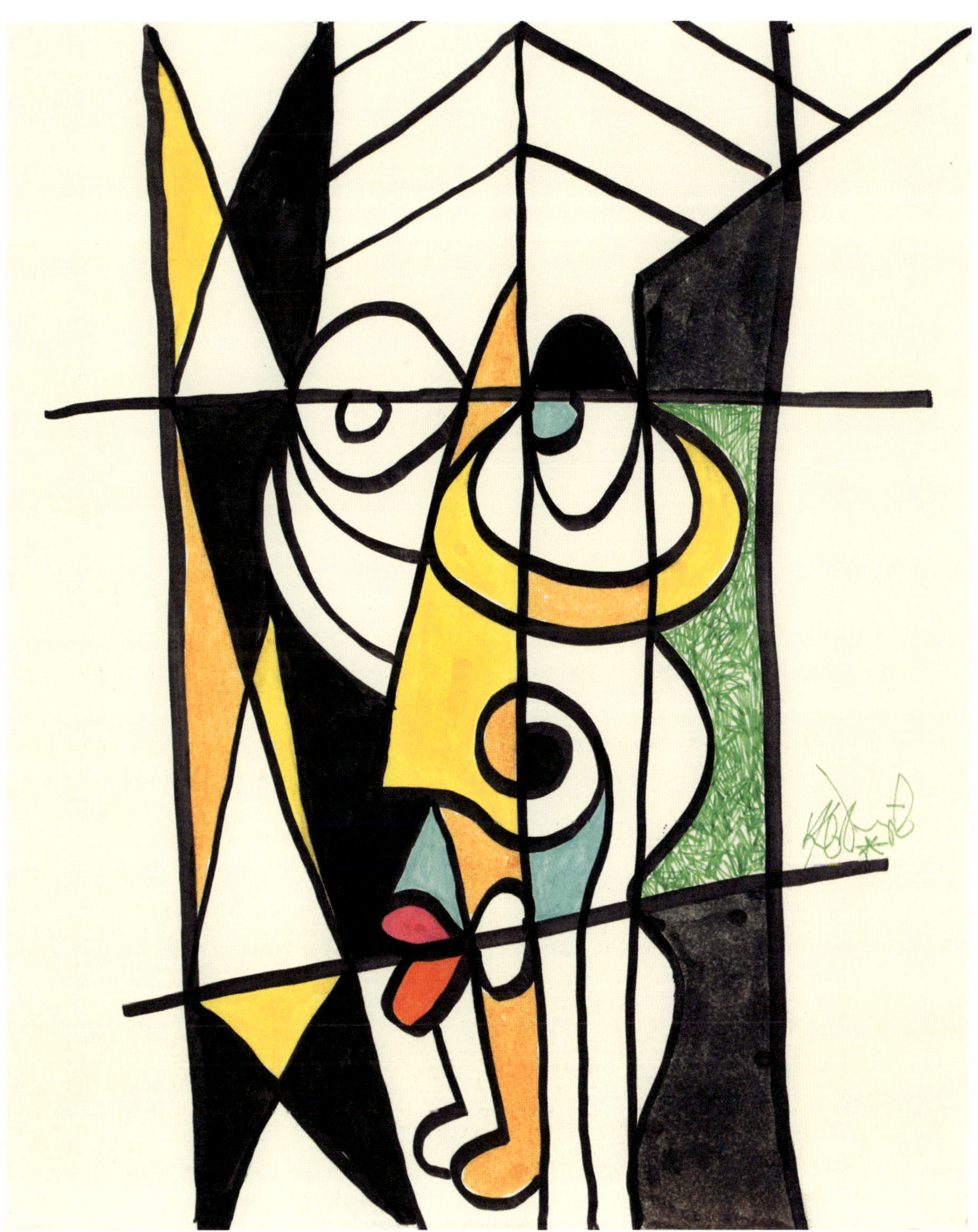

Untitled, n.d.

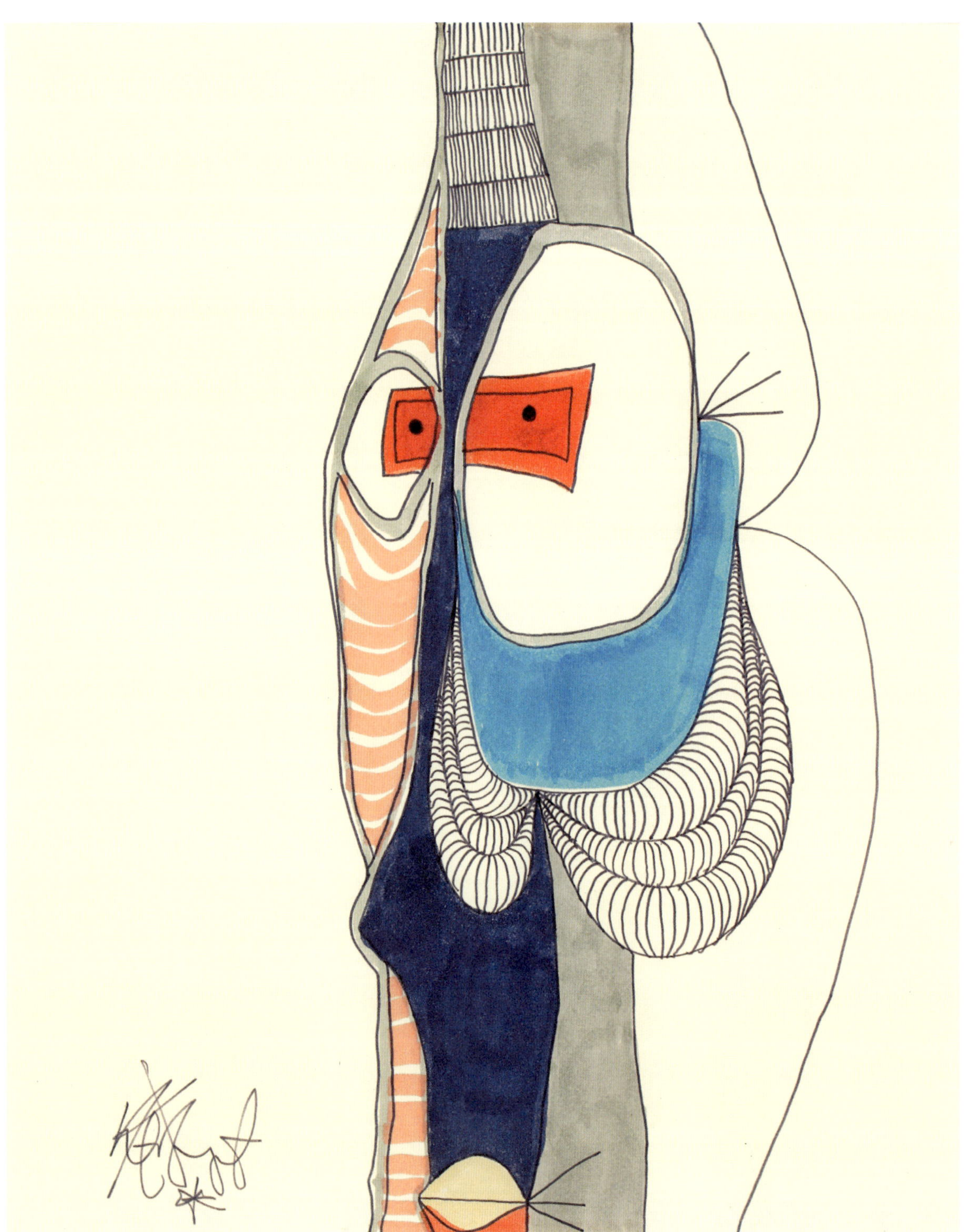

Untitled, n.d.

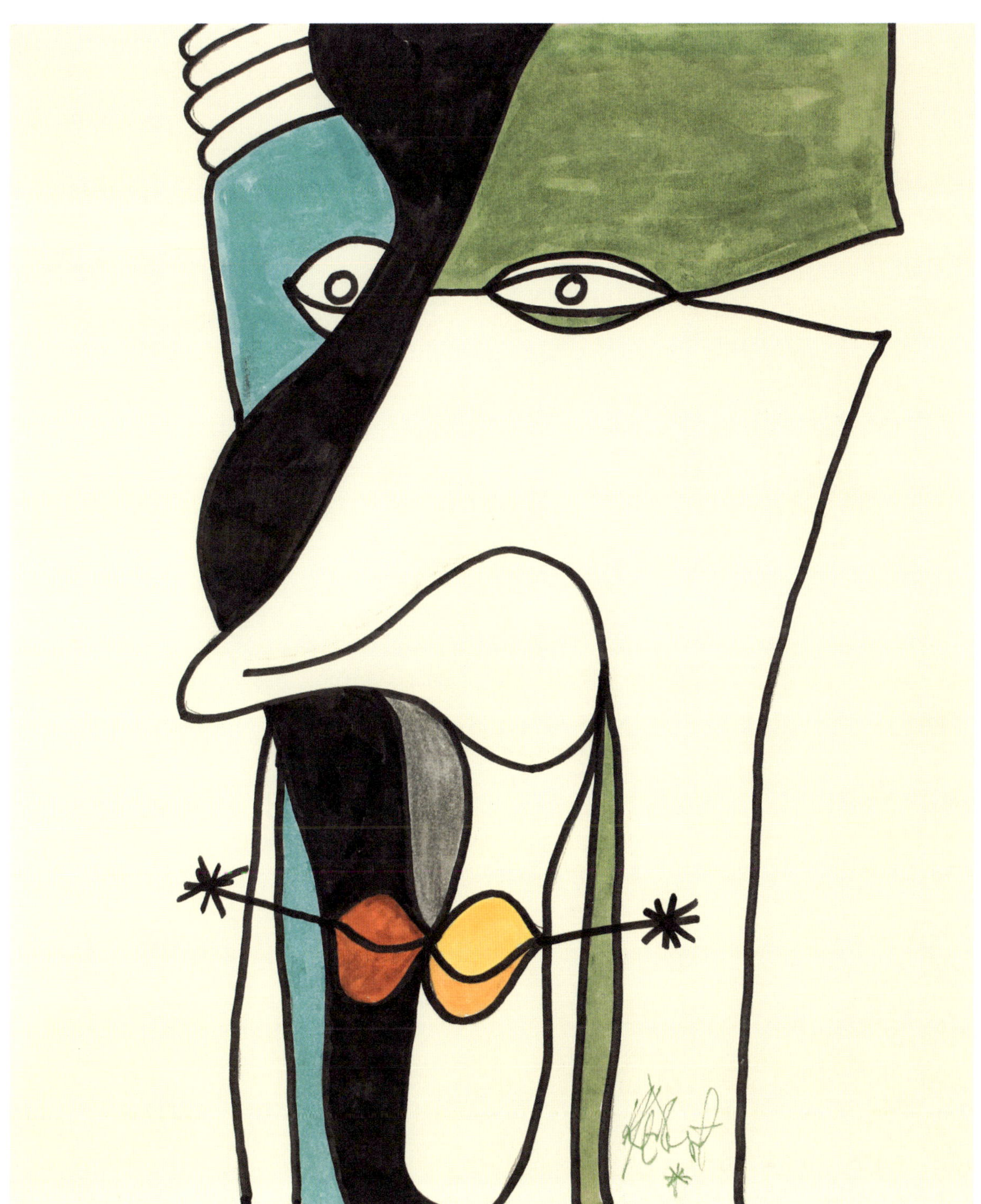

Untitled, n.d.

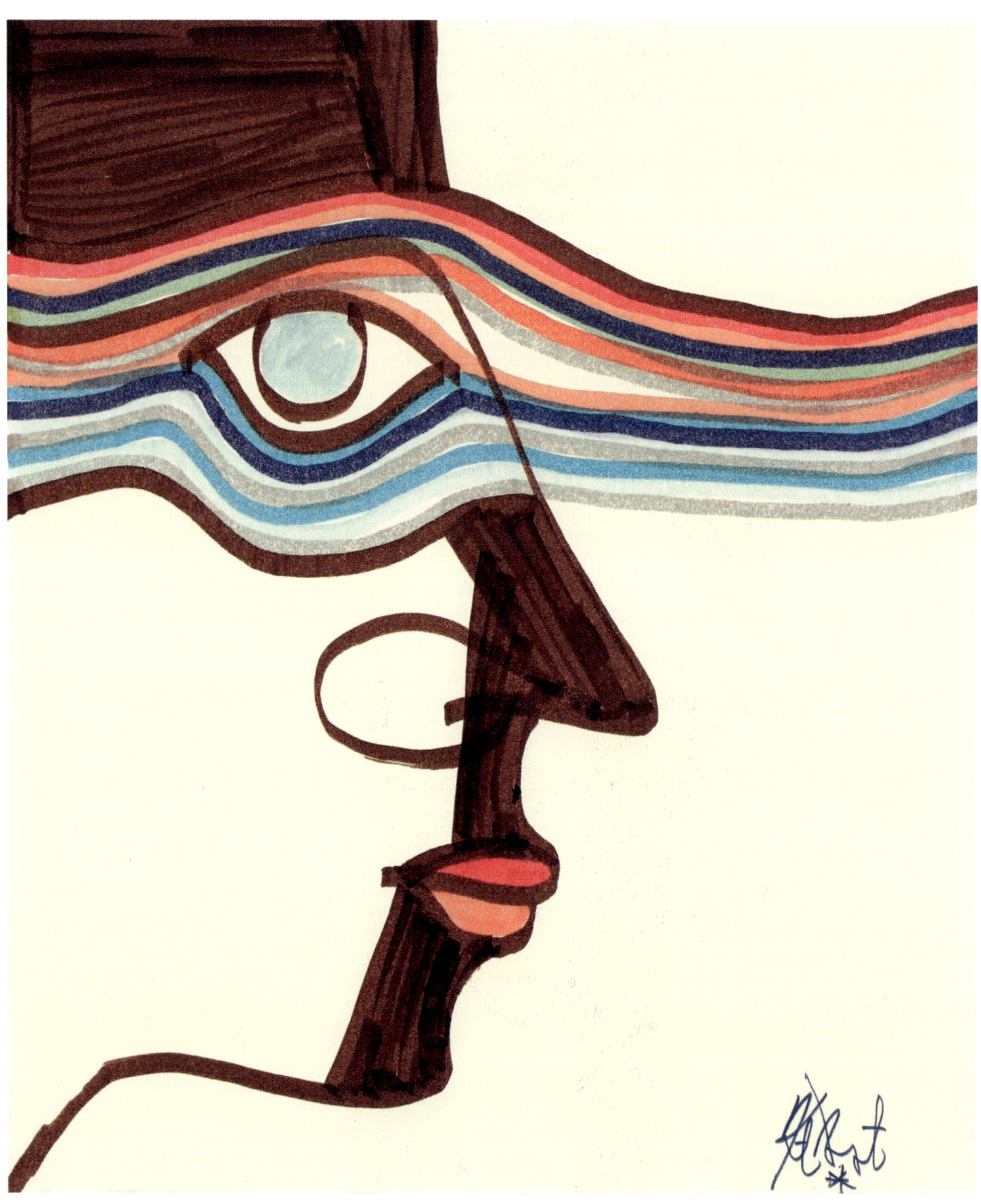

Untitled, n.d.

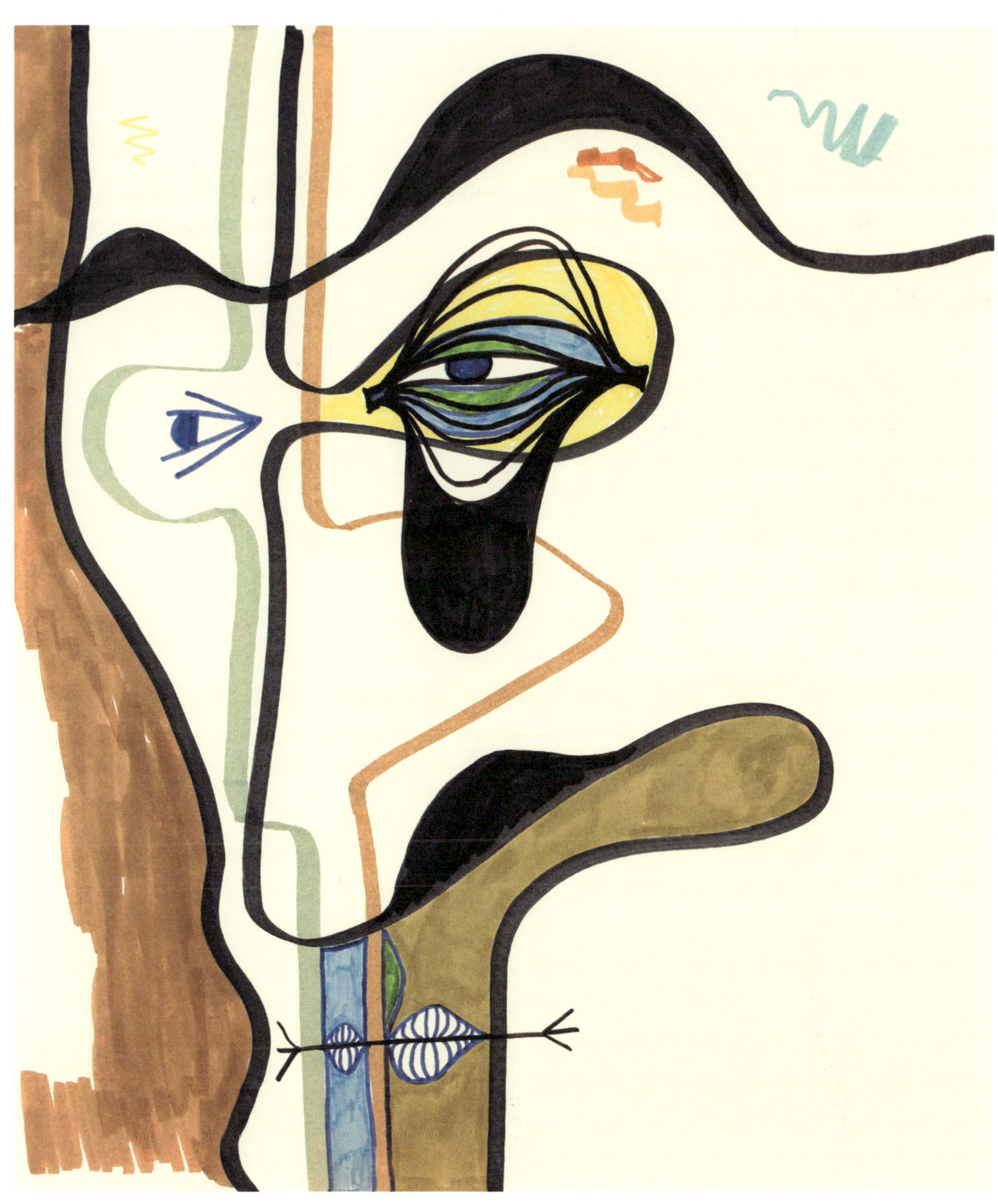

Untitled, n.d.

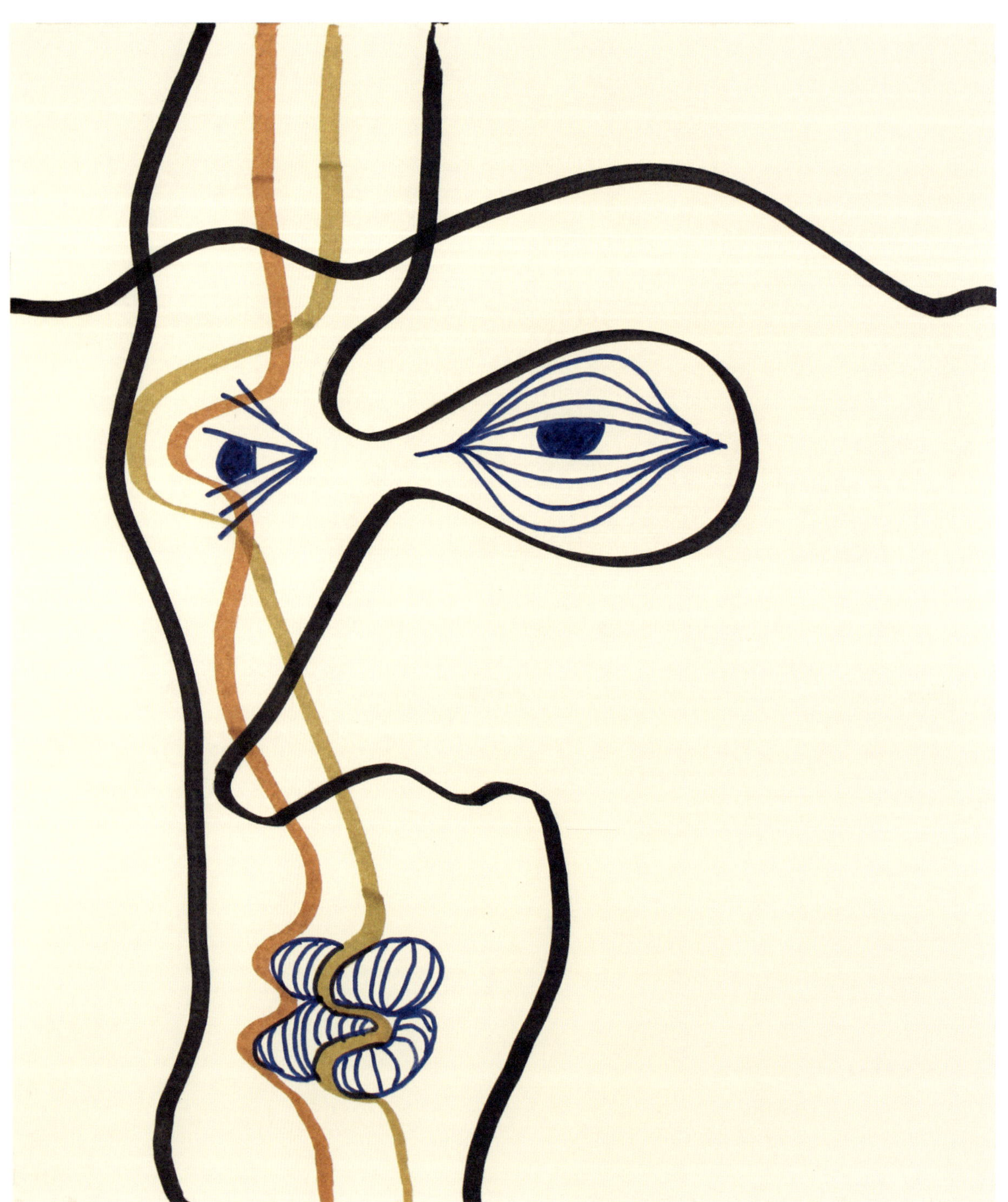

Untitled, n.d.

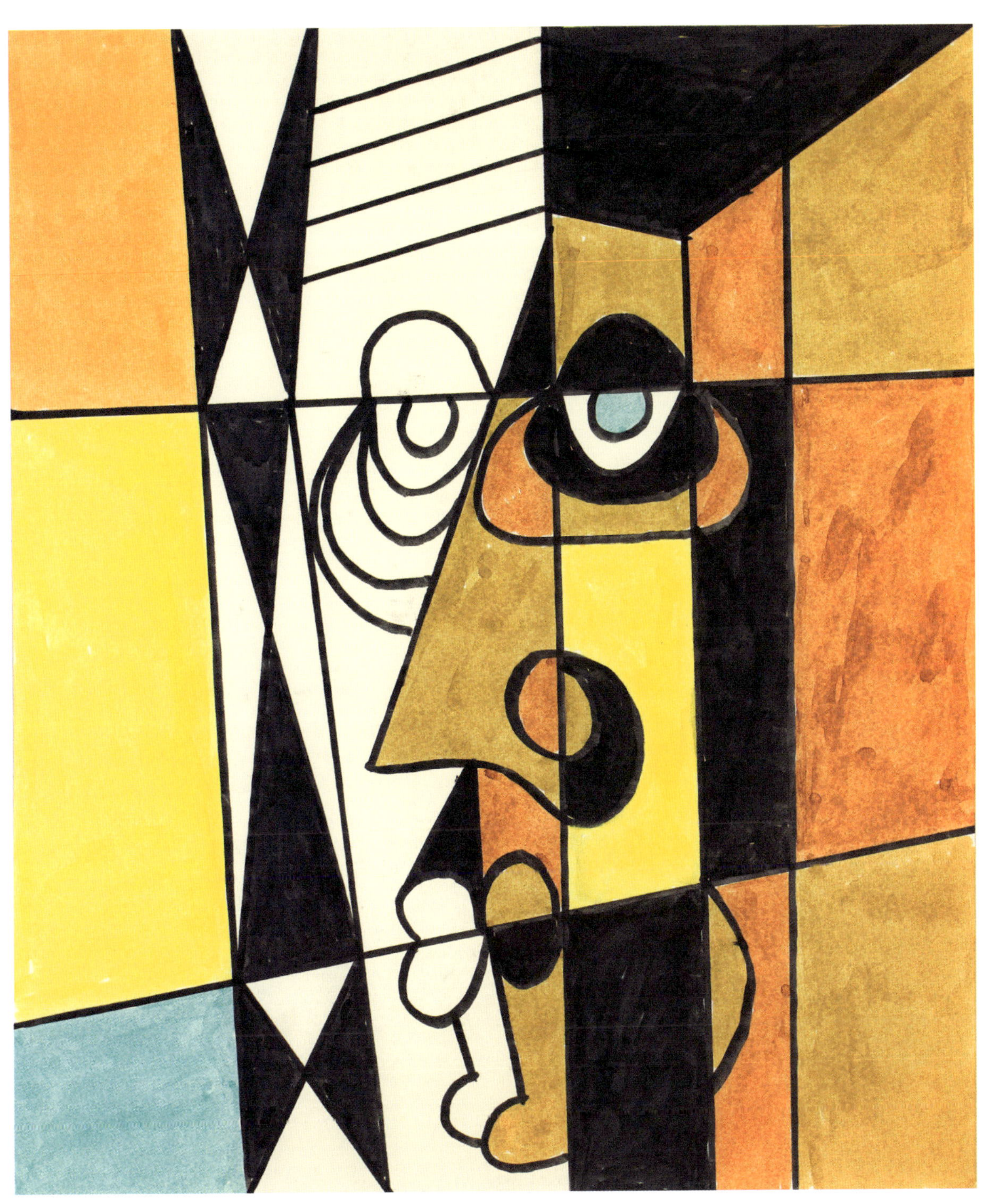

Untitled, n.d.

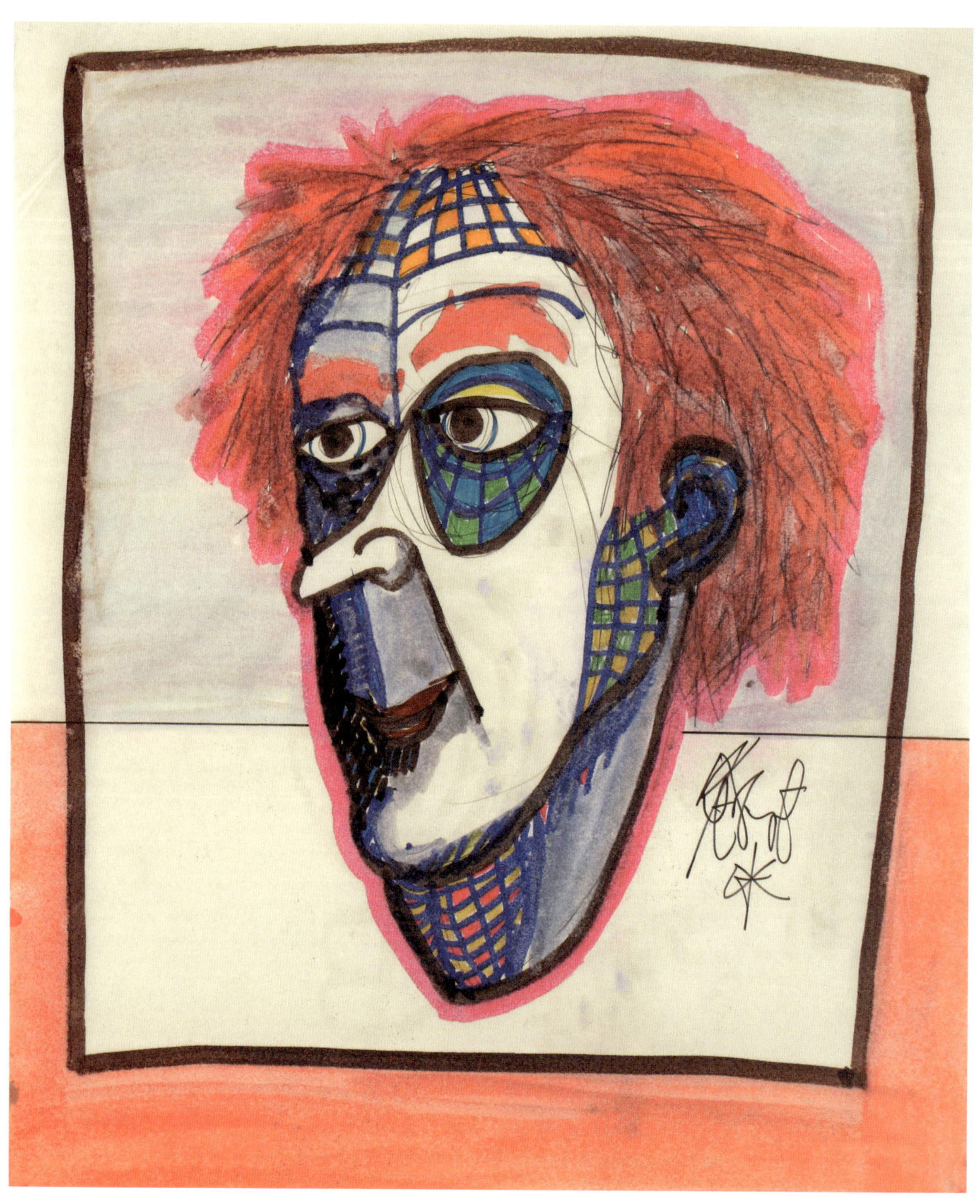

Untitled, n.d.

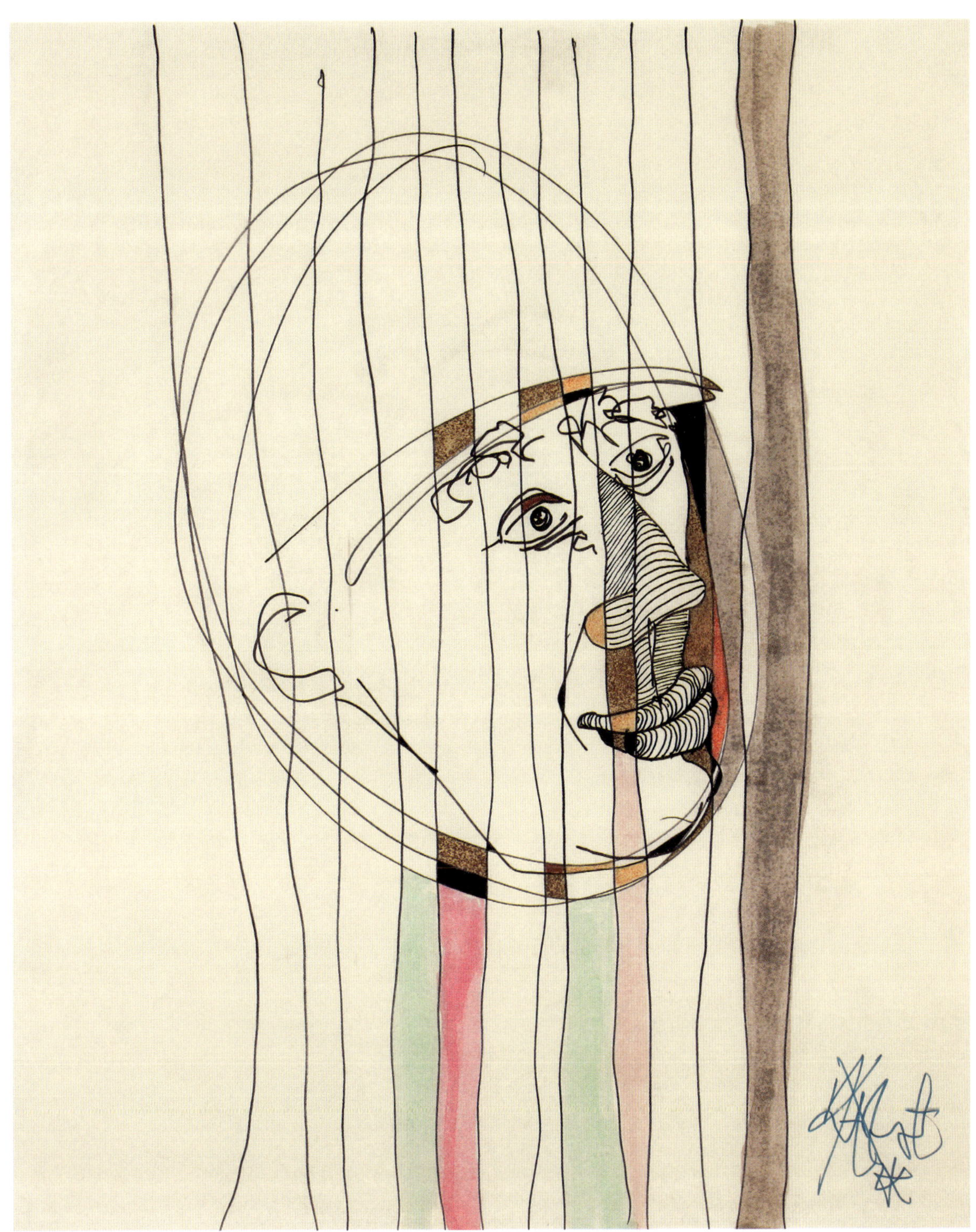

Untitled, n.d.

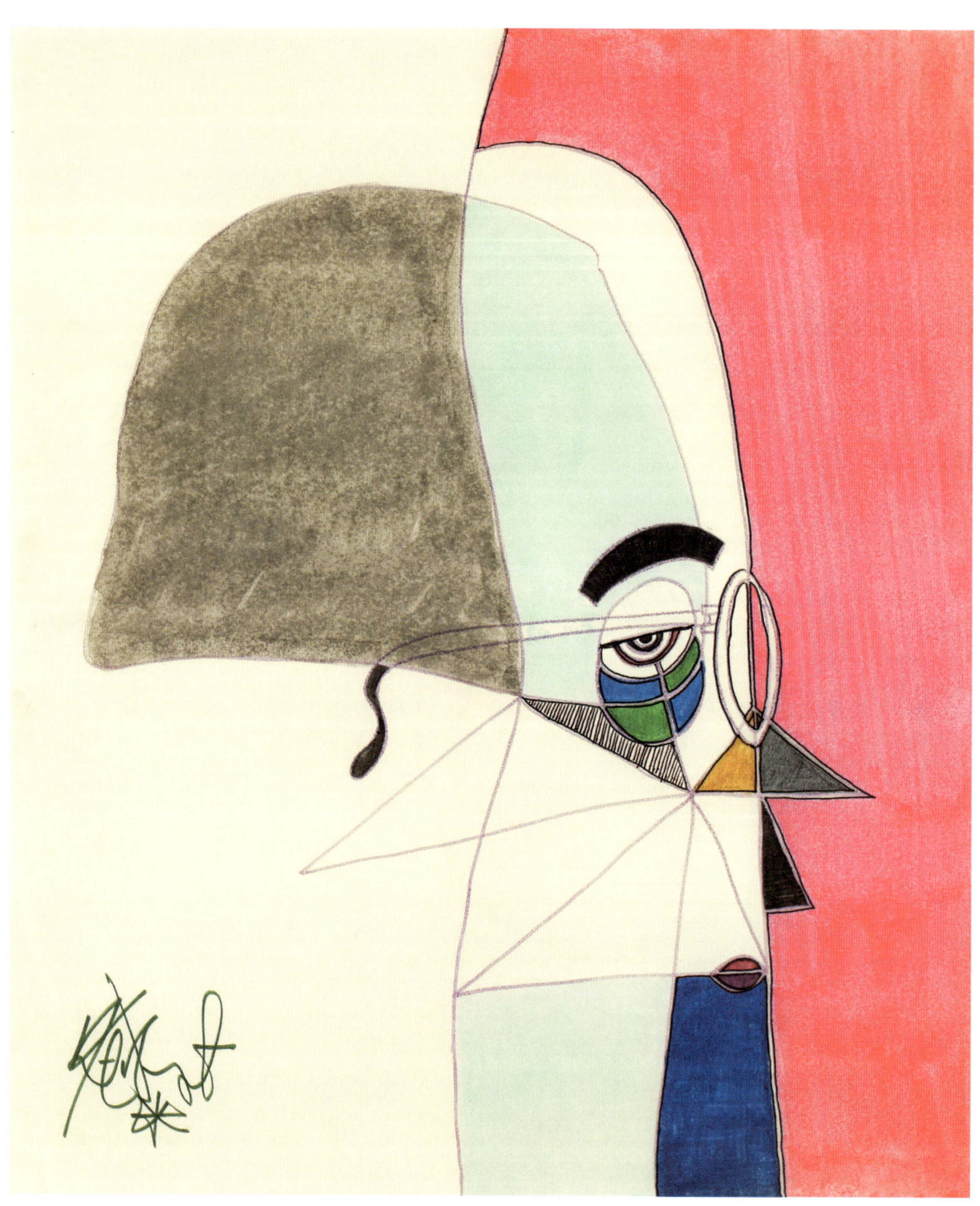

Untitled, n.d.

And may I say parenthetically that my own means of making a living is essentially clerical, and hence tedious and constipating. Intruders, no matter how ill natured or stupid or dishonest, are as refreshing as the sudden breakthrough of sunbeams on a cloudy day.

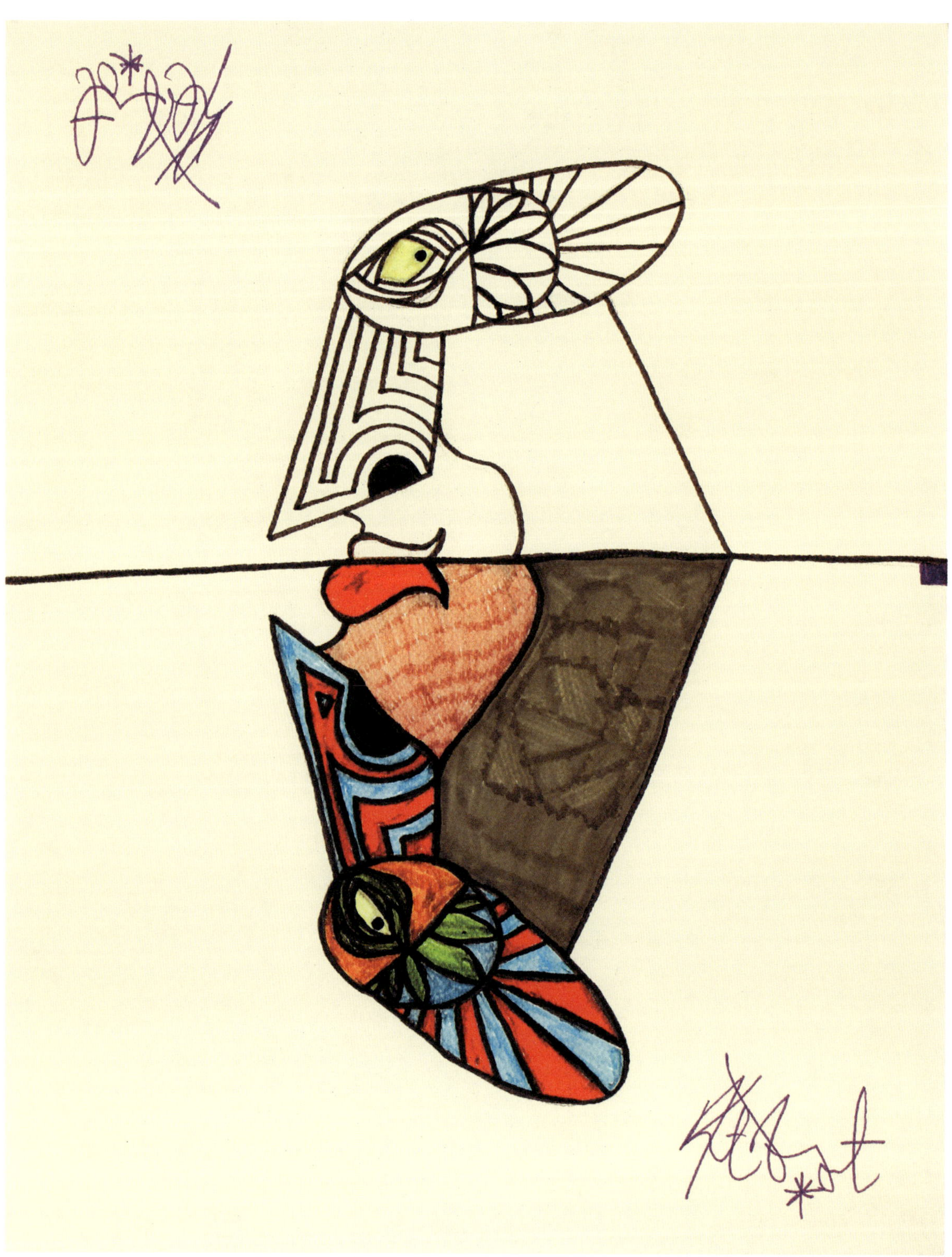

Untitled, n.d.

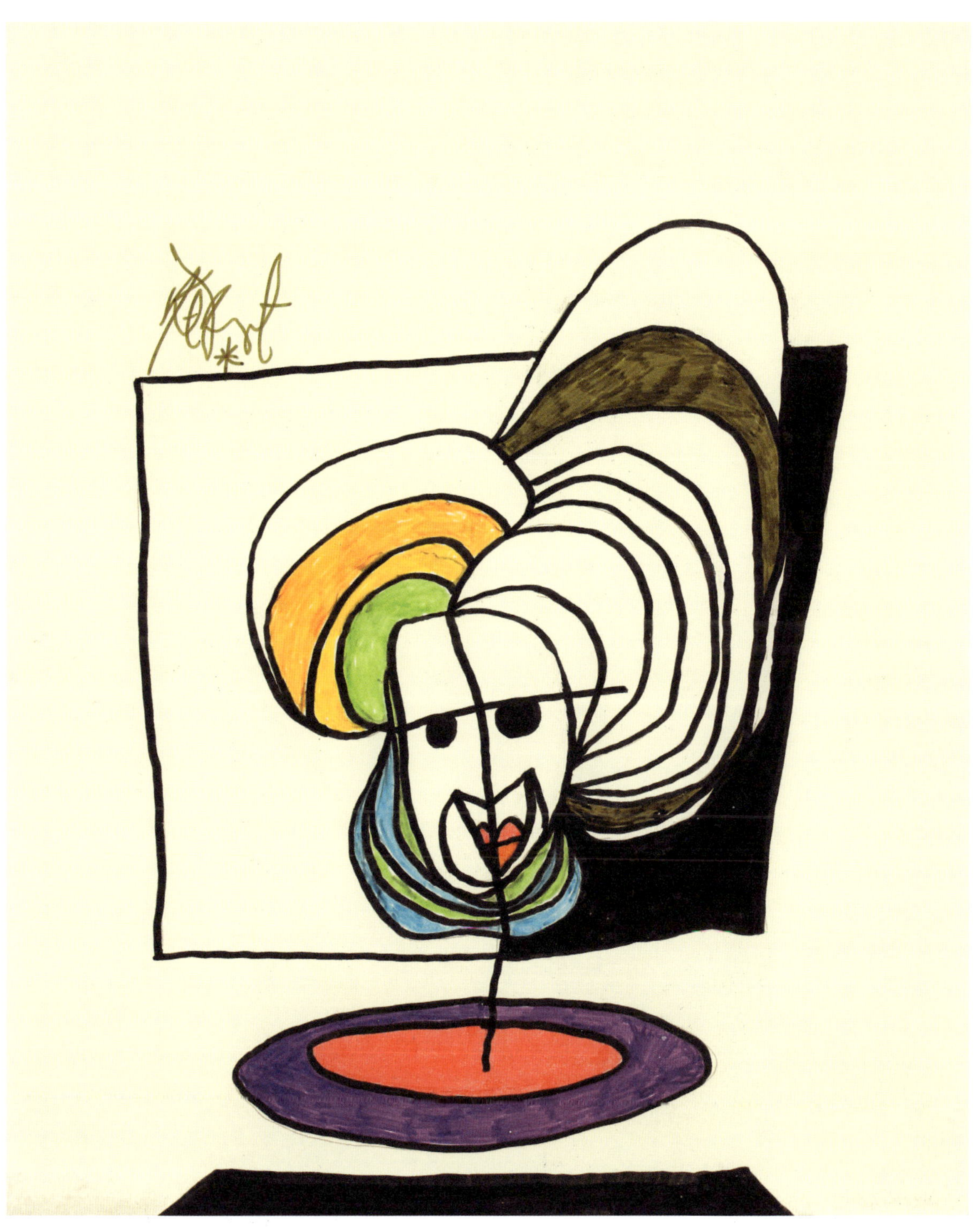

Untitled, n.d.

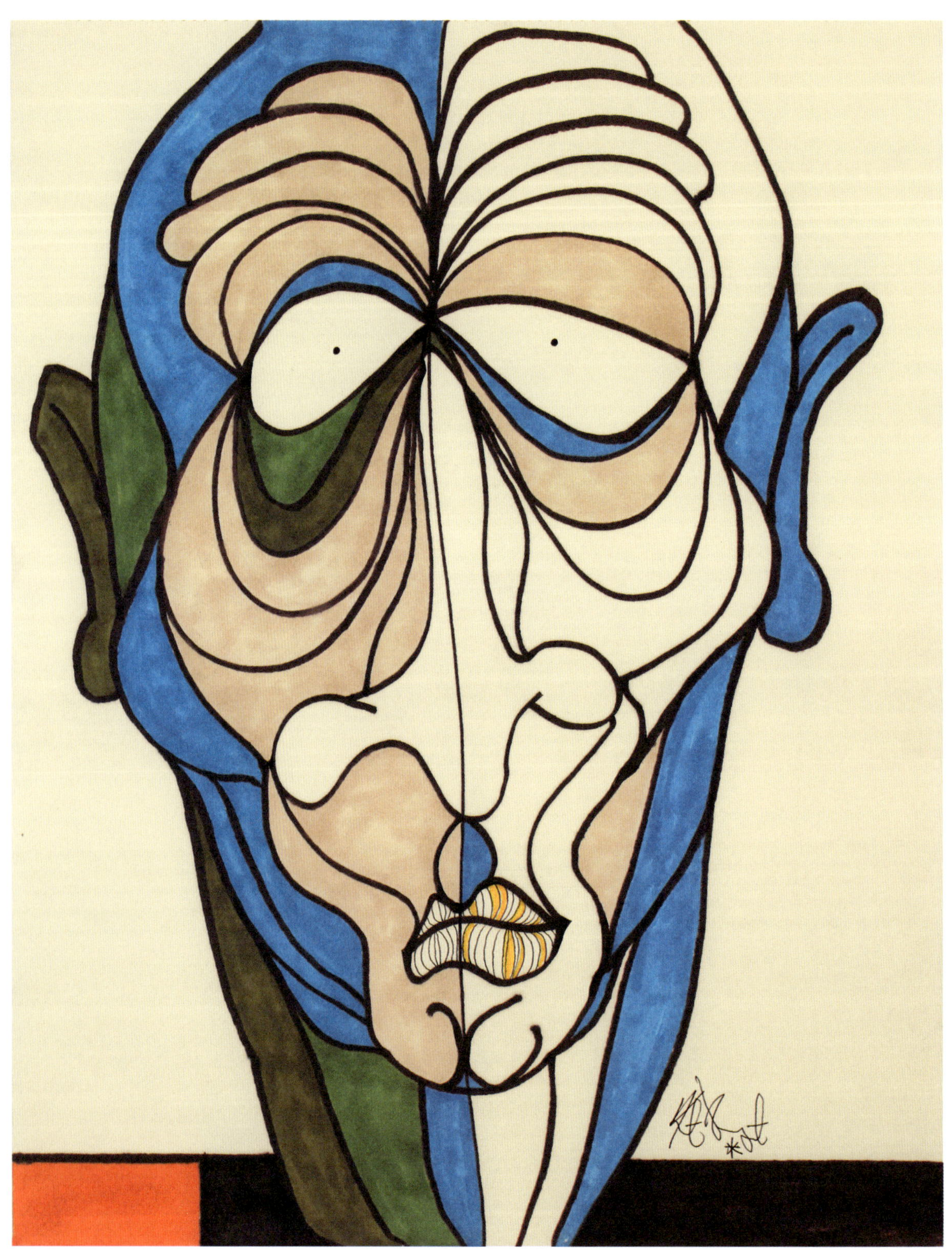

Untitled, n.d.

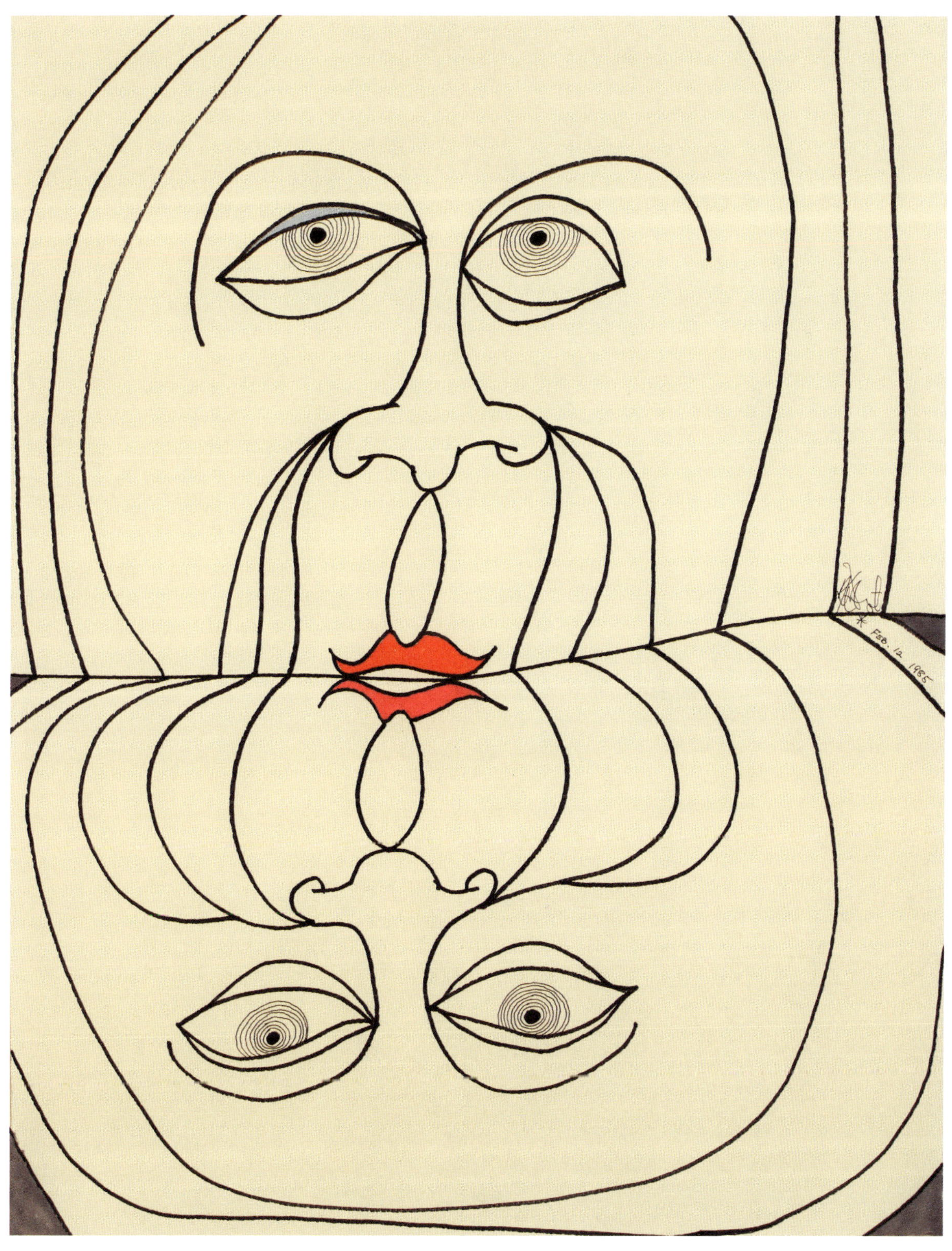

Untitled, February 12, 1985

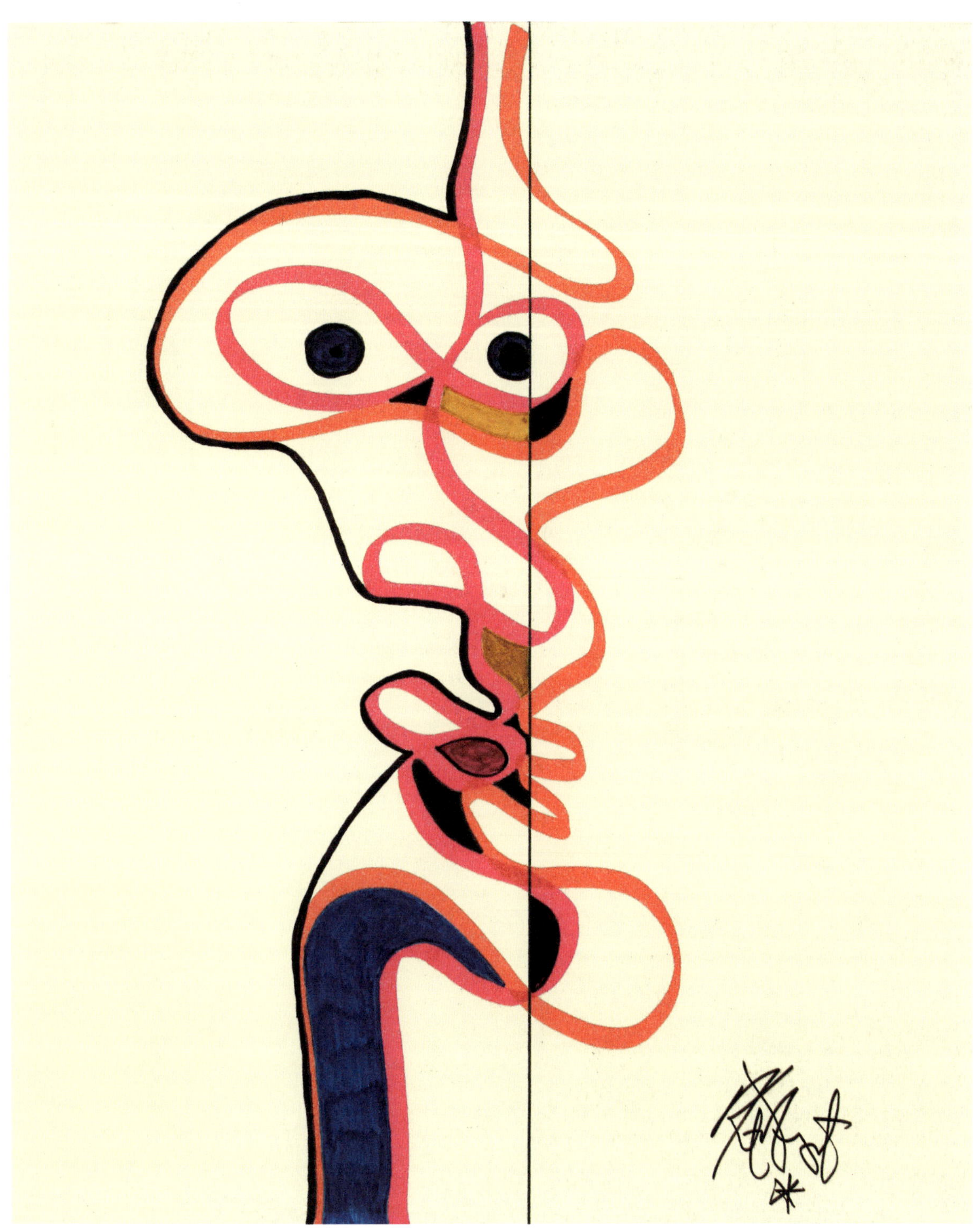

Untitled, n.d.

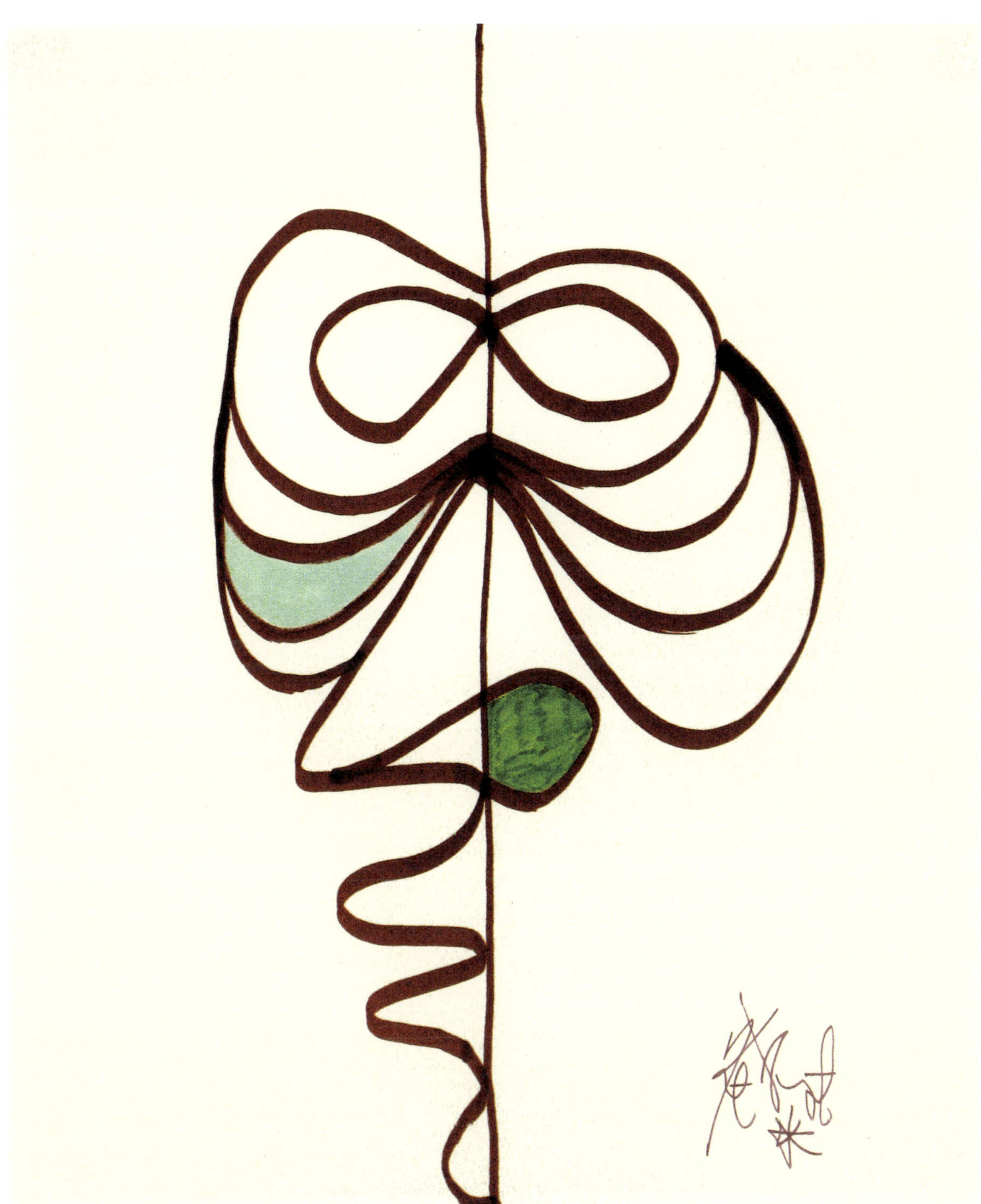

Untitled, n.d.

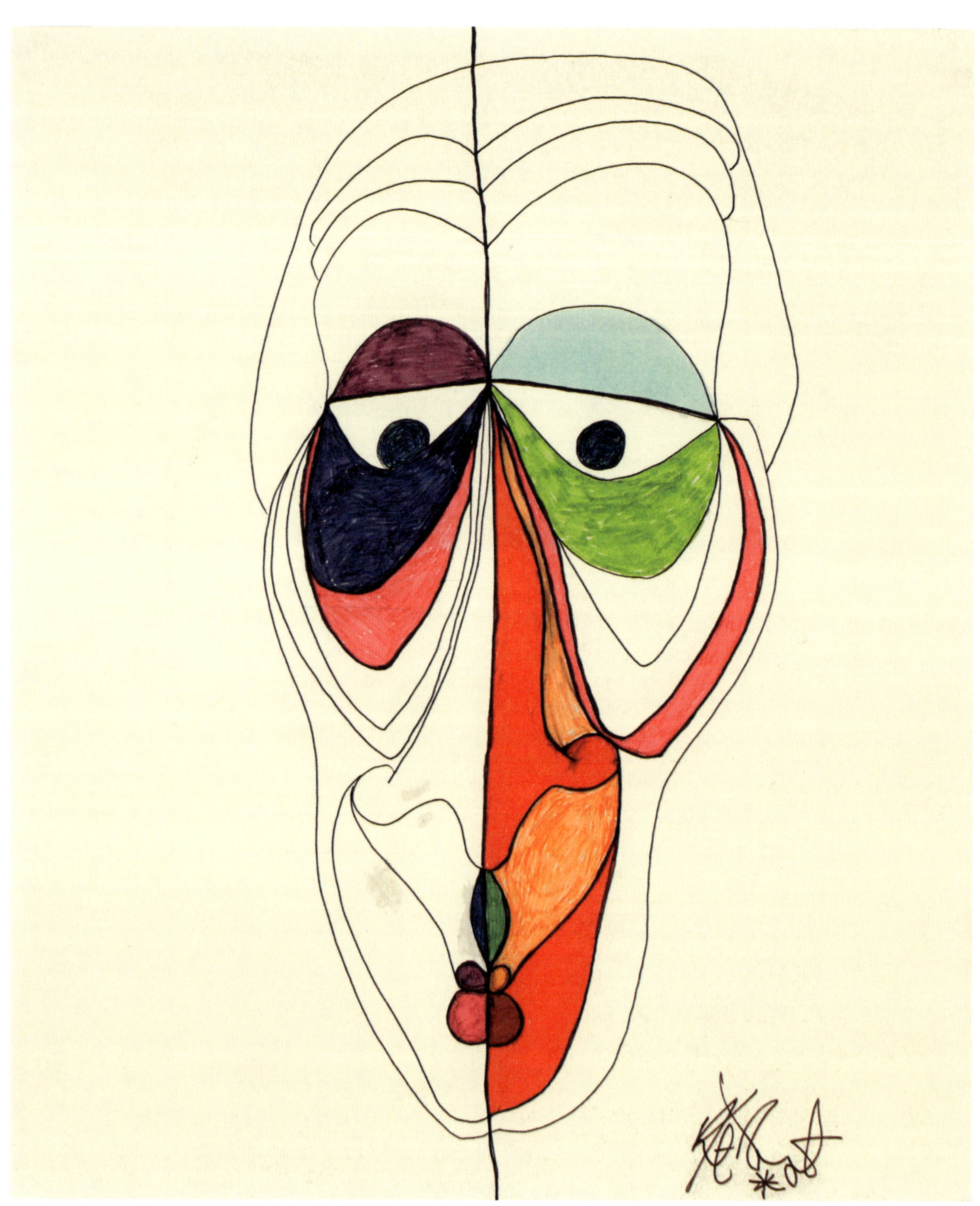

Untitled, n.d.

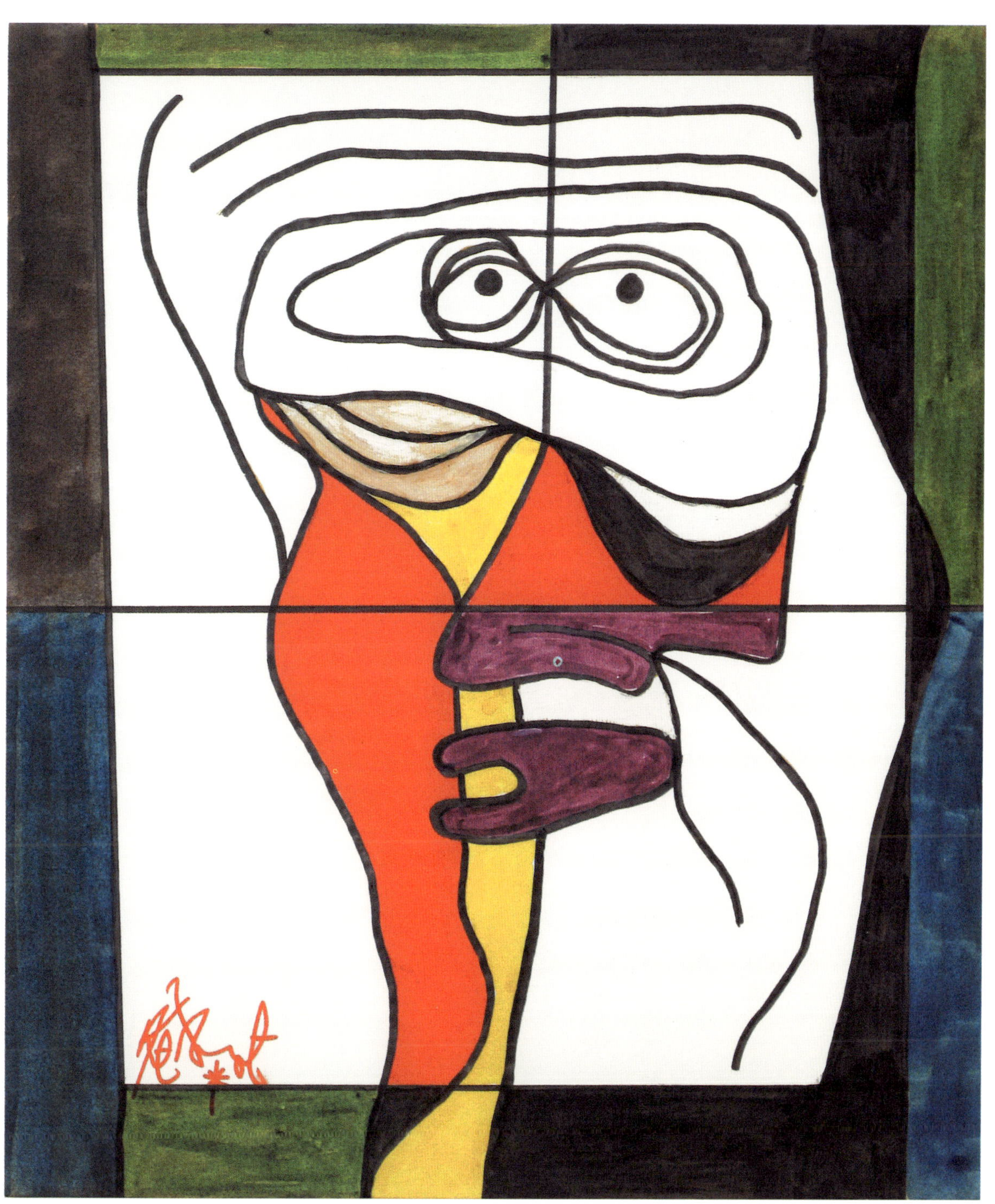

Untitled, n.d.

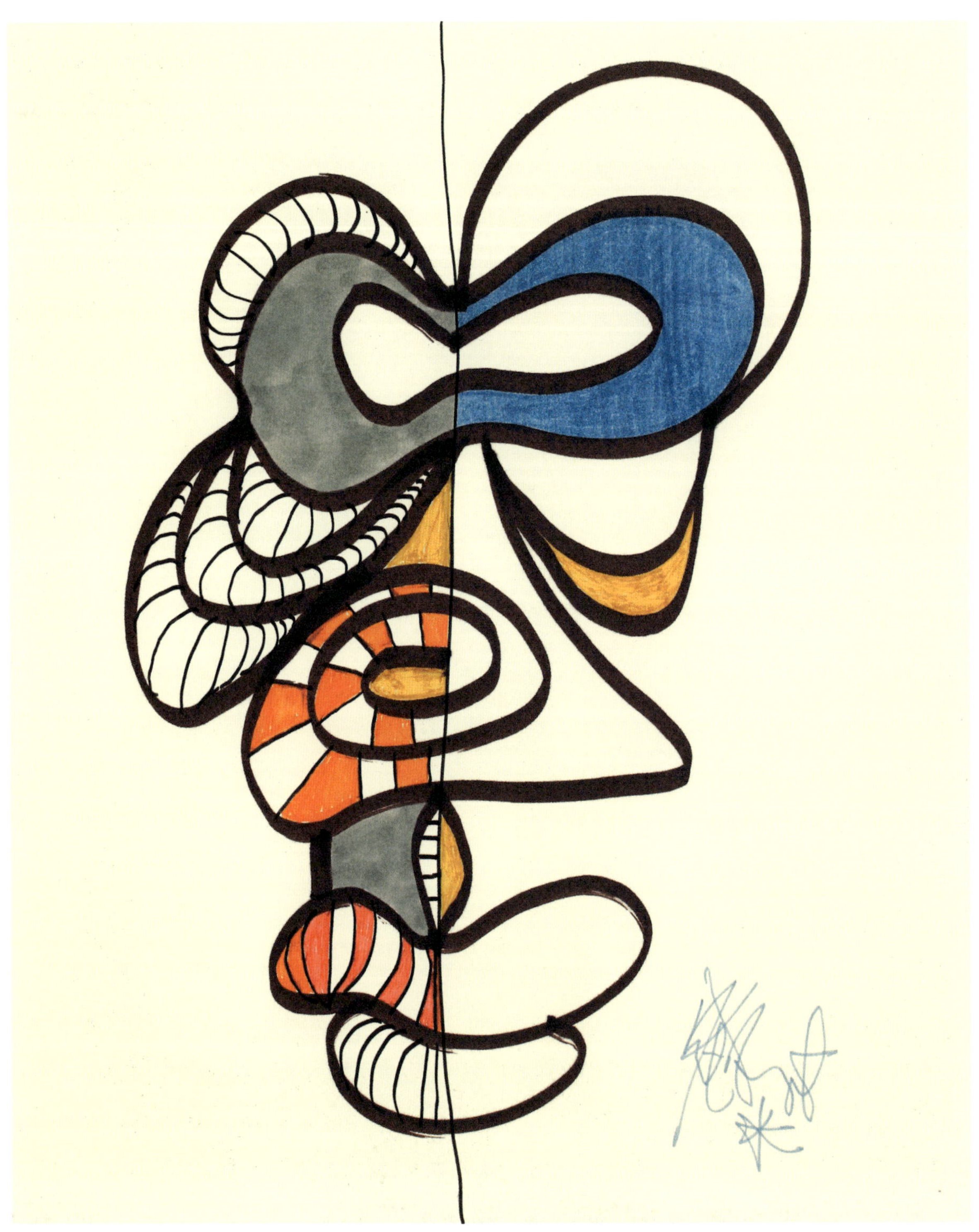

Untitled, n.d.

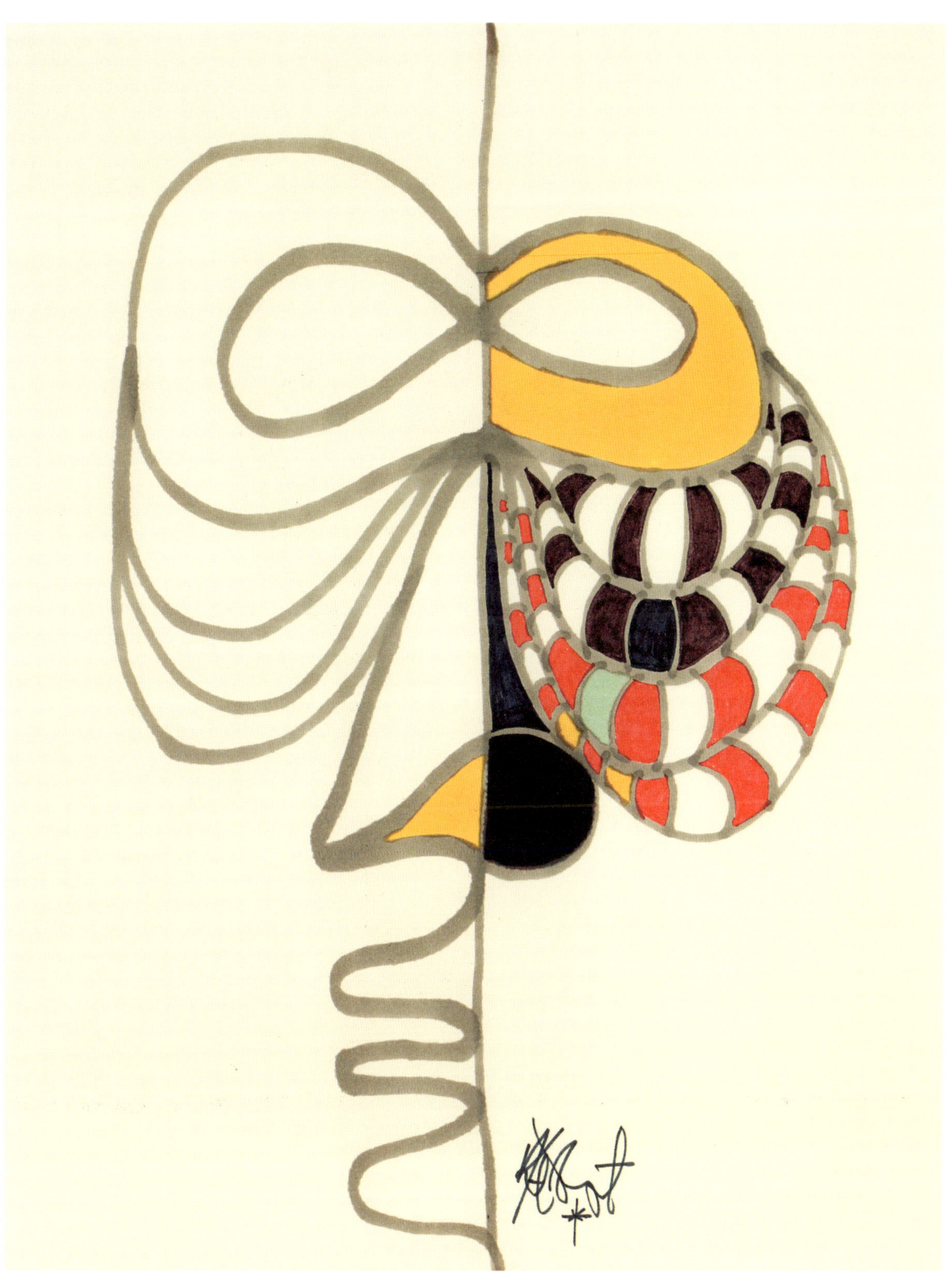

Untitled, n.d.

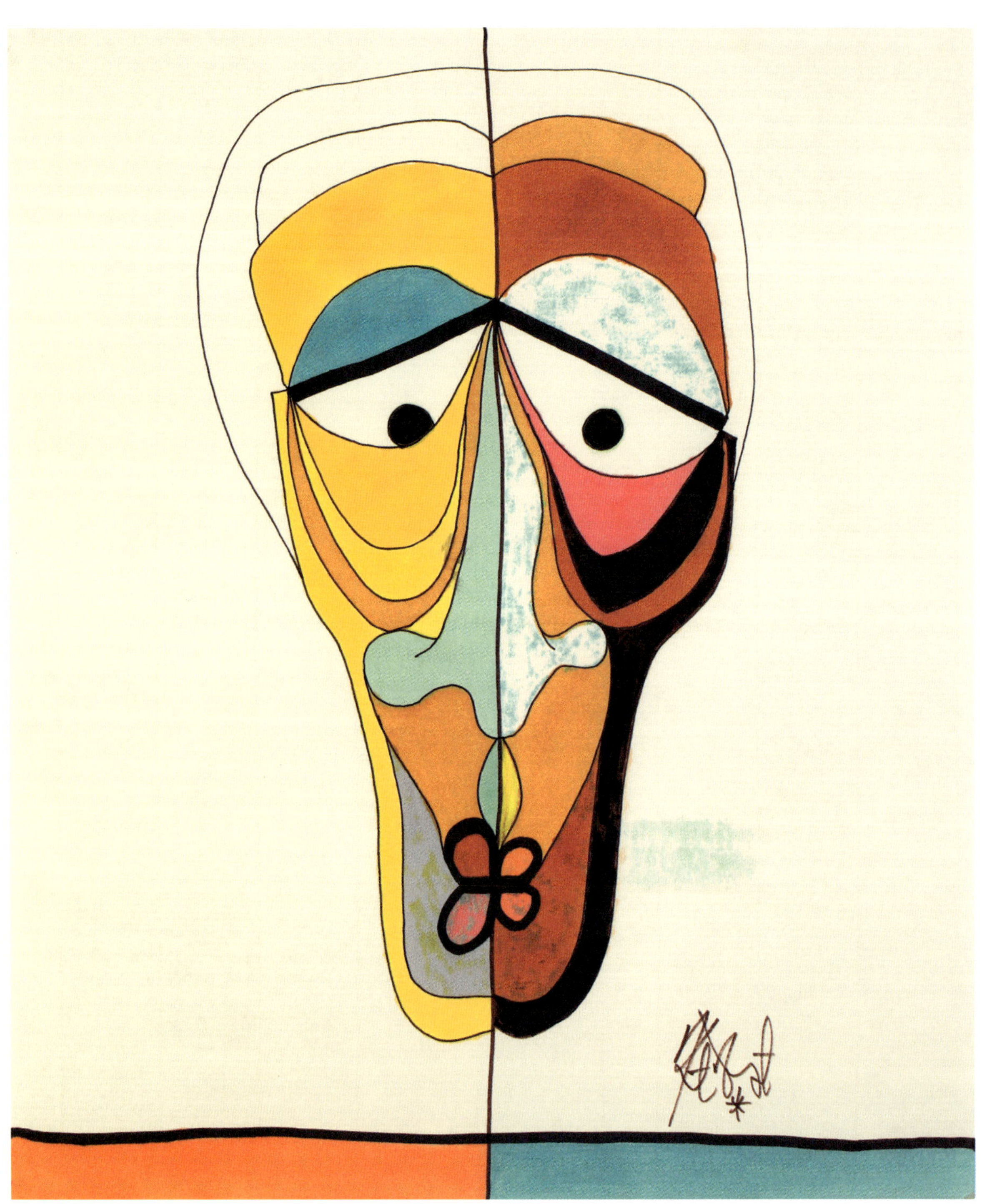

Untitled, n.d.

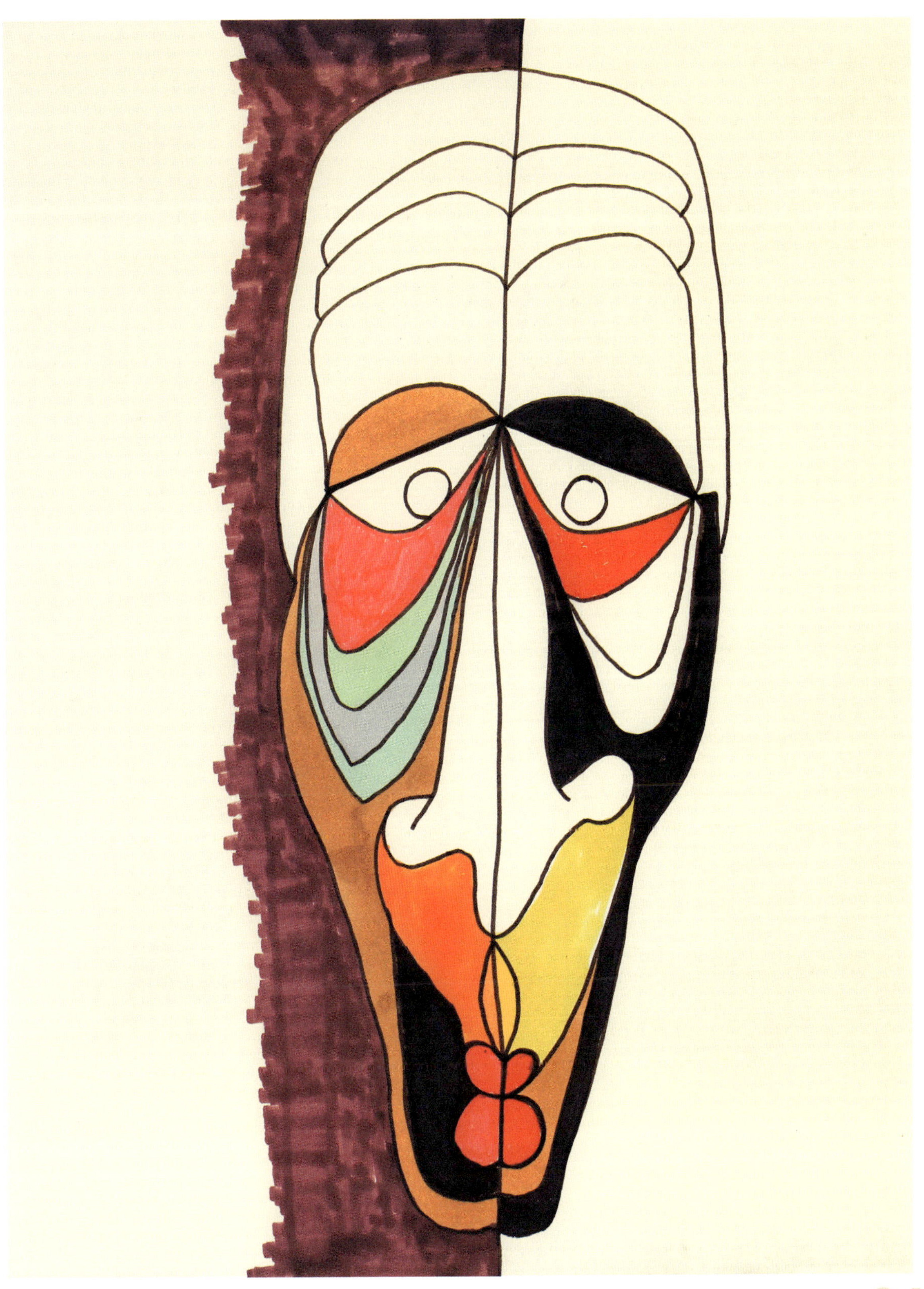

Untitled, n.d.

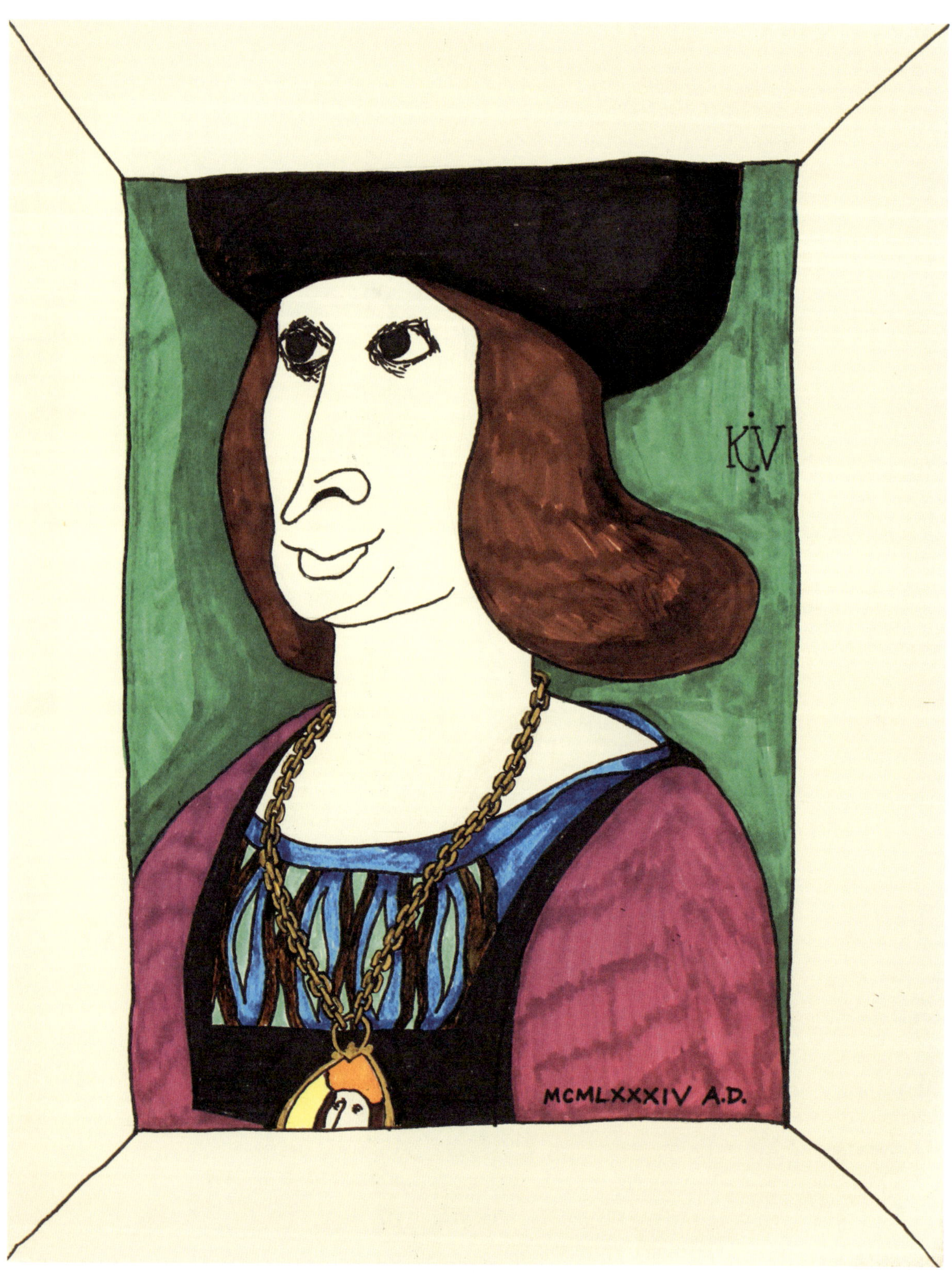

Untitled, 1984

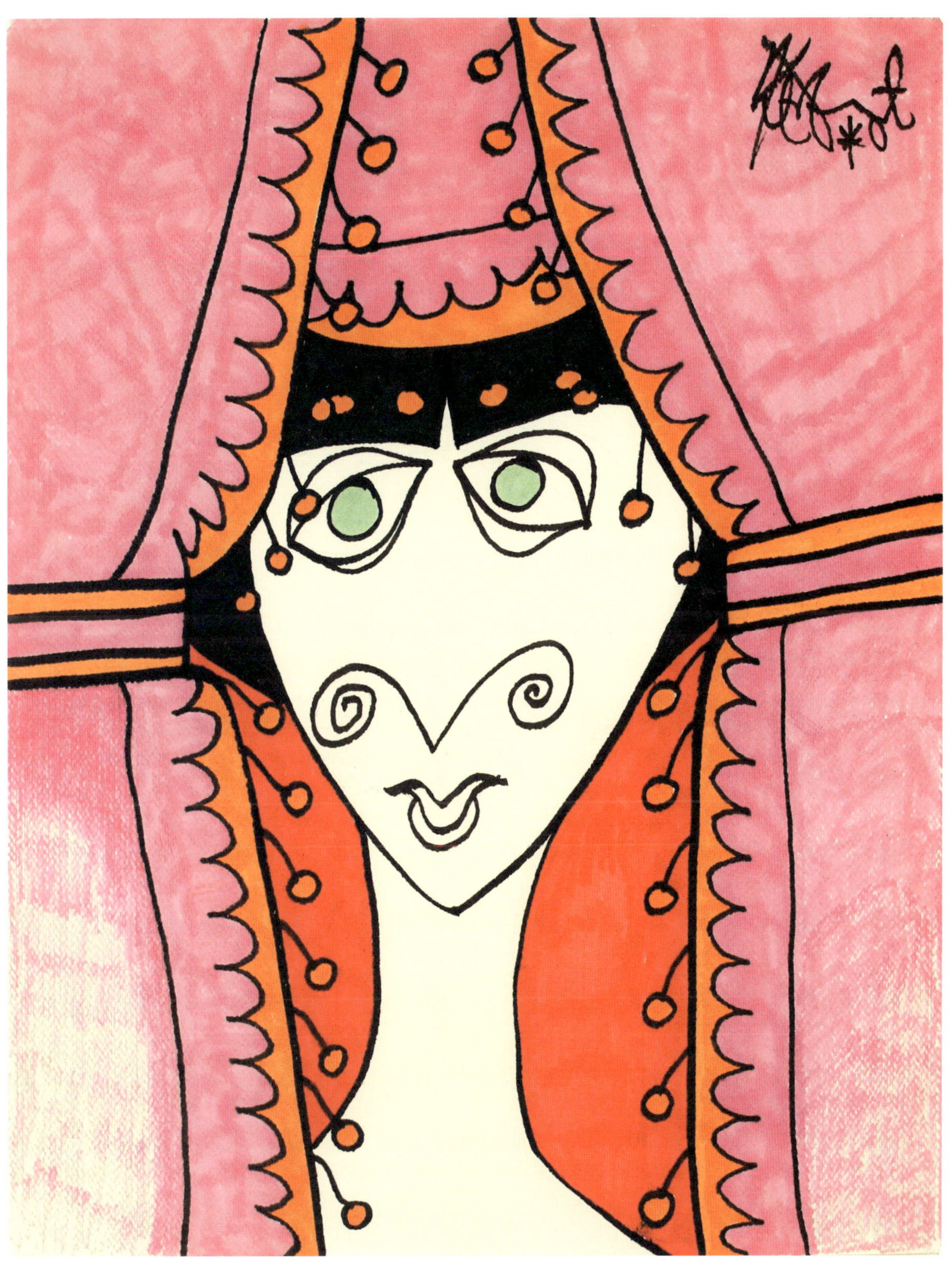

Untitled, n.d.

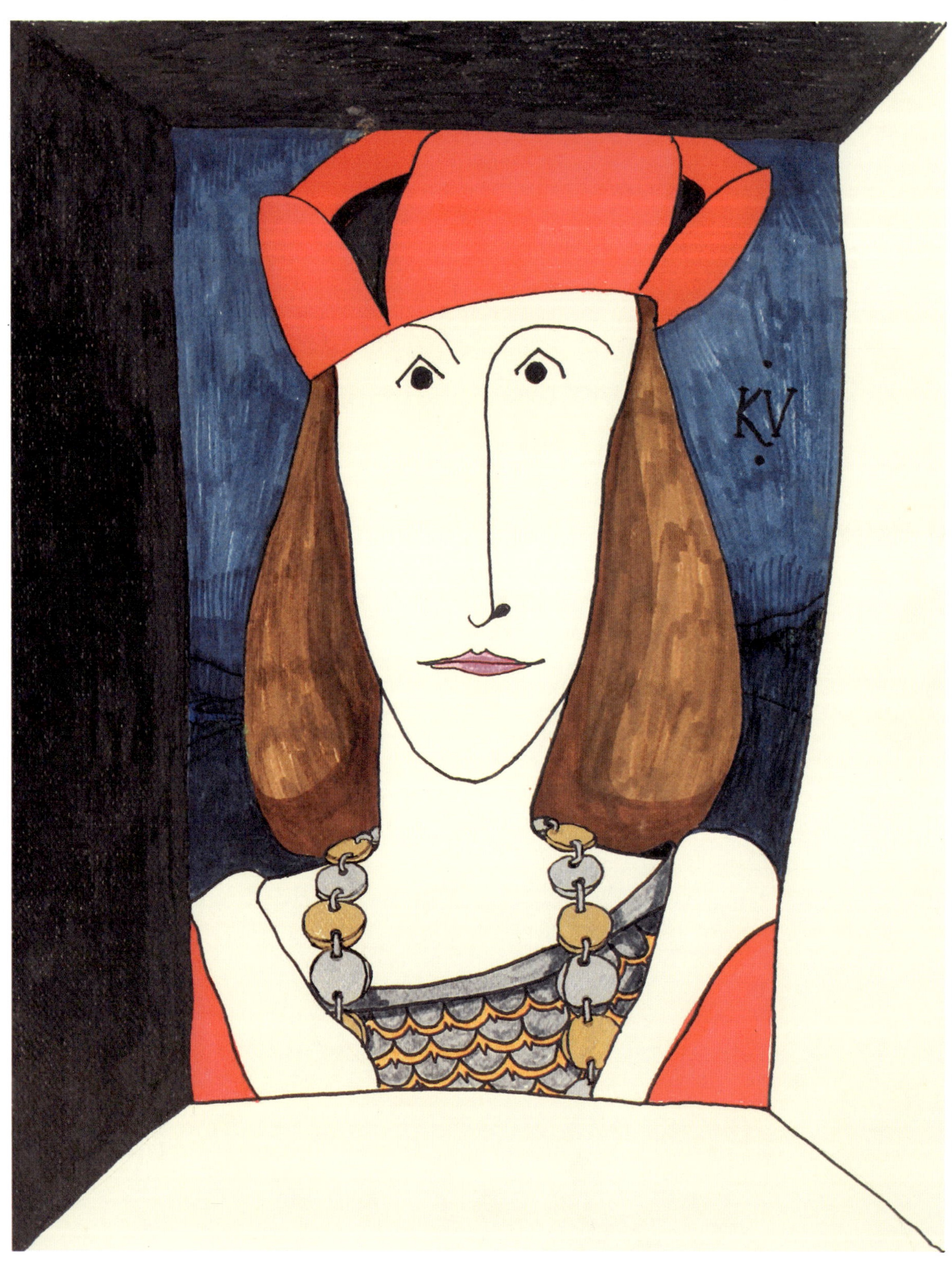

Untitled, n.d.

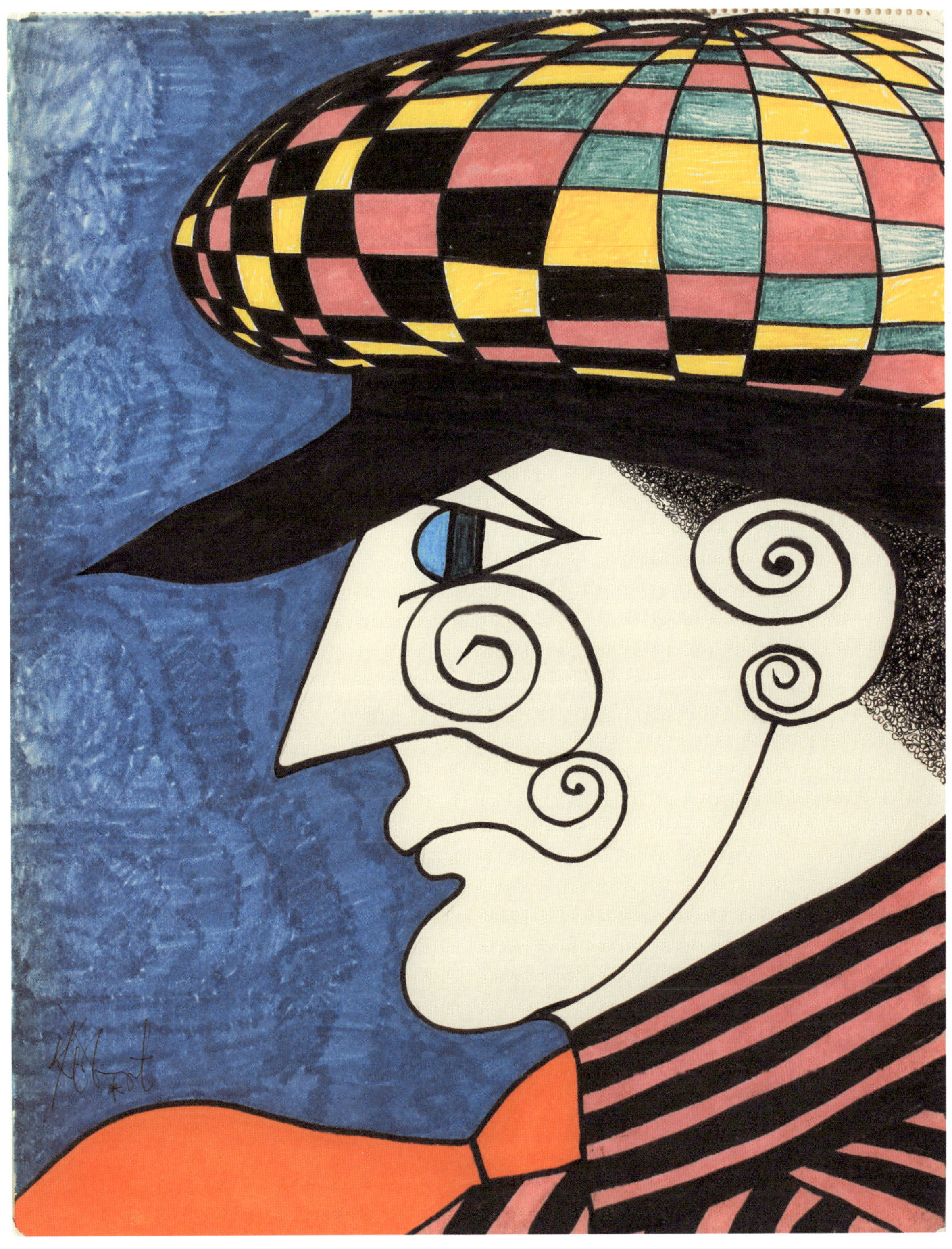

Untitled, n.d.

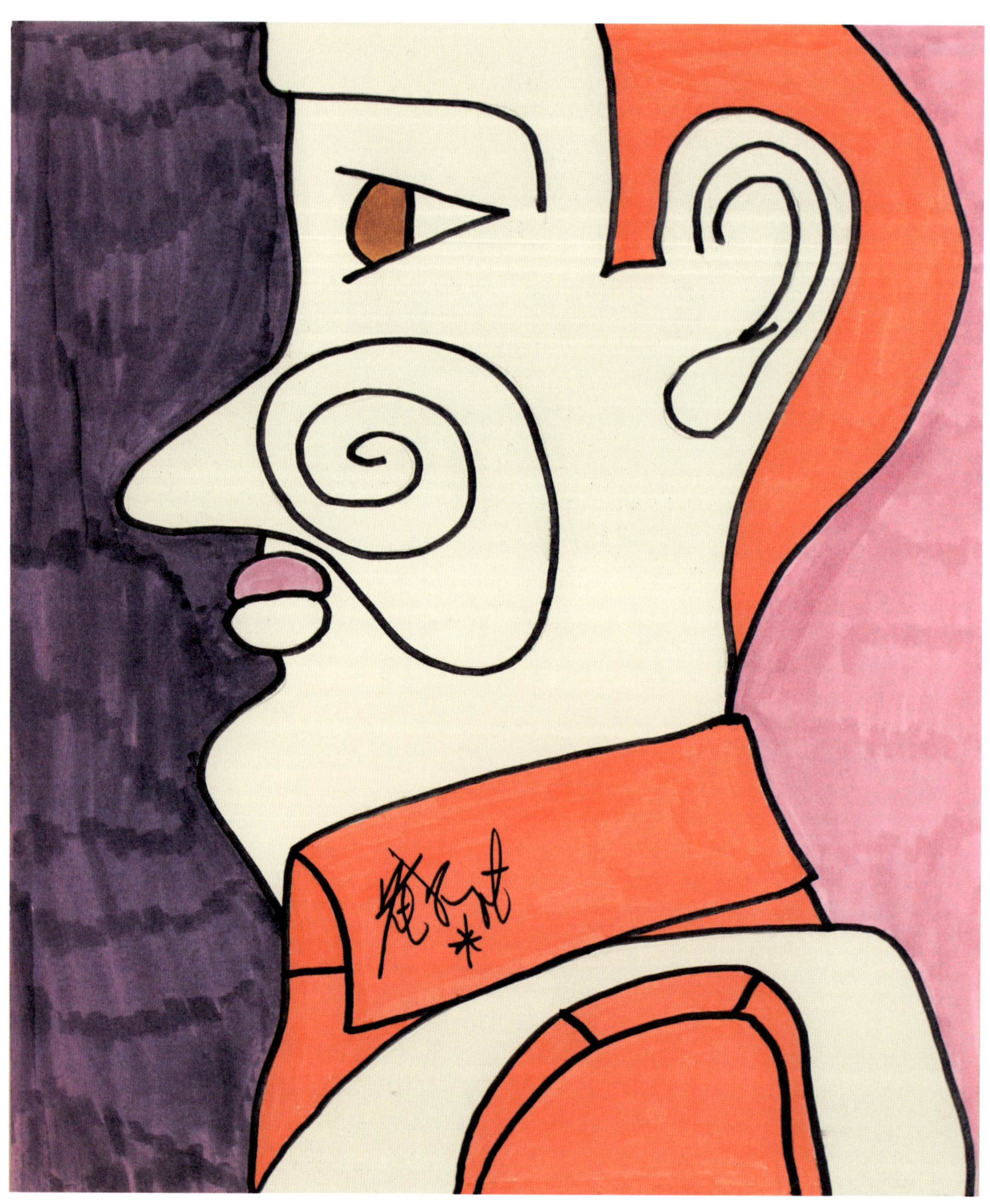

Untitled, n.d.

Paint and weapons have more in common than I previously realized. They both suggest to their owners surprising and possibly noteworthy things which might be done with them.

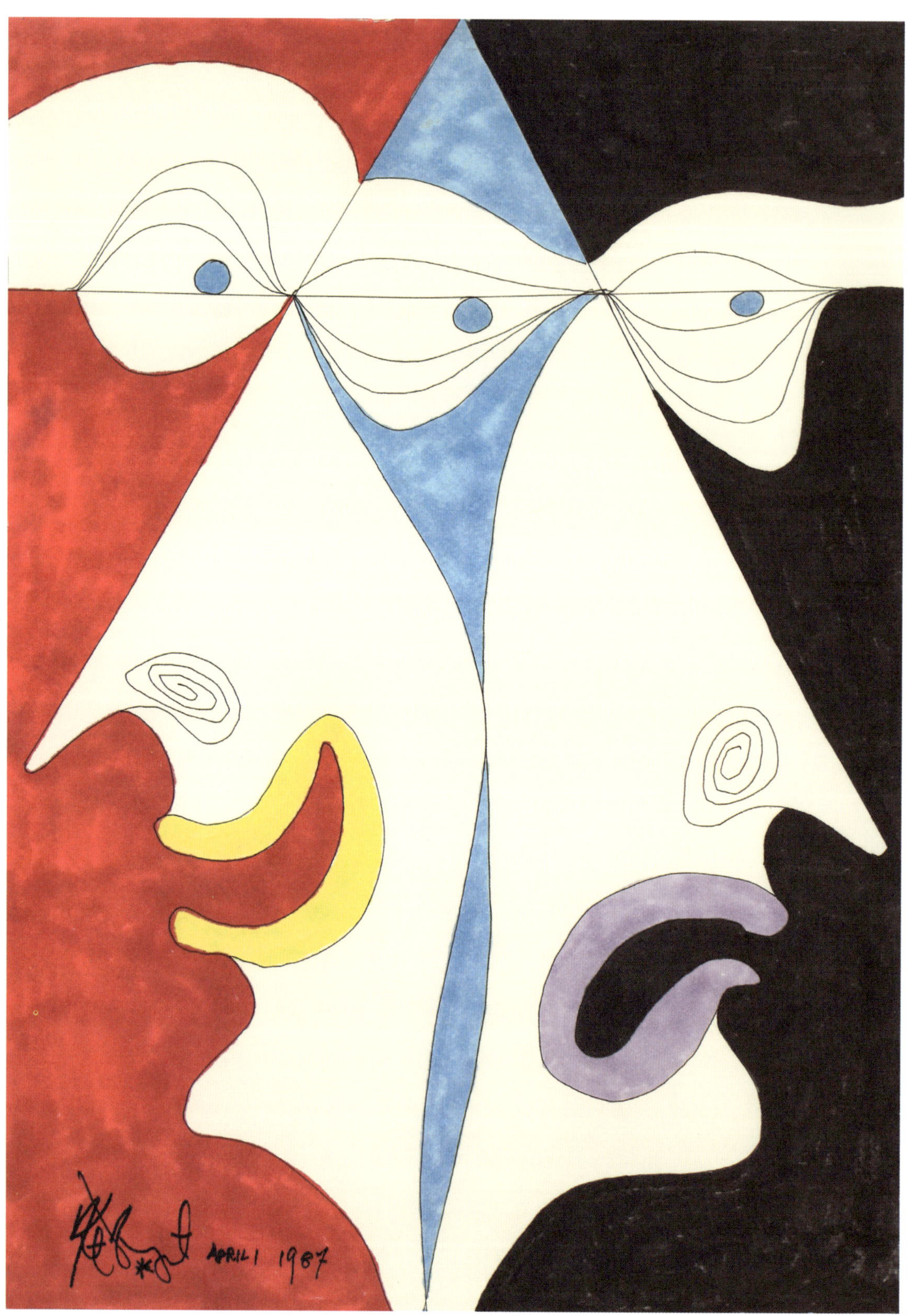

Untitled, April 1, 1987

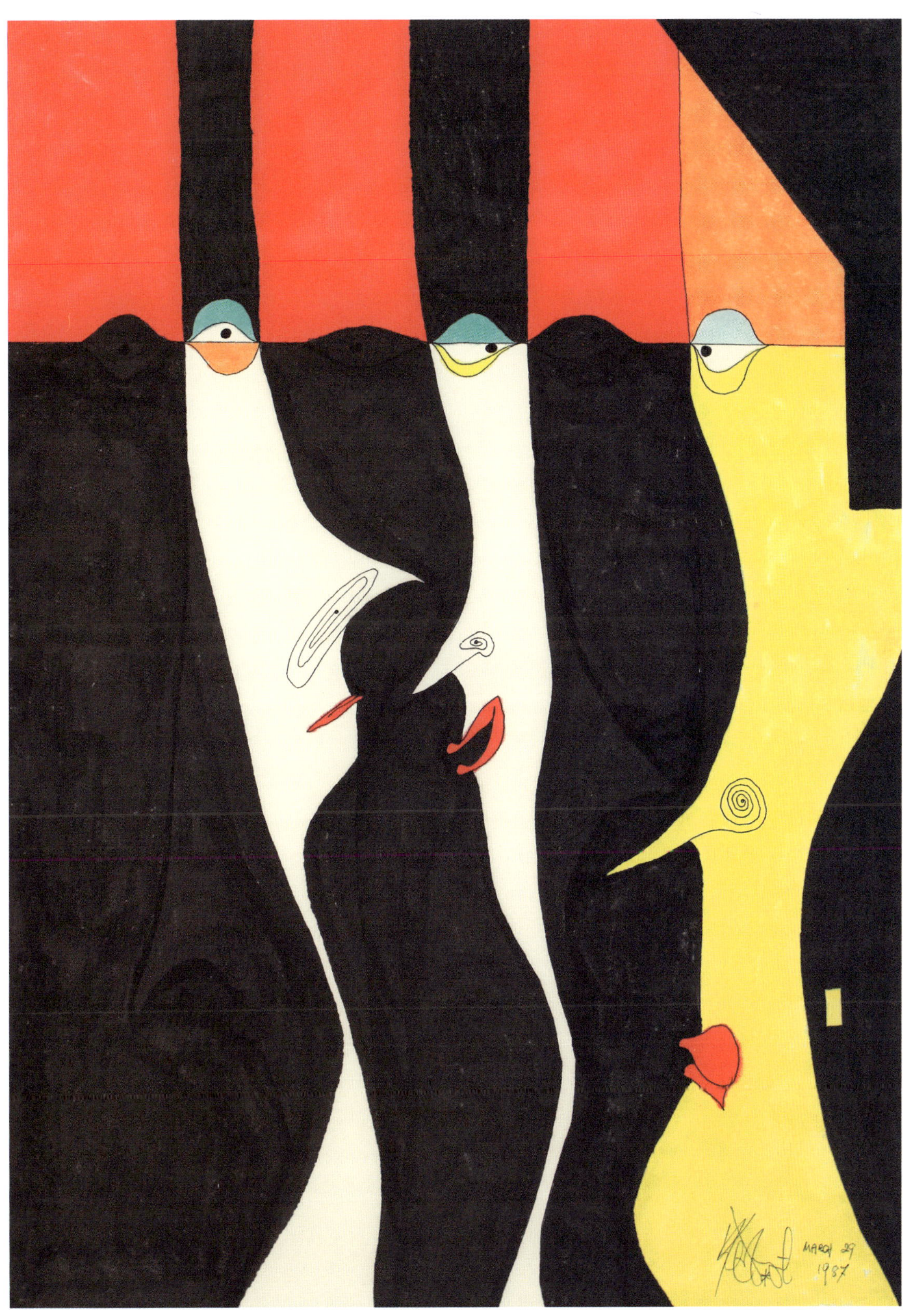

Untitled, March 29, 1987

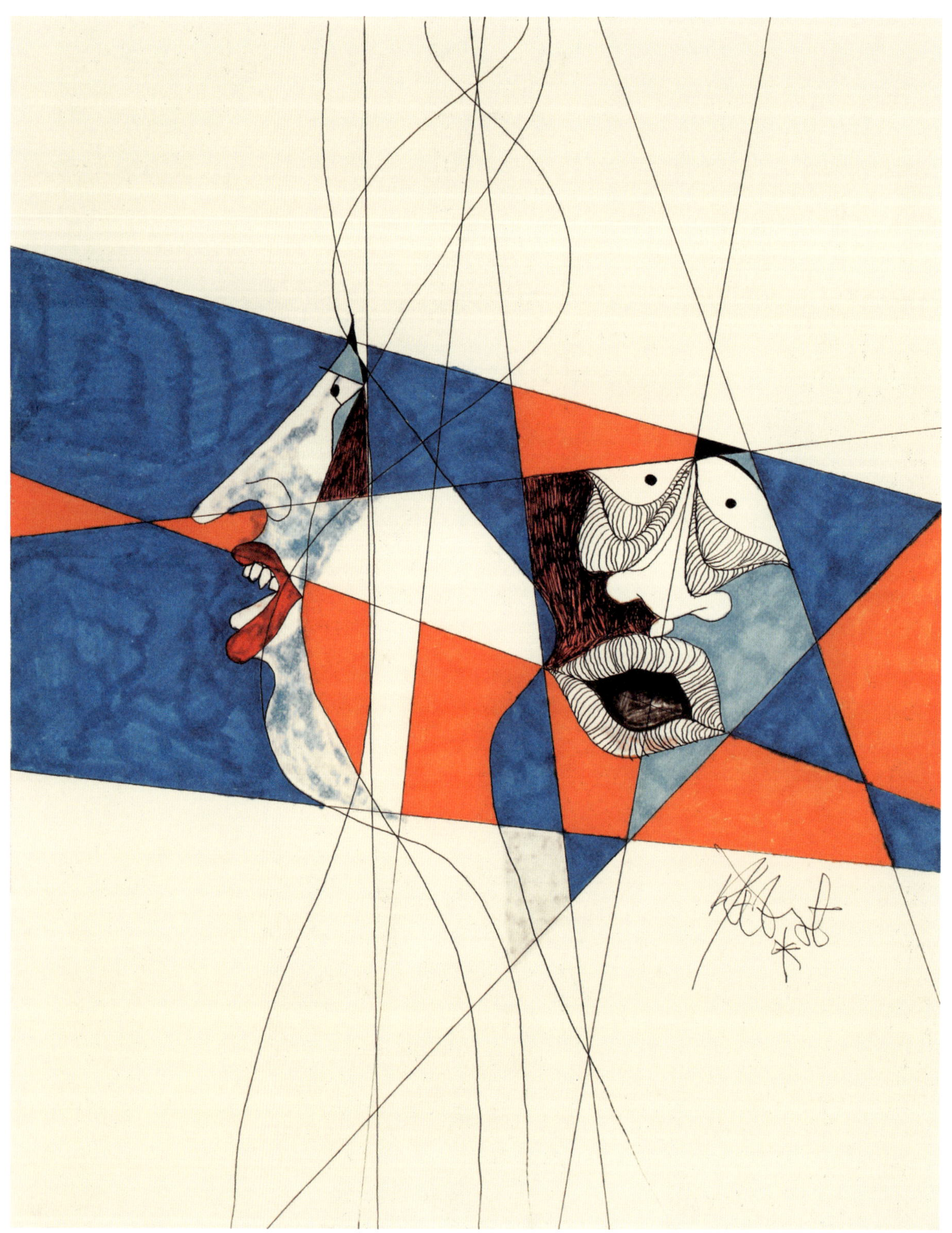

Untitled, n.d.

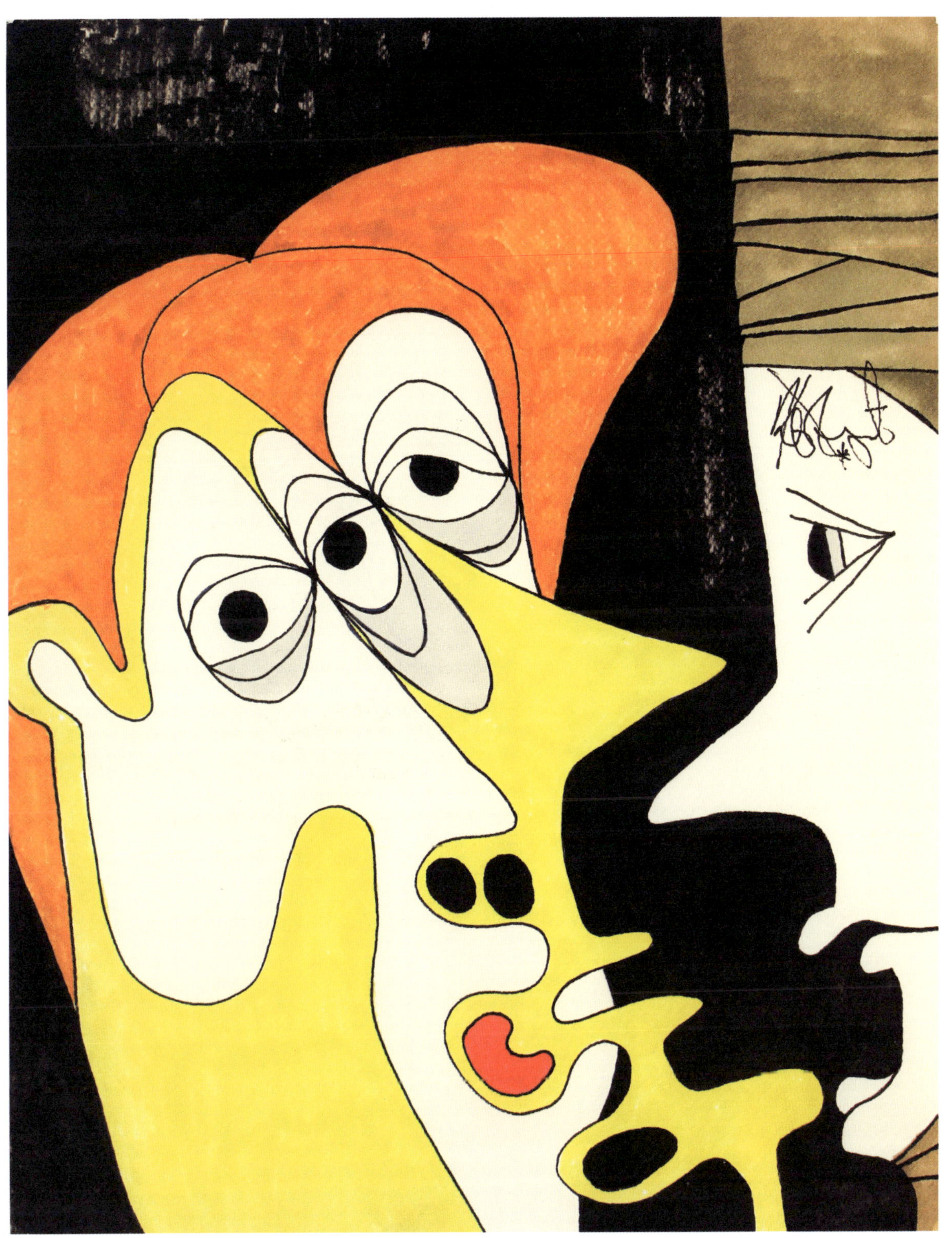

Untitled, n.d.

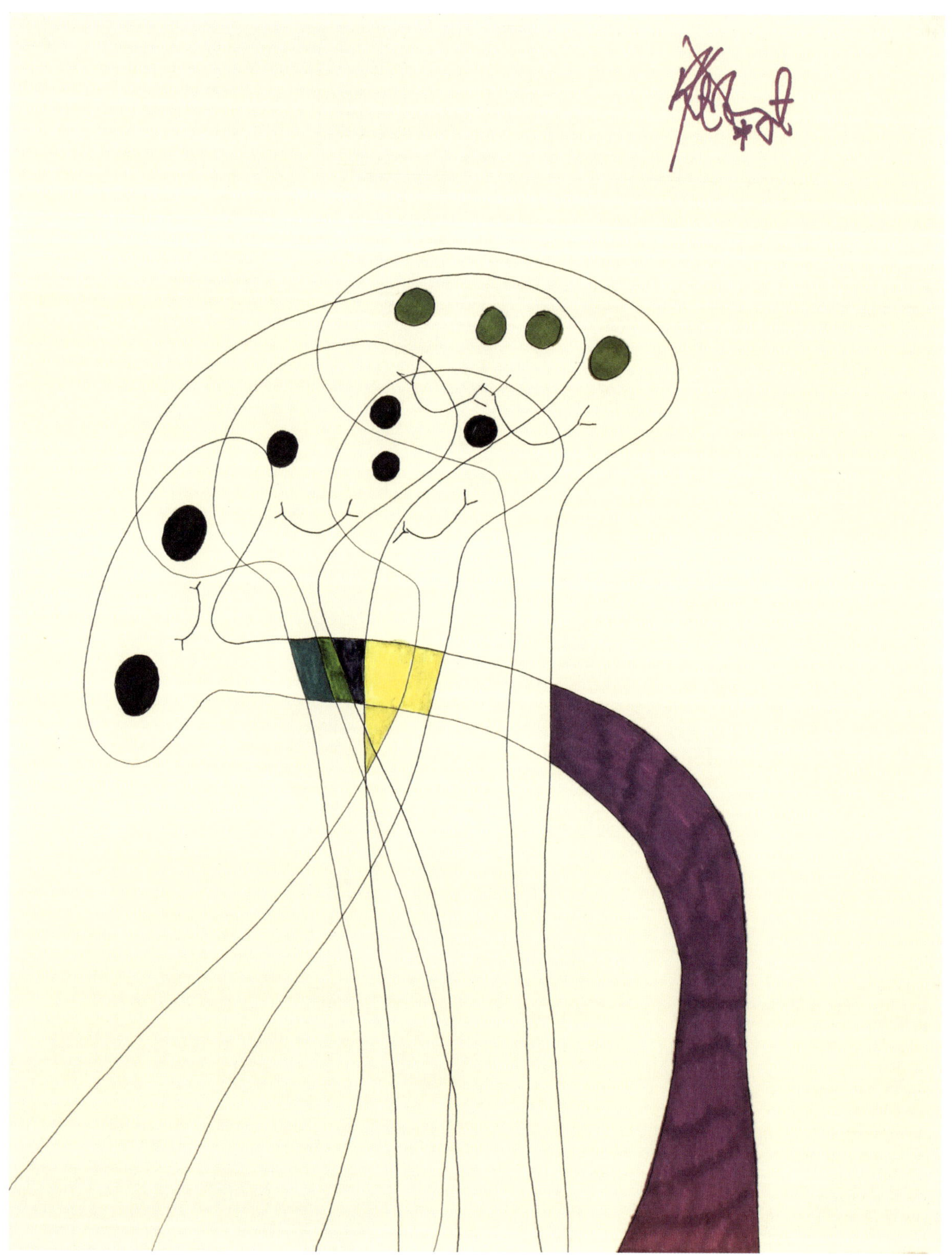

Untitled, n.d.

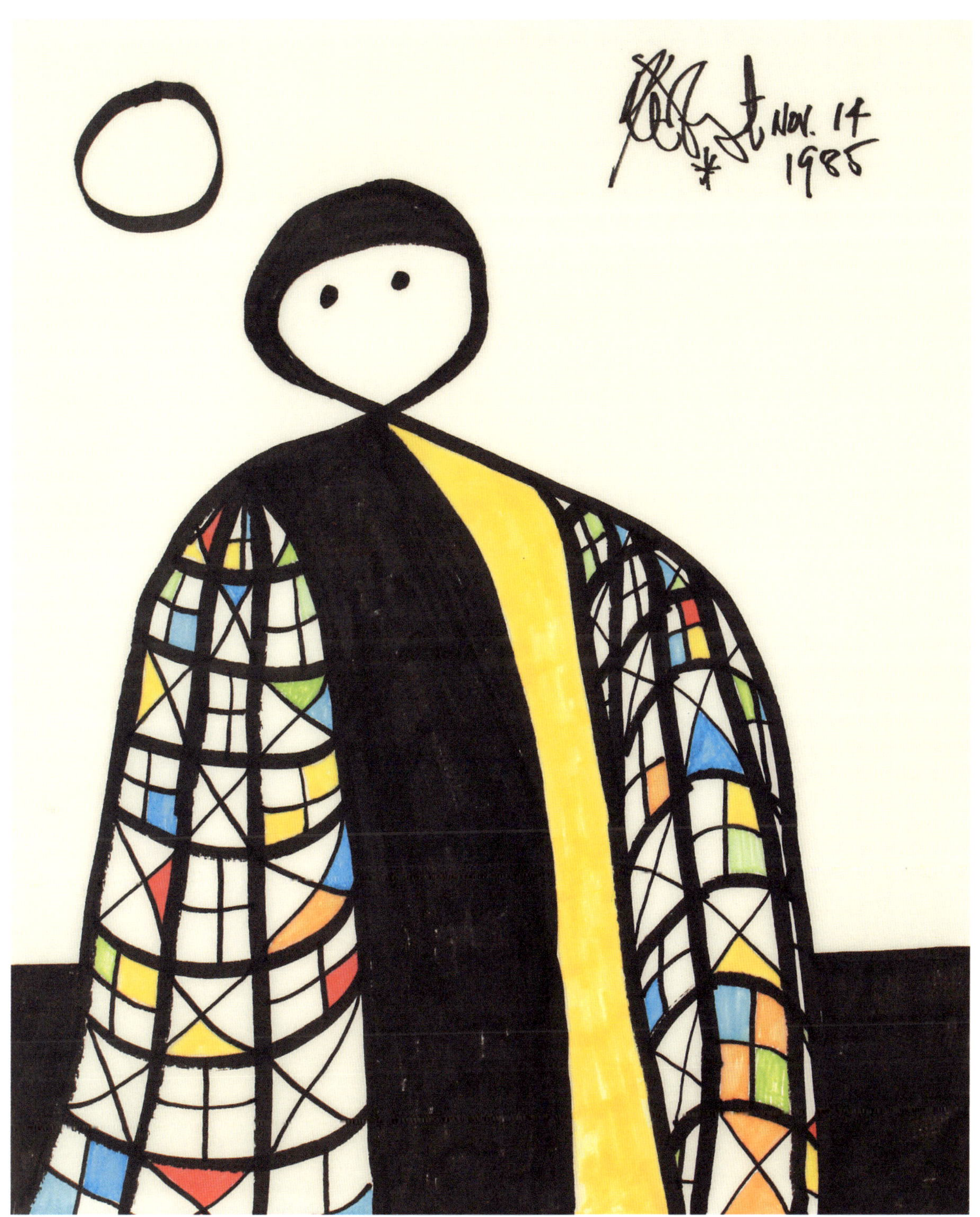

Untitled, November 14, 1985

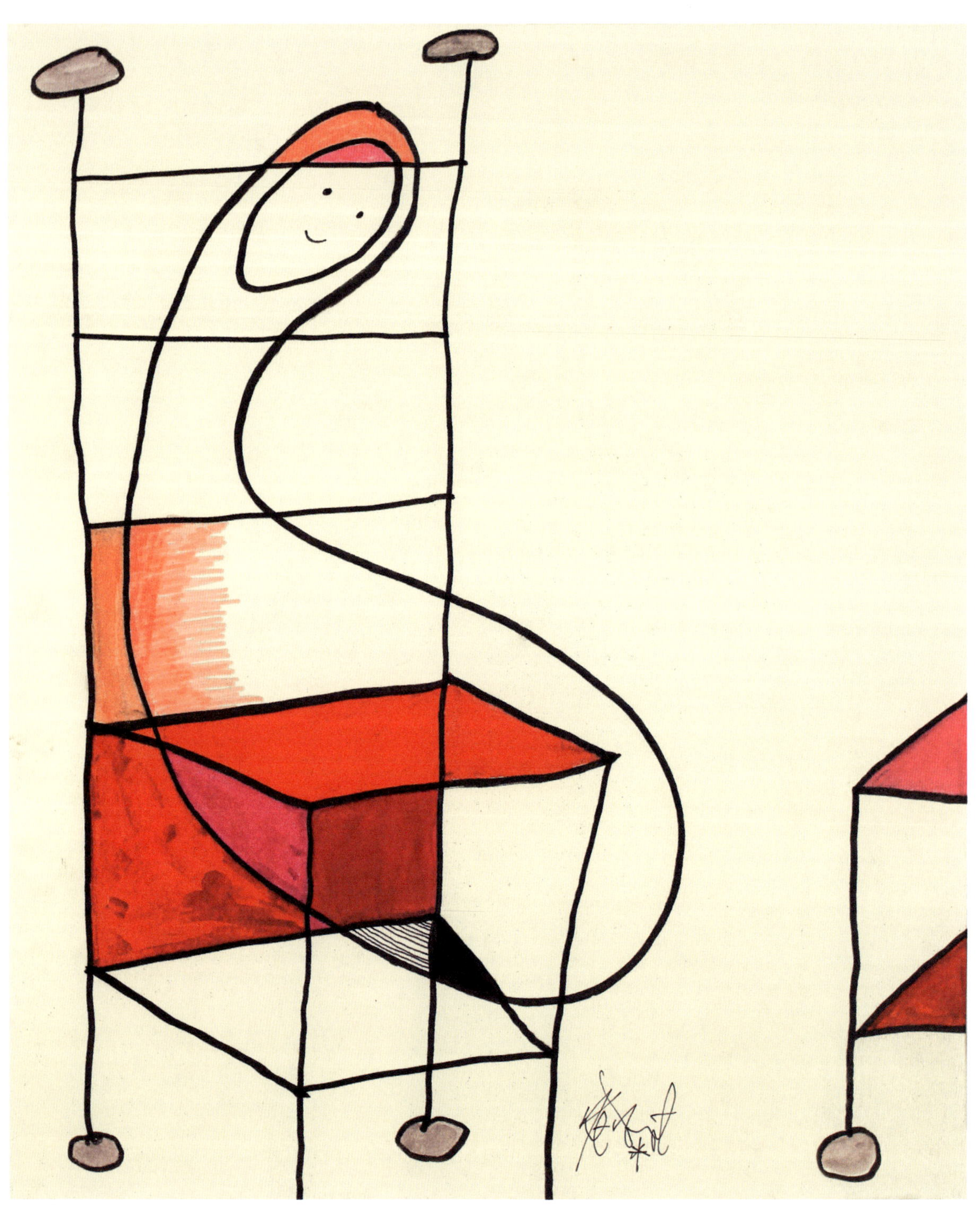

Untitled, n.d.

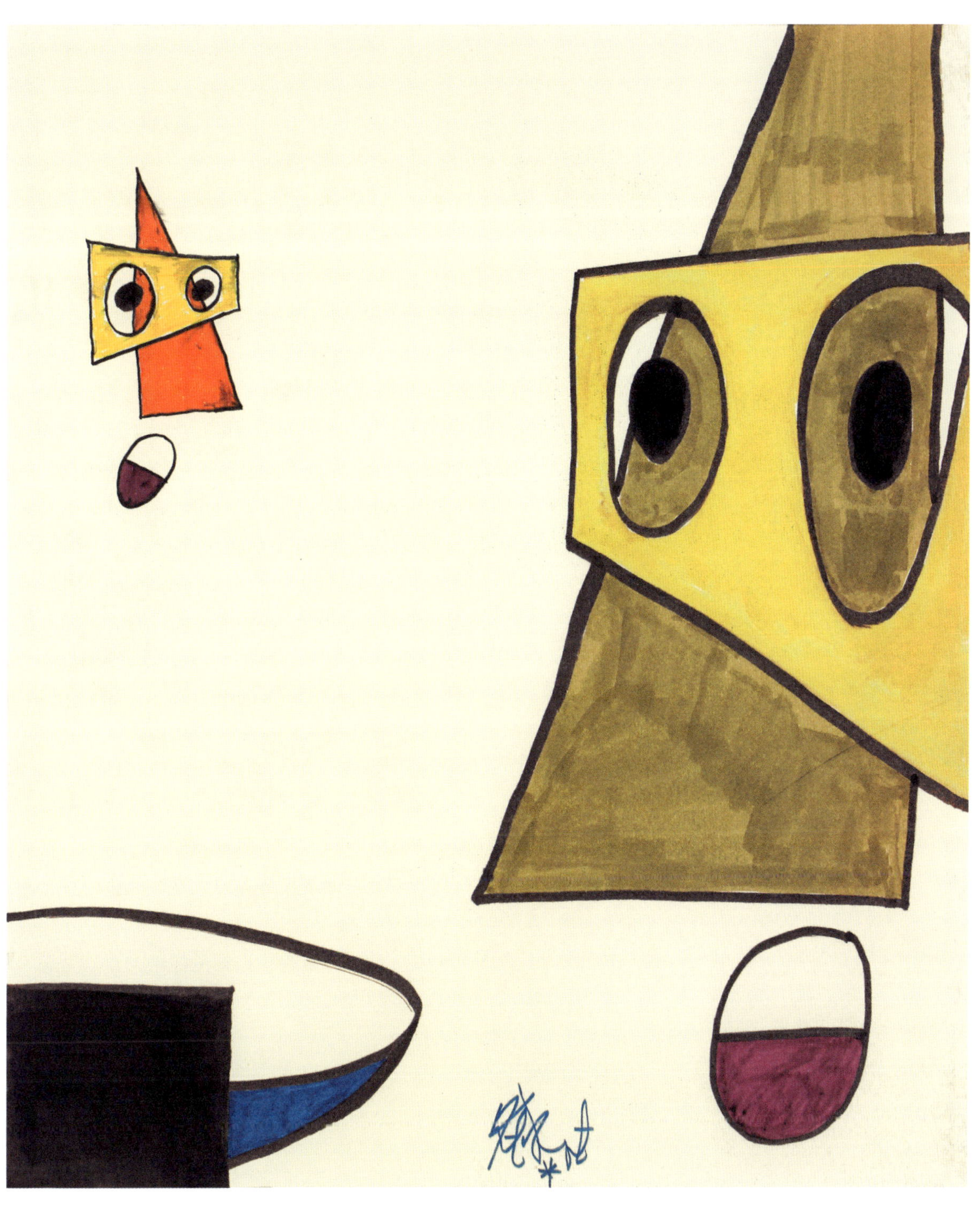

Untitled, n.d.

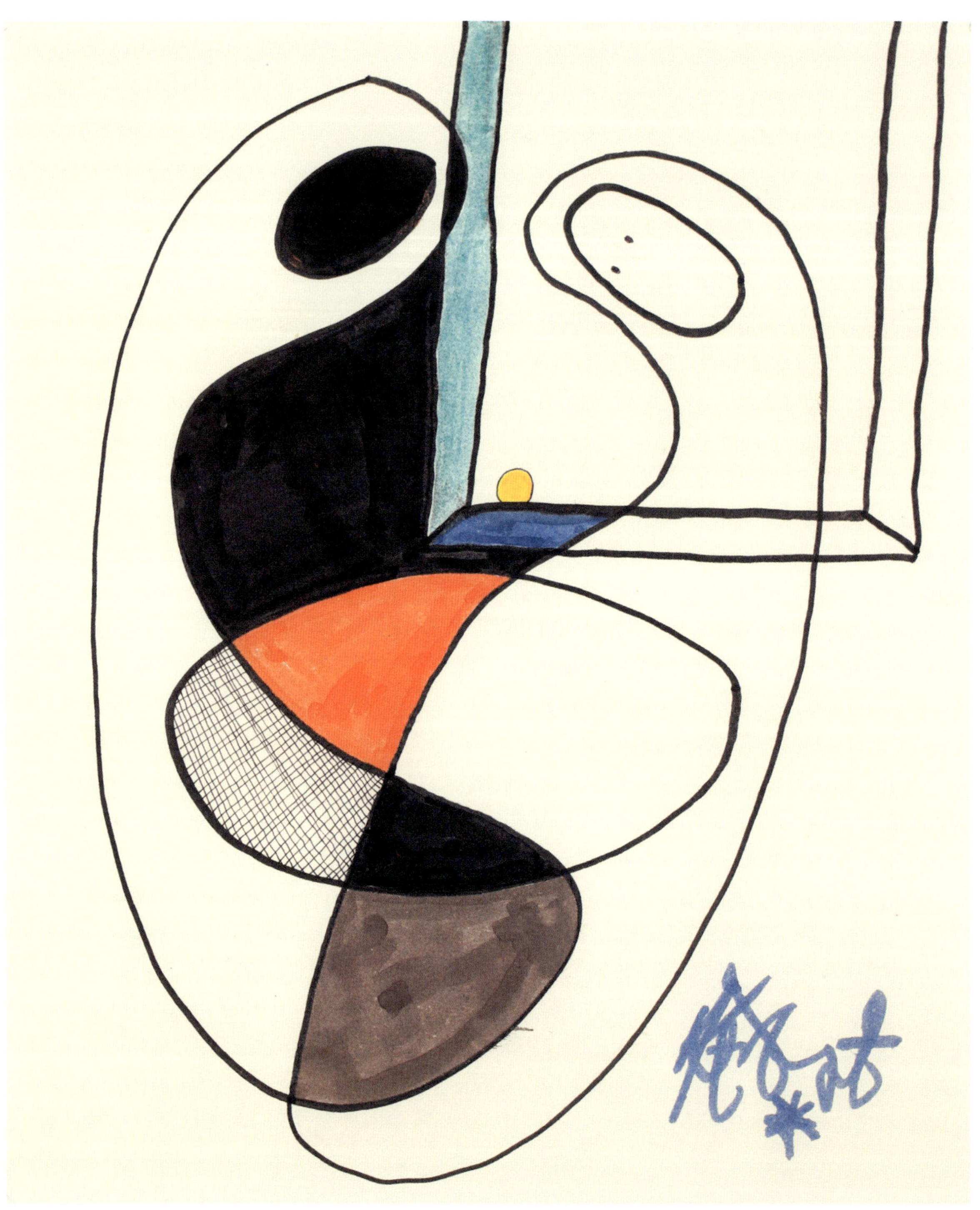

Untitled, n.d.

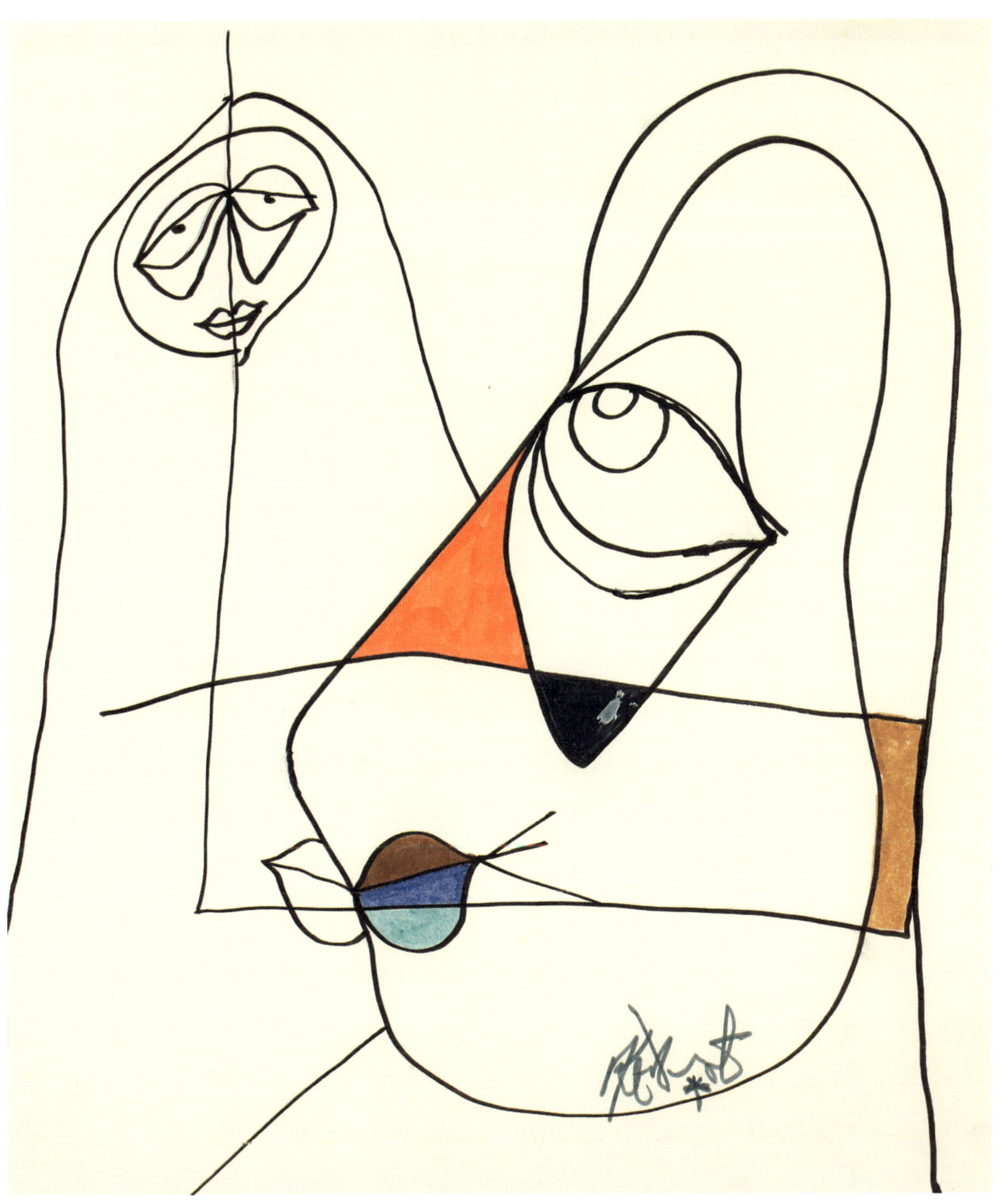

Untitled, n.d.

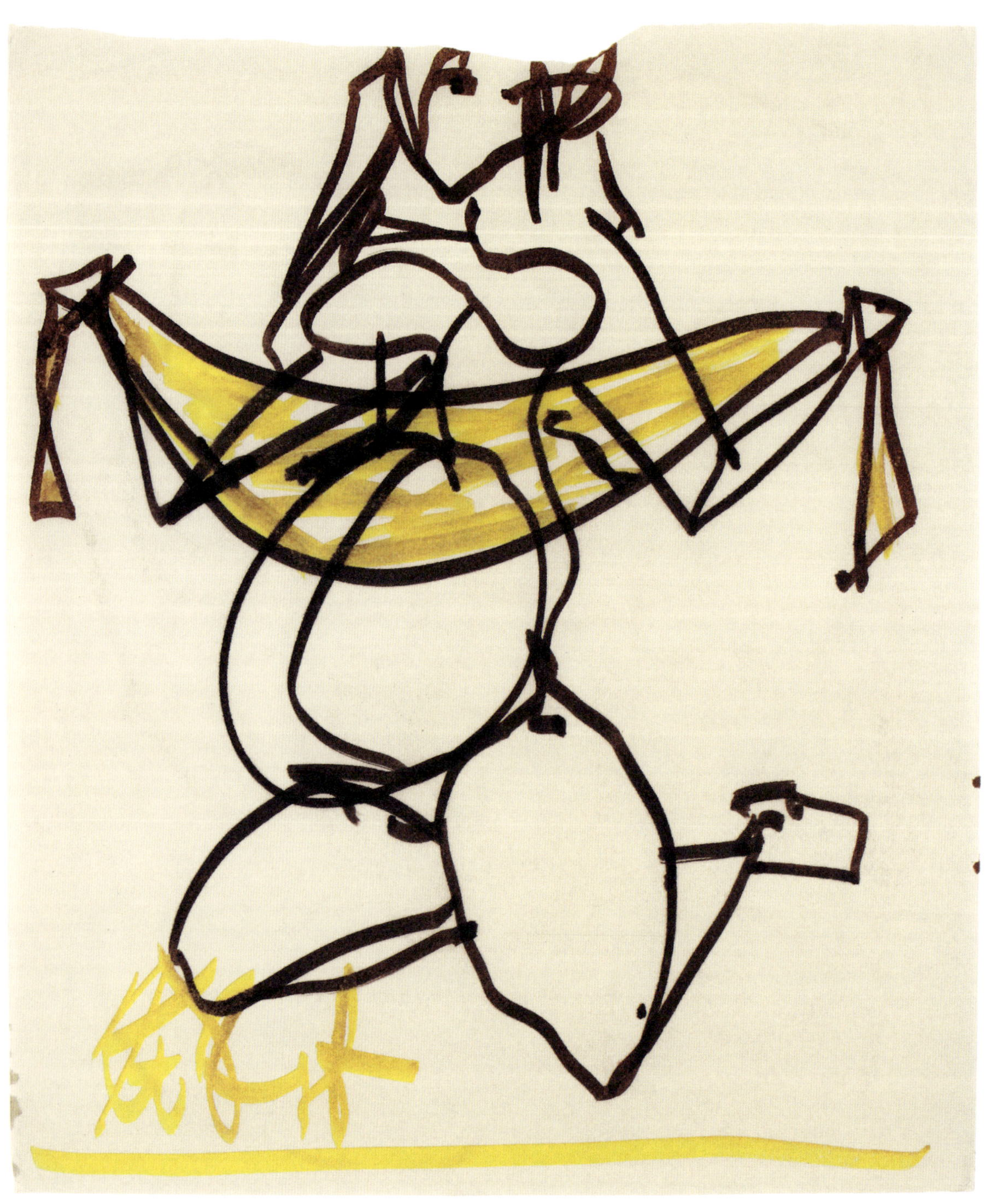

Untitled, n.d.

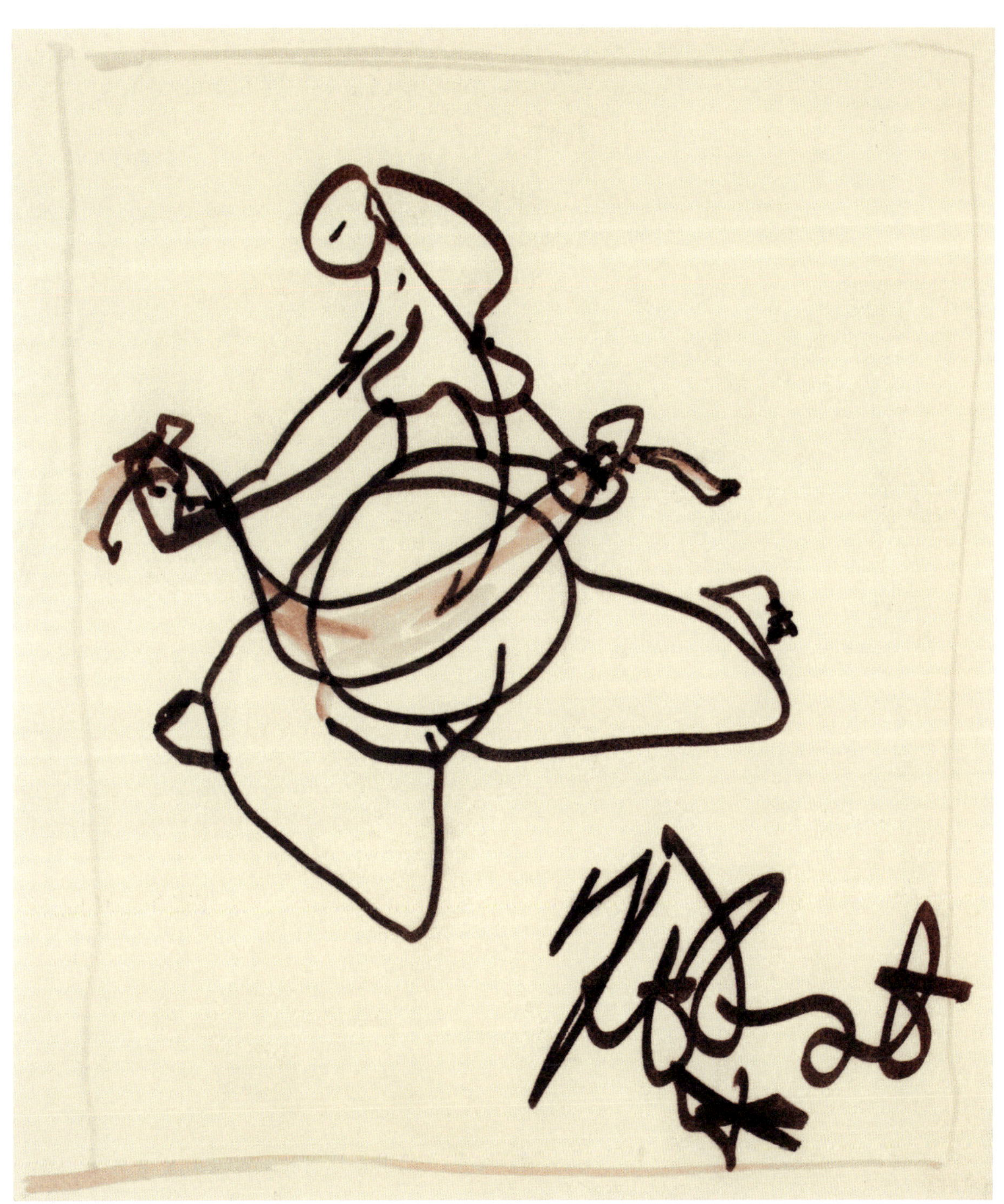

Untitled, n.d.

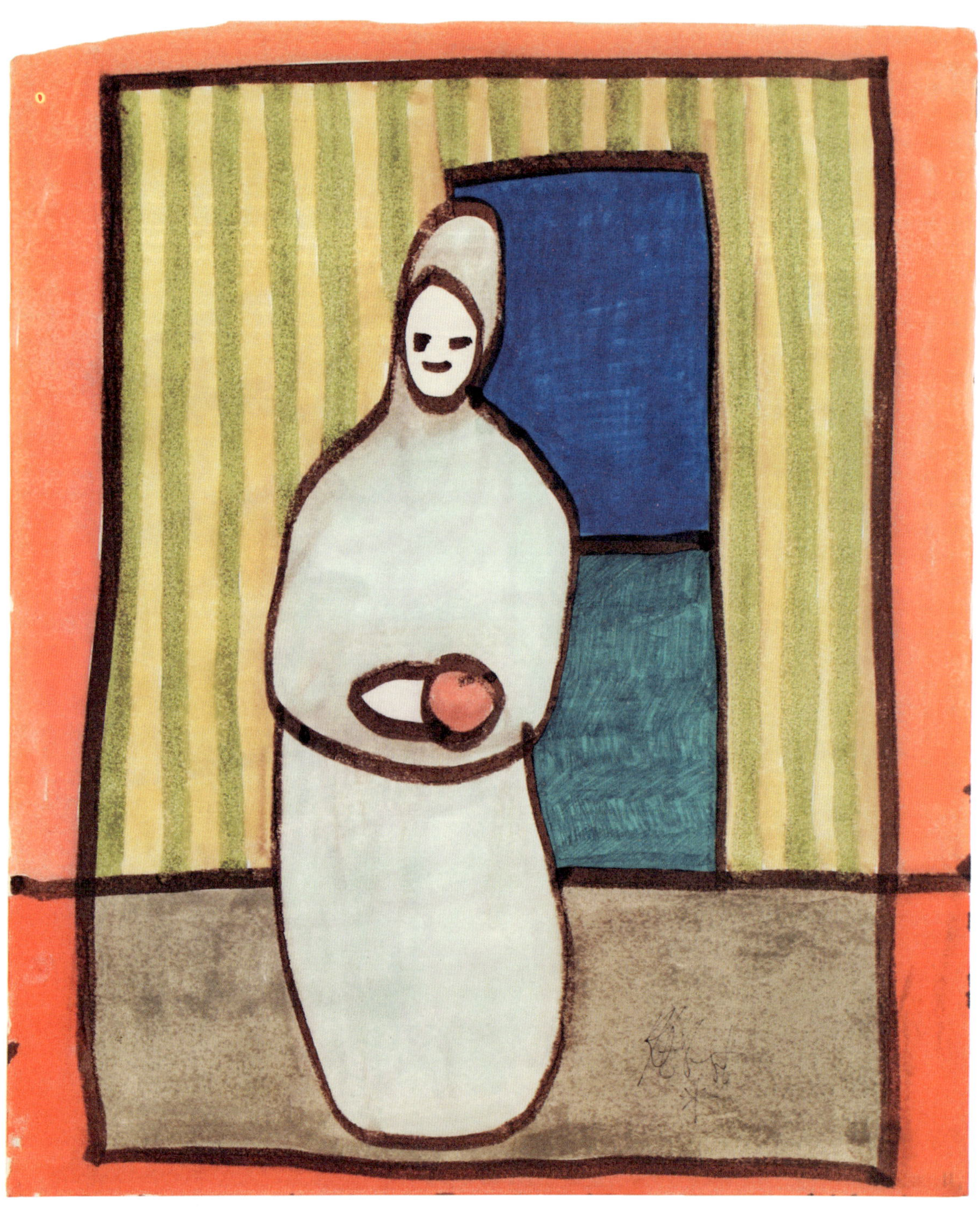

Untitled, n.d.

Both my grown daughters make pictures and sell them. But they wish they could keep them. It is the third player who forces them to put them up for adoption. And that player is full of vehement advice about how to make their pictures more adopt-able, how to run a successful baby factory, so to speak.

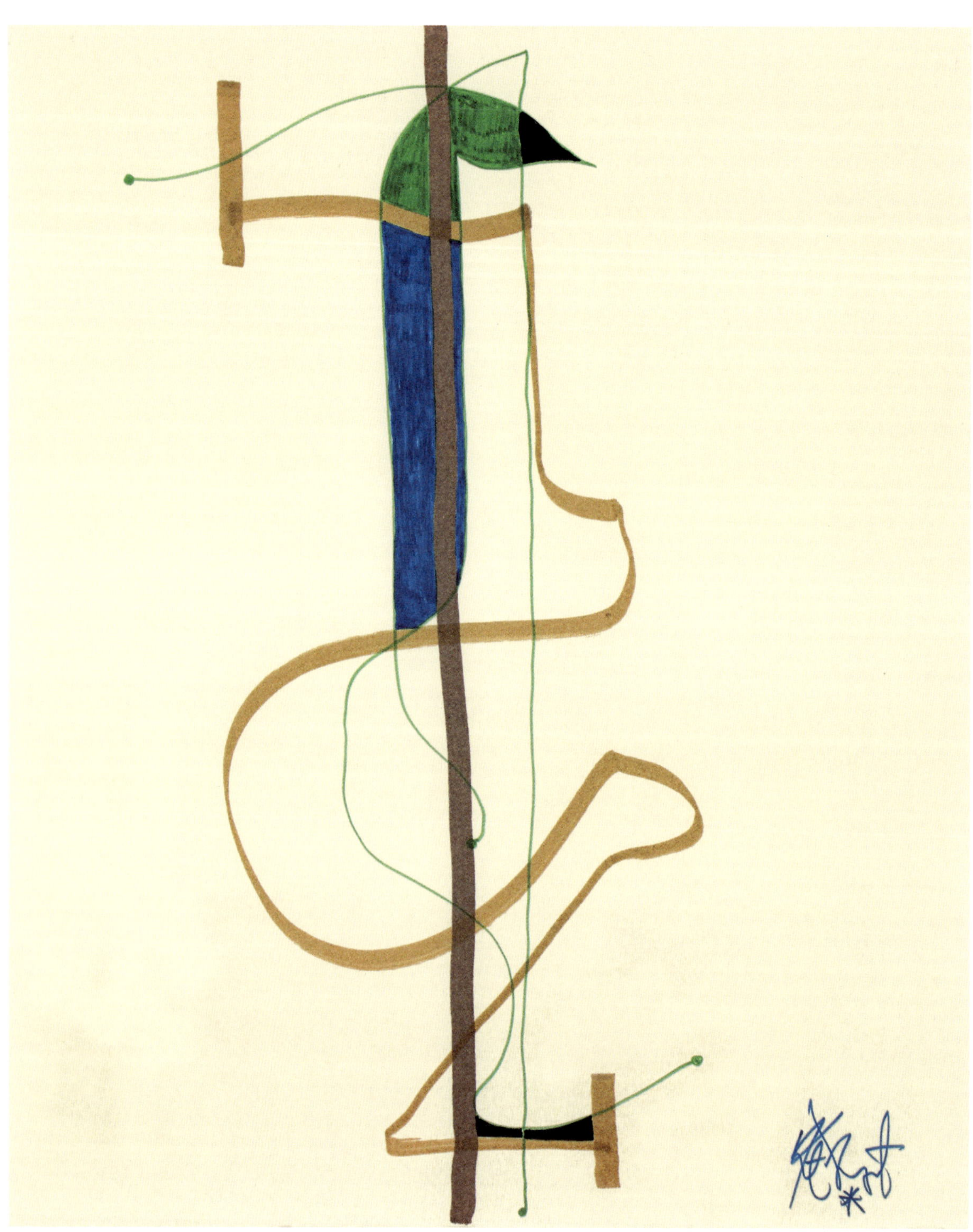

Untitled, n.d.

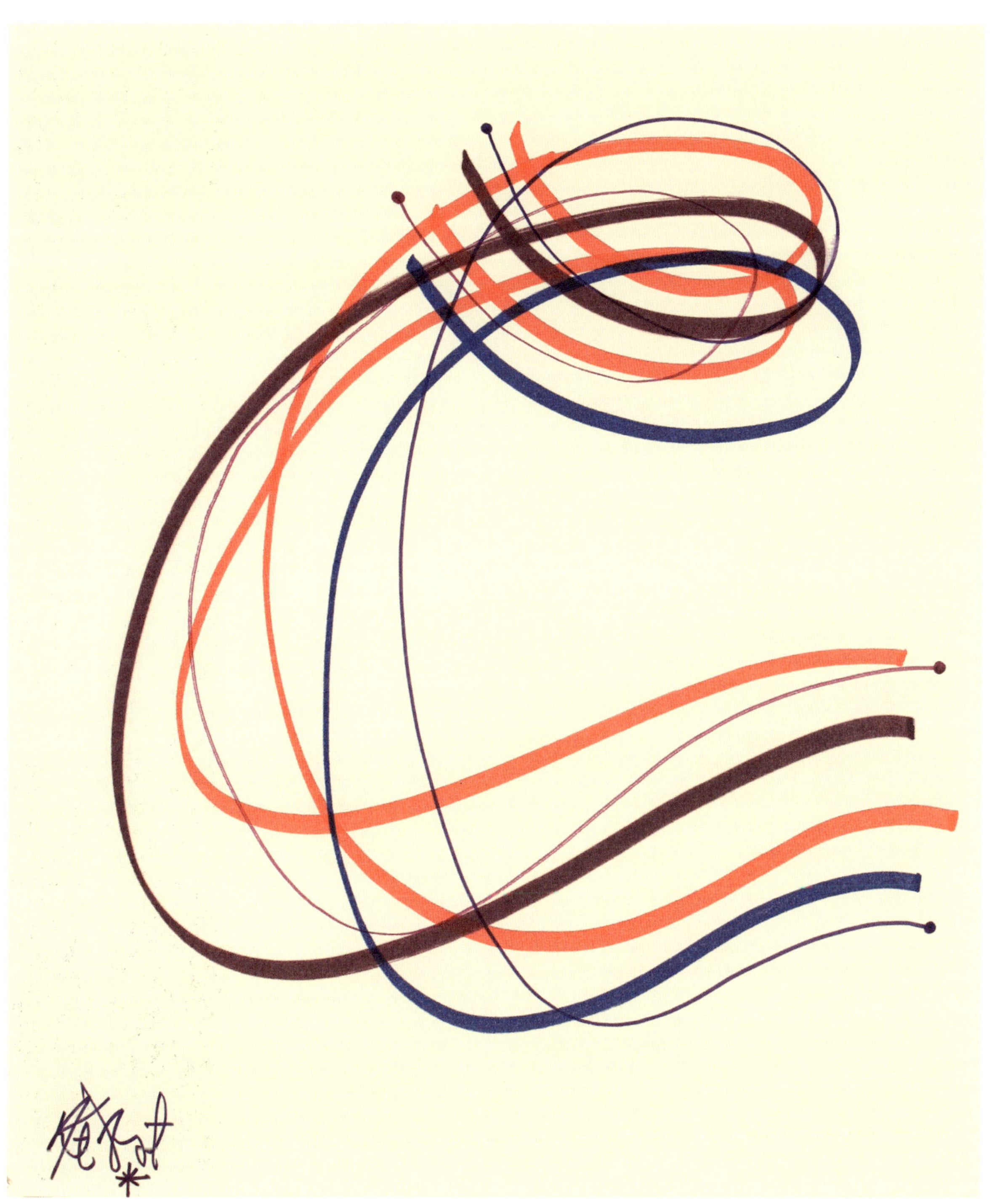

Untitled, n.d.

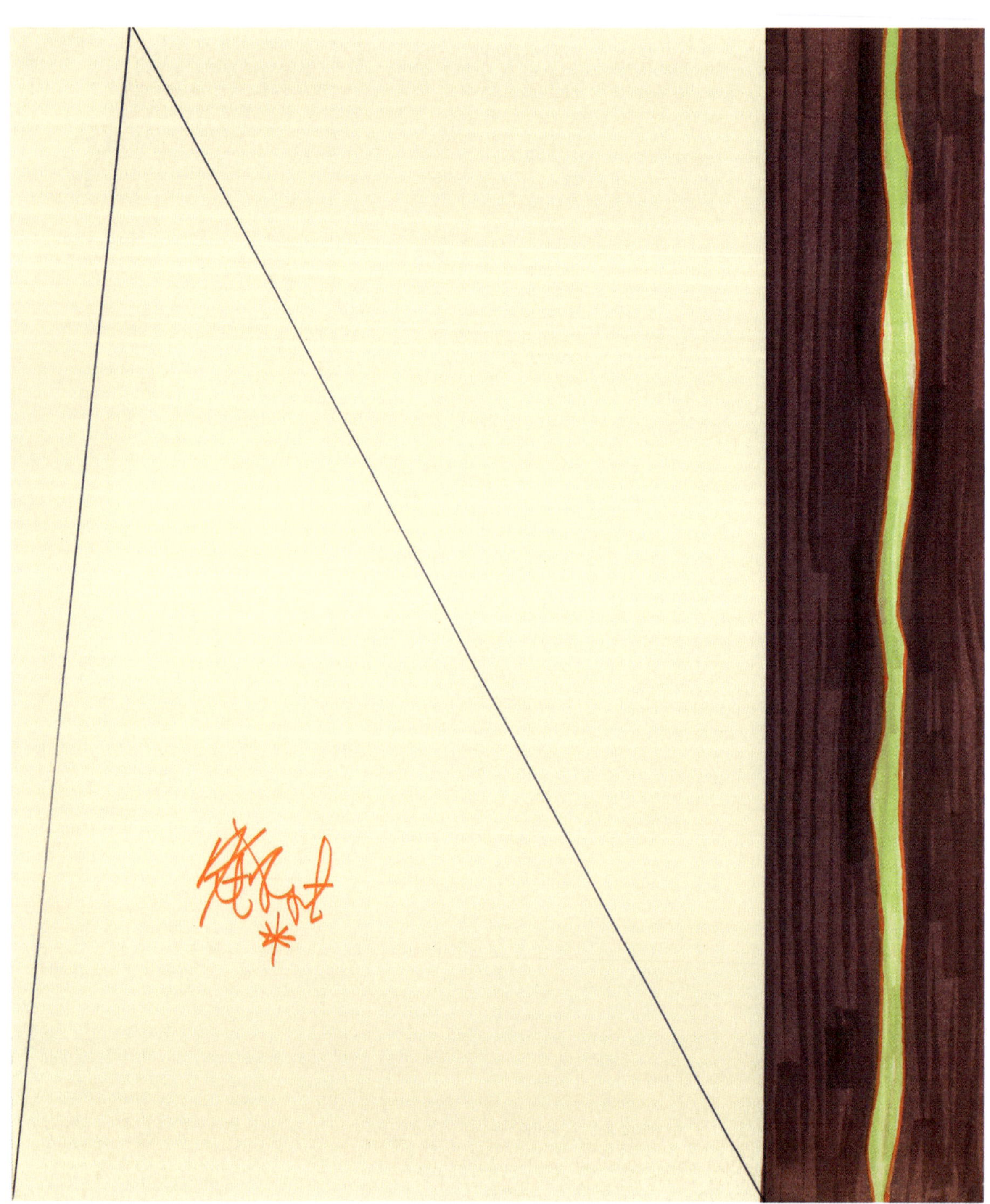

Untitled, n.d.

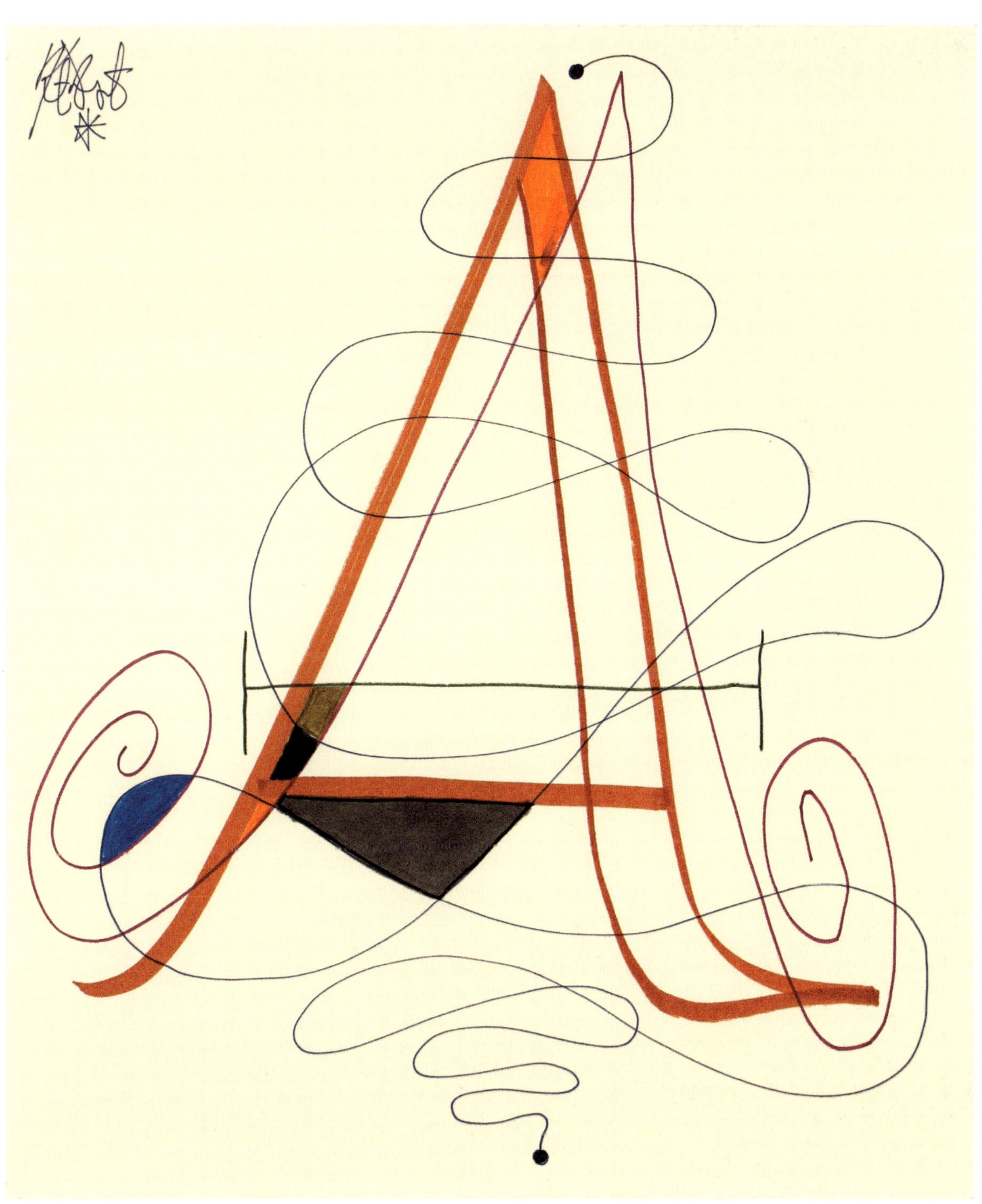

Untitled, n.d.

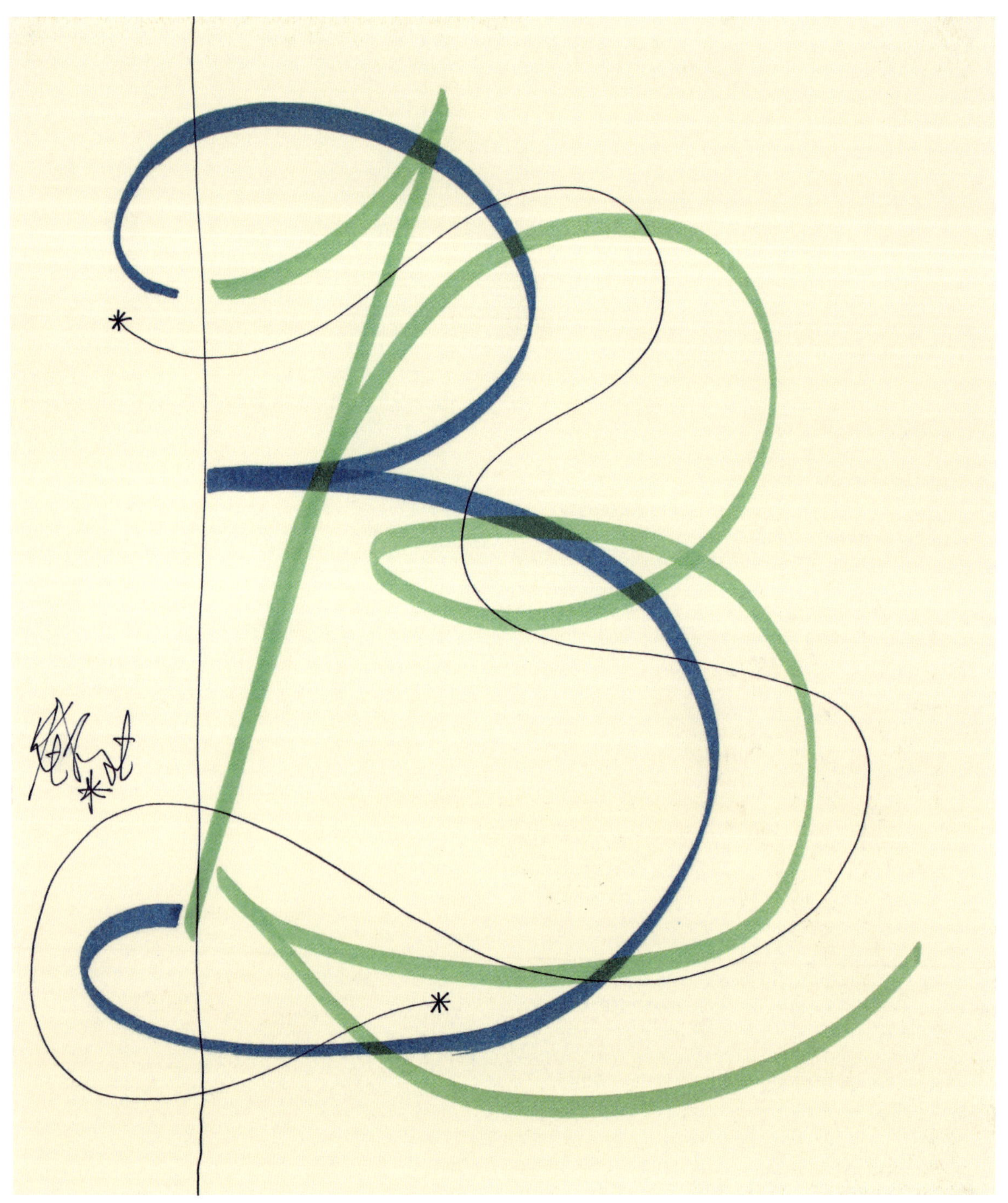

Untitled, n.d.

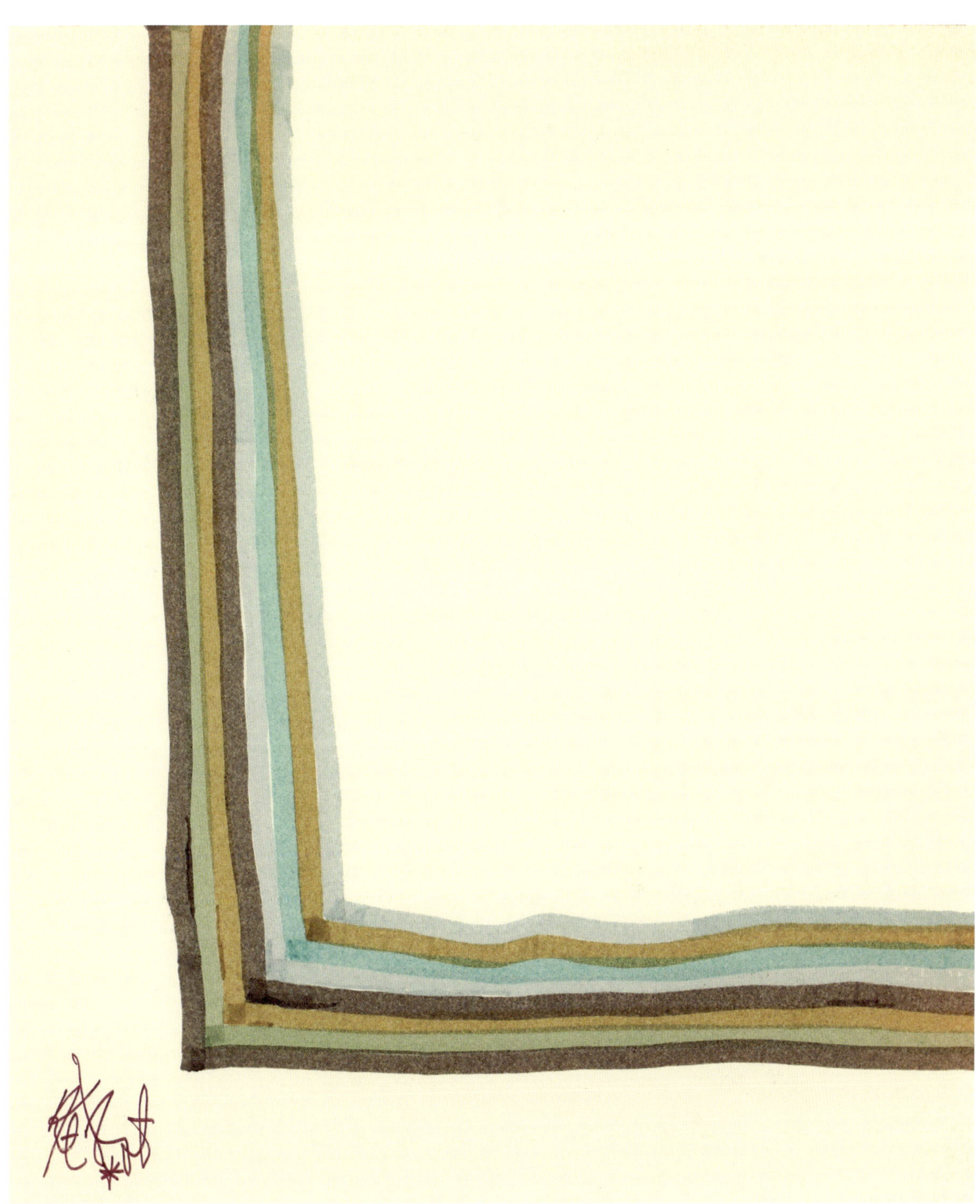

Untitled, n.d.

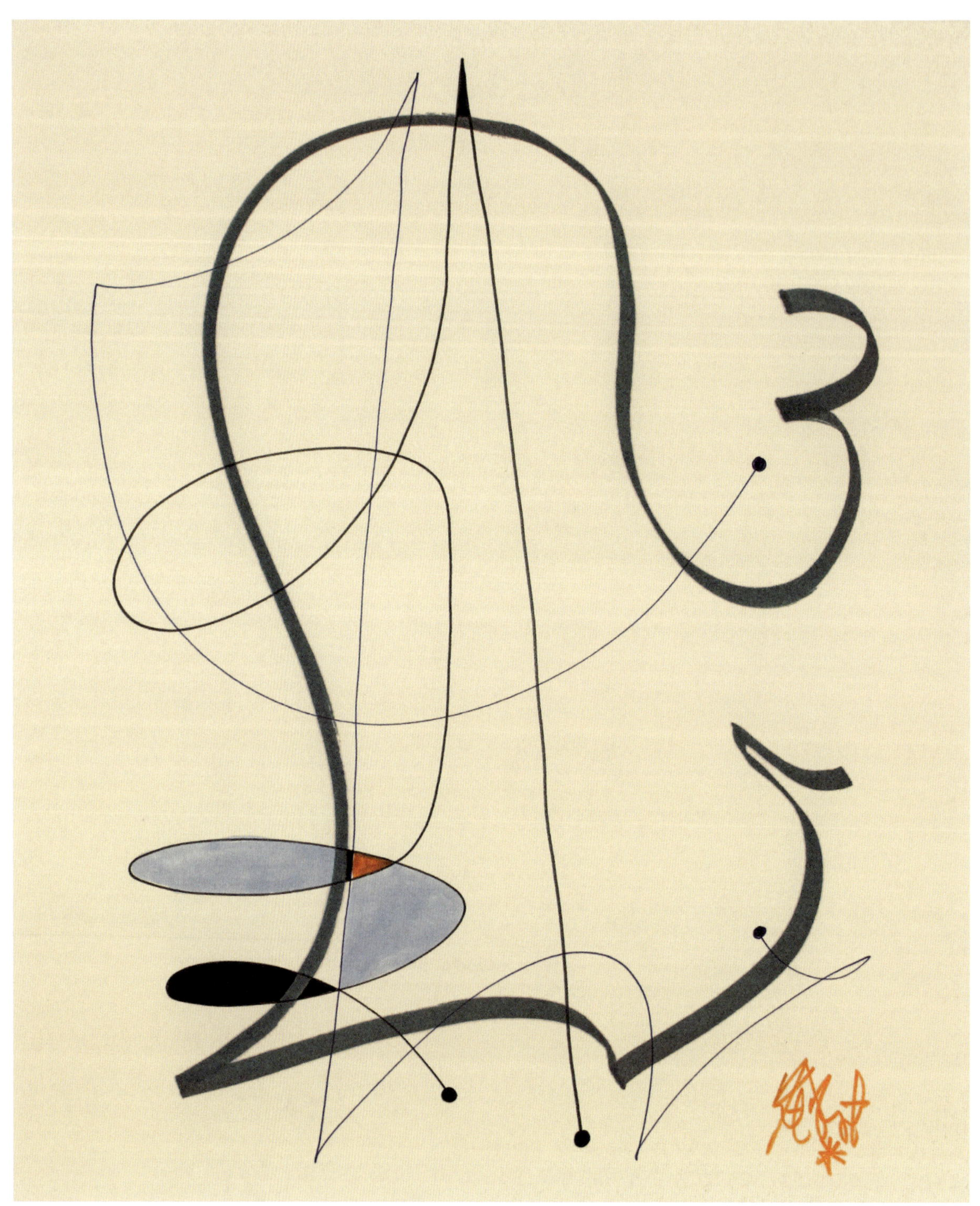

Untitled, n.d.

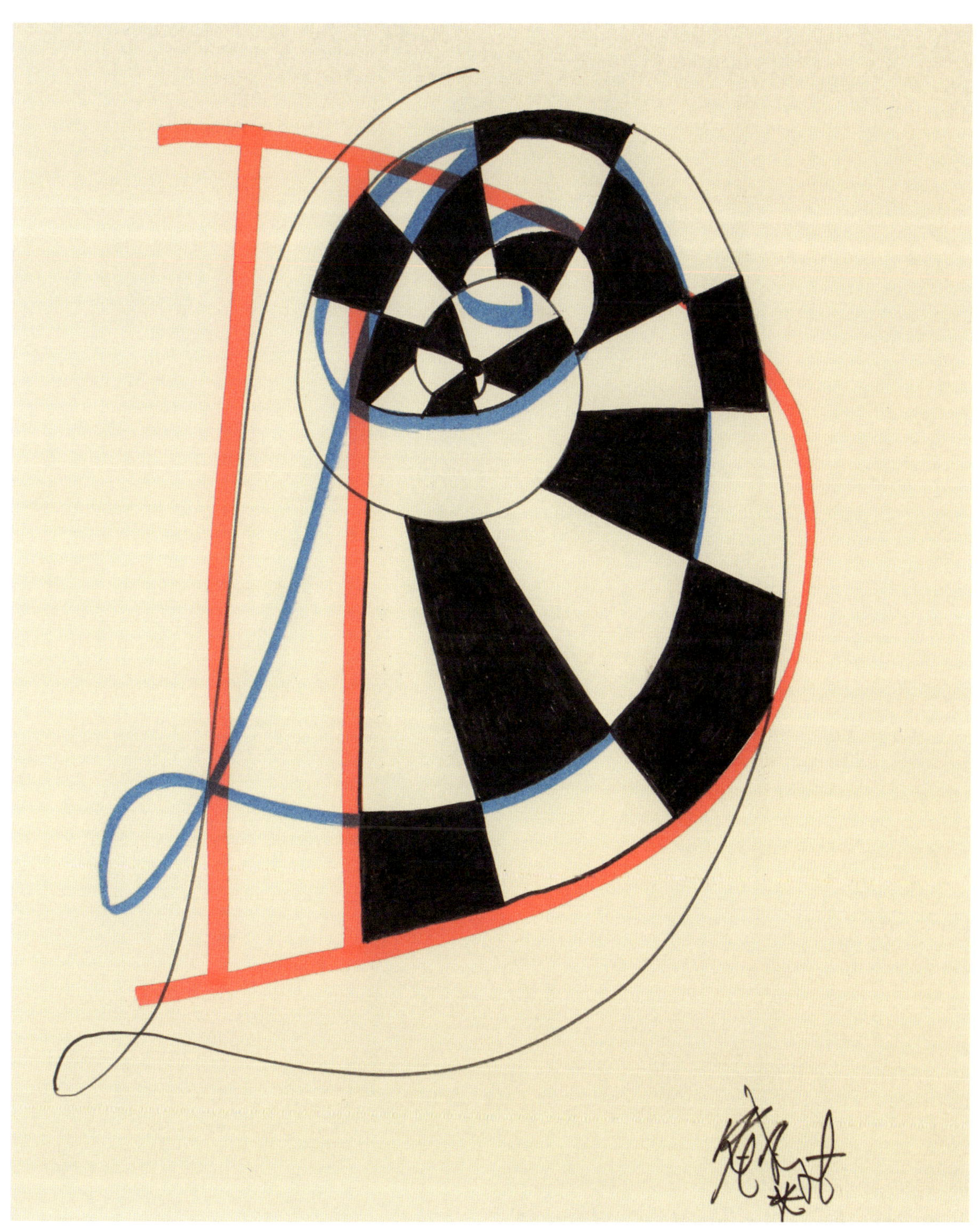

Untitled, n.d.

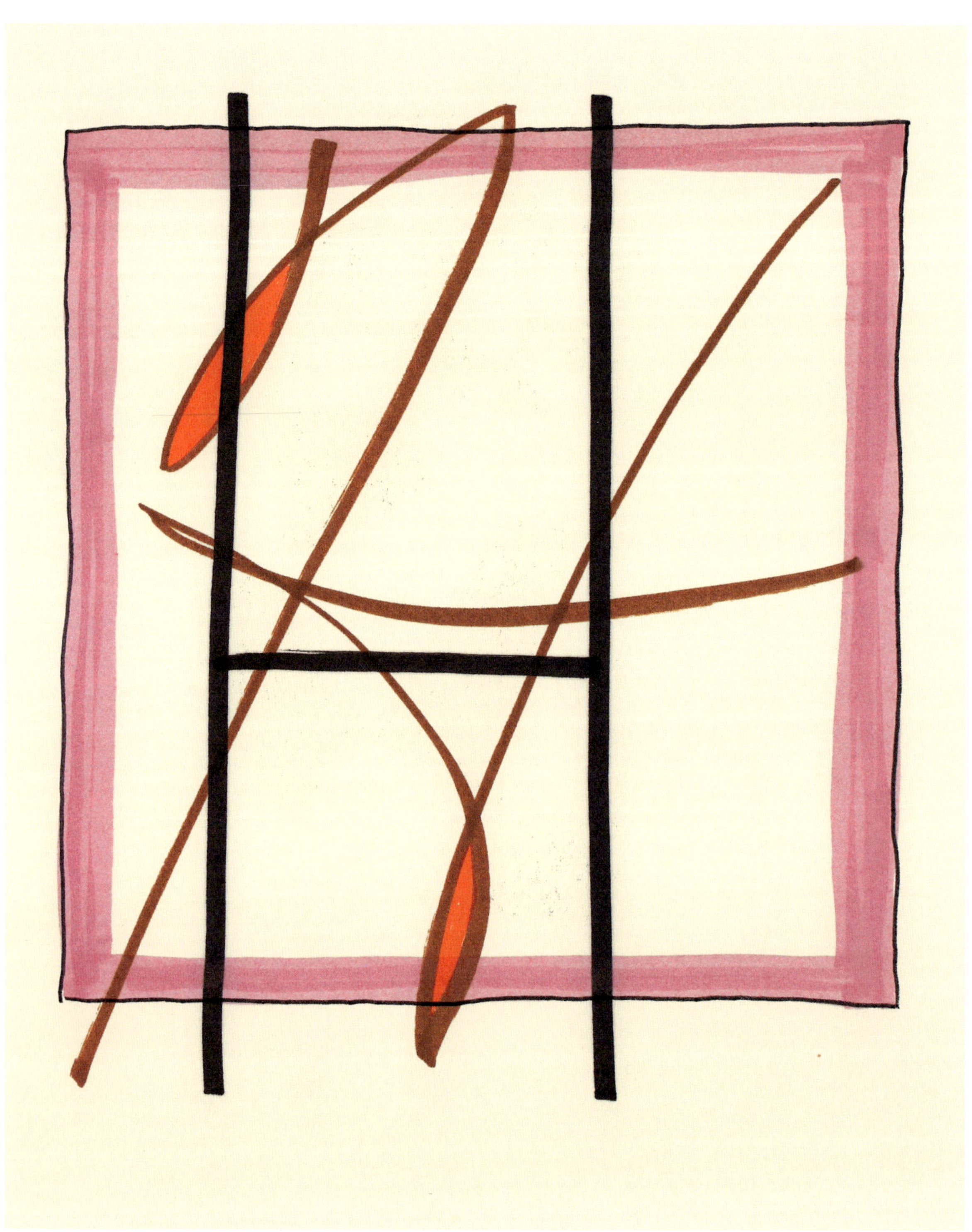

Untitled, n.d.